AFTER THE CONQUEST

AFTER THE CONQUEST

THE DIVIDED REALM 1066-1135

TERESA COLE

AMBERLEY

First published 2018

Amberley Publishing
The Hill, Stroud
Gloucestershire, GL5 4EP

www.amberley-books.com

British Library Cataloguing in Publication Data.
A catalogue record for this book is available from the British Library.

ISBN 978 1 4456 6778 2 (hardback)
ISBN 978 1 4456 6779 9 (ebook)

Map design by Thomas Bohm, User design.
Typesetting and Origination by Amberley Publishing.
Printed in the UK.

Contents

Genealogy trees   7

Maps   12

1 The Lion's Cubs (1054–1087)   15

2 King, Duke and Count (1087–1100)   39

3 An Arrow in the Forest (August–December 1100)   68

4 Robert the Hero (1101–1103)   91

5 Church and State (1101–1107)   112

6 The Conquest of Normandy (1102–1106)   132

7 Lion of Justice (1106–1111)   155

8 Prestige and Problems (1111–1120)   174

9 All the King's Children   202

10 The White Ship and After (1120–1125)   219

11 A Surfeit of Lampreys (1125–1135)   241

12 The End of an Era   261

A Note on Sources   274

Select Bibliography   279

Index   282

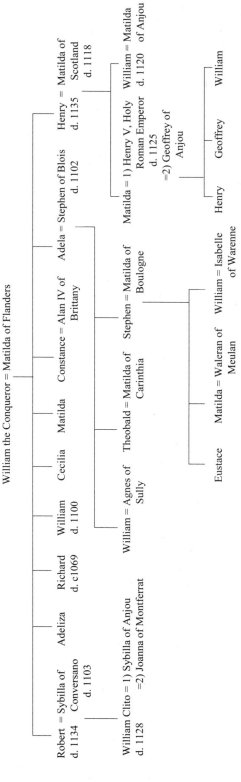

1. The family and selected descendants of William the Conqueror

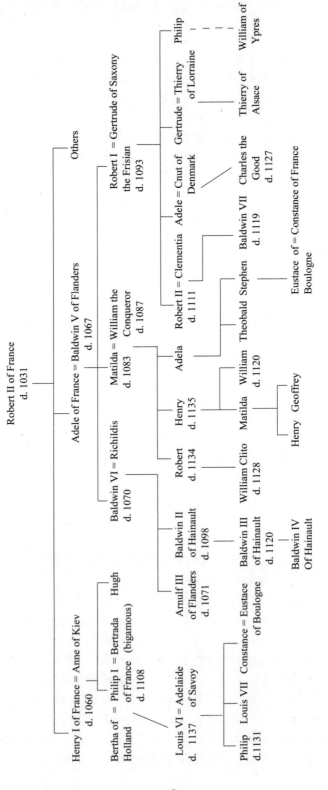

2. Selected connections: France, Flanders, Normandy & England

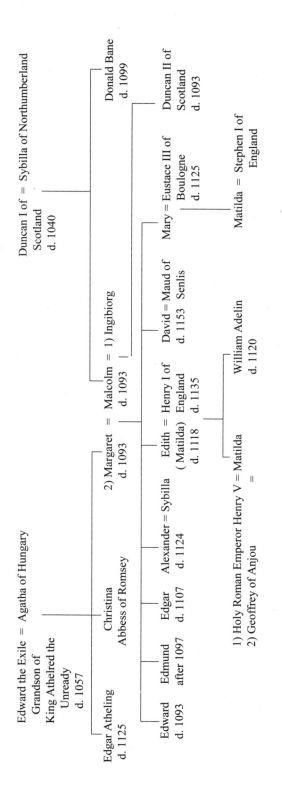

Edward the Exile = Agatha of Hungary
Grandson of
King Athelred the
Unready
d. 1057

Duncan I of = Sybilla of Northumberland
Scotland
d. 1040

Christina
Abbess of Romsey

Donald Bane
d. 1099

2) Margaret = Malcolm = 1) Ingibiorg
d. 1093   d. 1093

Duncan II of
Scotland
d. 1093

Edgar Atheling
d. 1125

Mary = Eustace III of
Boulogne
d. 1125

Edward   Edmund   Edgar   Alexander = Sybilla
d. 1093   after 1097 d. 1107 d. 1124

Edith = Henry I of
(Matilda) England
d. 1118   d. 1135

David = Maud of
d. 1153   Senlis

Matilda = Stephen I of
England

1) Holy Roman Emperor Henry V = Matilda
2) Geoffrey of Anjou   =

William Adelin
d. 1120

3. Selected Connections: Anglo-Saxon & Scottish

9

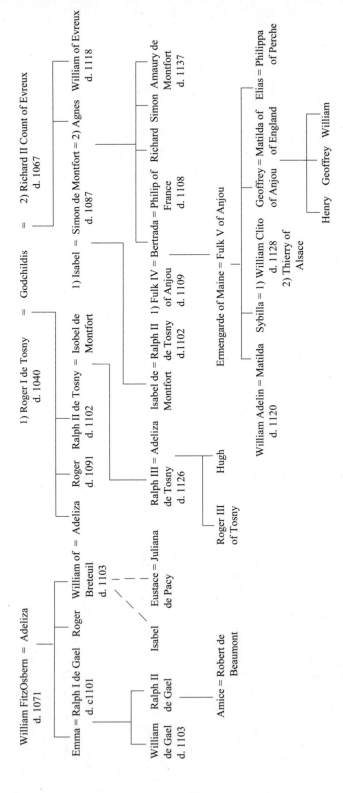

4. Selected Connections: Notable Norman Families

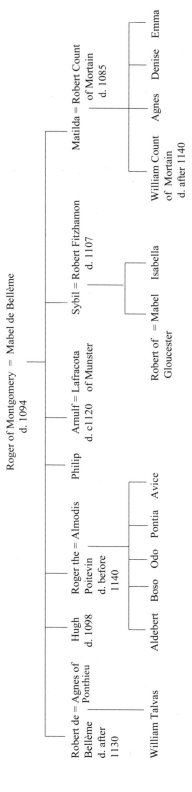

Roger of Montgomery = Mabel de Bellême
d. 1094

Robert de = Agnes of
Bellême   Ponthieu
d. after
1130

William Talvas

Hugh
d. 1098

Roger the = Almodis
Poitevin
d. before
1140

Aldebert   Boso   Odo   Pontia   Avice

Philip

Arnulf = Lafracota
d. c1120   of Munster

Robert of = Mabel   Isabella
Gloucester

Sybil = Robert Fitzhamon
d. 1107

Matilda = Robert Count
of Mortain
d. 1085

William Count
of Mortain
d. after 1140

Agnes   Denise   Emma

5. Selected members of the Montgomery Family

English Channel

Barfleur

Mont-St-Michel

Avranches

Carentan

Coutances

Bayeux

Mortain

Tinchebrai

Caen

Lisieux

Domfront

Almênêches

Argentan

Falaise

Pont-Audemer

Rougementier

R. Seine

Vatteville

Bourgtheroulde

Fecamp

St. Ceneri

Sées

L'aigle

St. Evroult

Montfort

Bec

Brionne

Harcourt

Conches

Evreux

Rouen

Pont-St-Pierre

Saint-Saens

Bures

Eu

Alençon

Bellême

Mortagne en-Thimerais

Verneuil

Breteuil

Nonancourt

Pacy

Brêmule

Tosny

Andely

Charleval

Lyons-la-Foret

Gournay

Aumale

Chateauneuf-en-Thimerais

Dreux

Ivry

Mantes

R. Seine

Montfort L'Aumary

Neufles

Gisors

Normandy in the eleventh/twelfth century

12

England and Wales

1

The Lion's Cubs
(1054–1087)

From the death of William the Conqueror to that of the last of his sons was a span of some forty-eight years. For about twenty of these, the sons fought each other in turn to obtain supremacy in the lands their father had conquered, while the victor spent a further twenty-two years trying to hold on to what he had gained. Small wonder, perhaps, that he provided only a single legitimate male heir to inherit the whole of his achievements, but even that plan was overthrown by a totally unexpected and freakish tragedy.

Throughout this time of struggle, Normandy suffered by far the worst of the violence, with neighbouring lands of France, Flanders and Anjou drawn into the fray at different points in the conflict. The Holy Roman Emperor and even the pope were also involved. England, though more peaceful, bore the brunt of paying for the fighting, albeit with an incidental benefit of developing a smooth-running system of administration and justice that operated well, even in the prolonged absence of her king.

A turbulent family, then, that of the Conqueror, though no doubt it would be foolish to expect anything else, given the background of the man at its head. William, bastard son of Robert Duke of Normandy and a tanner's daughter, had been thrust into the limelight at the age of six or seven when his father nominated him as his heir before departing on a pilgrimage to Jerusalem. When Robert died on the way home the following year, the child became, in name at least, Duke of Normandy. Thereafter, however, despite the Norman nobility having sworn oaths of loyalty to him, he had to fight, and fight hard, to make that title a reality. Further fighting would turn the name of William the Bastard into William the Great, and ultimately William the Conqueror, but it left its mark on a man most frequently described as grim, stern and formidable.

He had to struggle, too, for his wife, Matilda, daughter of Count Baldwin of Flanders and niece of the French king, Henry. The very fact that William asked for her hand in marriage shows the boldness of the young duke, only just secure himself in his duchy. It was certainly a prestigious match and something of a surprise when her father consented, but an alliance of Flanders, Normandy and France had advantages for all at the time, when the perceived enemy was the Holy Roman Emperor. The marriage, however, was forbidden by the pope, himself a German and no doubt well aware of the interests of the German Emperor, even if they were not explicitly stated. The excuse given was that William and Matilda were too closely related. Looking at their ancestors, it is hard to see how the pope could come to this conclusion, even though it was a common ploy at the time to prevent an inconvenient marriage. The sole connection seems to be that William's aunt was the second wife of Matilda's grandfather. Matilda herself, though, was descended from the first wife.

With or without the pope's permission, William went ahead with the marriage. Forbidden in 1049, it may have happened as early as the following year when Matilda's name first appeared as witness to a Norman charter. It was certainly a fait accompli by the time the prohibition was quietly withdrawn in 1053, at which time the pope himself was effectively a prisoner of the Normans from southern Italy, and at least three children of the marriage had been born before it was formally approved by a new pope in 1059. The penance demanded for the initial disobedience is still readily visible today in William's favourite city of Caen. The Abbaye aux Hommes, founded by William, stands a few hundred yards away from the Abbaye aux Dames, founded by Matilda, a testimony in stone to a partnership that was equally solid and long-lasting.

Although certainly a diplomatic triumph, there may even have been a little love there right from the start. It has been suggested that

William first laid eyes on Matilda at the court of her uncle, Henry of France, which is plausible, though the story attached to this – that she turned him down, that he pursued her to Flanders and that he dragged her from her horse by her braided hair to persuade her to marry him – is definitely not. William of Malmesbury, a monk who chronicled the times, says her 'obedience to her husband and fruitfulness in children, excited in his mind the tenderest regard for her,' which is a distinctly monkish view of the blossoming of love. It clearly was a loving relationship, however, and he adds that, when she died, William, 'weeping most profusely for many days showed how keenly he felt her loss.'

Fruitful, too, is a good description of the marriage. Four sons and at least five daughters were produced by William and Matilda over a period of about eighteen years, and though some are rather shadowy figures, a good number appear as strongly defined characters. Robert was the eldest son, born either in 1051 or 1054 depending on which account of the marriage is believed. He was probably followed by a daughter, Adeliza, who may be the one some Norman accounts declare was to marry Harold Godwinson, though she could only have been around twelve years old at the time. The next few years saw the arrival of Richard, William, Cecilia, Constance and possibly Matilda. Then there was something of a gap before the birth of Adela, around 1067, and Henry in 1068.

Daughters of the nobility had two possible career paths open to them, either to be married off in order to form territorial alliances, or to follow the life of a nun. Orderic Vitalis, based in Normandy, was another monk who produced a chronicle. It is he who names Adeliza as the prospective bride of Harold Godwinson, but he then muddies the waters in a later book by declaring that the daughter concerned was Agatha, a lady not mentioned elsewhere. This may simply be a mistake in the names, since he acknowledges at one point that he can't remember the names of all William's daughters. He does, however, add the circumstantial detail that after this marriage fell through, Agatha was betrothed to Alfonso, King of Leon and Castile, but didn't want to marry him because she had seen and loved Harold. The story goes that she prayed so hard to avoid the marriage that her prayers were answered and she died on the journey to meet her husband. On the other hand, another source suggests that Adeliza became a nun after her matrimonial disappointment, which is quite plausible but makes a less romantic ending to her story.

Cecilia, probably born in the later 1050s, was given as a child oblate to the Abbey of the Holy Trinity, the Abbaye aux Dames, founded by her mother. Giving a child to God was seen as a noble sacrifice at the time, and the presentation of Cecilia in 1066 might possibly be seen as some sort of bargain with the Lord for a happy outcome to William's planned conquest of England. Brought up at the abbey, she became a fully professed nun in 1075 and was later abbess. After her death in 1126, her tomb was apparently built into the walls of the abbey, with no way of accessing it, though for whatever reason we don't know.

The next daughter, Constance, was probably born around 1060. She was reputed to be the most gifted and her mother's favourite. This might account for her rather late marriage to Alan, Duke of Brittany in 1087. William had previously been at war with Brittany, and the marriage was intended to cement the friendship of the new duke. Sadly, Constance died childless a few years later, and there were rumours at the time that she had been poisoned.

Of Matilda we know almost nothing except that she was named in the Domesday Book as being William's daughter. The last daughter, Adela, on the other hand, comes across as a distinctly strong character. Born around 1067, she was married to Stephen, Count of Blois, again to form a territorial alliance, but she was to play a considerable role in the fortunes of her family.

The three eldest sons of William the Conqueror, Robert, Richard and William, would all have been born, like their sisters, in Normandy. We have no exact details of where they were born, though Rouen or Caen are the most likely places, and their birthdates are usually given as 1051, 1054 and 1058 respectively. These are only approximates, however, based on their later activities and the ages ascribed to them at their deaths.

With the last son, Henry, we can be a little more precise both as to the date and place of his birth. One thing that is certain is that Henry was born in England. Not only is this stated in a number of accounts and nowhere contradicted, but he used this to his own advantage when claiming the crown for himself. Traditionally his birth is given as sometime in the autumn of 1068, the evidence for this coming from chronicles written some fifty years later, but more importantly from the activities of his parents around this time.

William, of course, was engaged at the Battle of Hastings in October 1066, and further action kept him away from Normandy until March 1067. Matilda remained as his regent in Normandy during this time. For a large part of 1067 William and Matilda were together in Normandy, but early in December he returned to England, sending for his wife to join him the following Easter, which in 1068 fell on 23 March. Henry cannot have been born, then, before March 1068 since that is the first time his mother was in England, and he can only have been conceived before December 1067 or after March 1068.

Matilda was crowned Queen of England at Westminster on Whitsunday, 11 May 1068, and though one chronicle declares that she gave birth not many days later, it would seem unlikely that she would have risked a Channel crossing while heavily pregnant. The account of Orderic Vitalis, however, is open to different interpretations. Writing in Latin in the 1120s, he says, 'Being now crowned Queen, Matilda before a year was ended, gave birth to a son named Henry.' However, another translation has it as, 'before *the* year was ended,' giving rise to a debate as to whether Vitalis meant before 1068 had ended, or before a twelvemonth had passed from the date of Matilda's crowning.

Unlikely as it may seem, the town of Selby in Yorkshire has always claimed for itself the honour of being Henry's birthplace. Indeed, for centuries visitors were directed to a particular room where this event was said to have taken place. Unfortunately neither that room nor that building existed at the time. However, in 1068 there was a monk in Selby, newly arrived from Auxerre in France. There he had had a vision of St Germain telling him to go to Selby and build an abbey. At that time he had got no further than erecting a large wooden cross and perhaps a temporary wooden building but in 1069, he received a royal charter giving him the land on which to build his abbey and extremely generous grants of lands and privileges for its support. The only other abbey founded in England by William was at Battle, near Hastings, in commemoration of the victory won at that place. Furthermore, it is clear the foundation at Selby was made jointly by William and Matilda, the first and only time this occurred. It is true William might have wanted a religious house in the north to signify his conquest of the whole of England, but there seems little reason why Selby should have been chosen unless the place itself had some importance in the minds of the royal couple – such as the birthplace of a son.

The joint foundation is commemorated today in the twentieth-century south-transept window at Selby Abbey, where the monk, Benedict, is shown between William with his sword on one side, and Matilda with a piece of needlework on the other. Close inspection reveals that Matilda is stitching, not at baby clothes, however, but at the Bayeux Tapestry.

In 1068 William was drawn to the north of England to deal with an insurrection led by the Anglo-Saxon earls, Edwin and Morcar. The revolt collapsed as soon as he drew near with an army, but William spent some time in and around York, strengthening its defences and negotiating peace with northern lords and the Scottish king. It is quite possible that Matilda accompanied or followed him, at least as far as Selby, and there gave birth to her son. It seems most likely, then, that the traditional story is true, and that the youngest child of the Conqueror was born sometime in the autumn of 1068 at Selby in Yorkshire.

With three older brothers already bearing the names customarily associated with Norman dukes, this boy was named Henry, and tradition says he was named by his mother after her uncle, the French king. Though William's relationships with his French overlords had been stormy at times, he had received assistance at a crucial time from Henry, and was no doubt grateful enough for that earlier support to approve the choice of name.

It seems unlikely that the brothers would ever have been close, though we know little of the relationship between Robert and Richard. As the 'heir and a spare' they would probably have had a similar upbringing, acquiring the skill at arms expected of the sons of a Norman duke, and probably, too, being initiated at an early age into the running of a court and the administration of a duchy. They would have been 'educated', at least to the standard of the day, as we are told all the Conqueror's children were educated, even the girls. That might have involved little more than an ability to read and possibly write Norman French and perhaps a little Latin, though Robert at least seems to have been reasonably literate. There is a suggestion that at the end of his life he even learnt Welsh and was able to compose poems in that language. Like many boys, however, he may have been initially resistant to learning. In a later row with his father, he exclaims that he doesn't need a sermon from him, having had more than enough of them from his teachers.

It is possible that the third son, William, might originally have been intended for the Church. This was a common career path for younger sons, and many noble families produced a bishop or two, whether or not they had any real inclination towards the religious life. A prime example would be William's uncle, Odo, Bishop of Bayeux, and half-brother to the Conqueror. Although a bishop, he was certainly present at the Battle of Hastings, and though his apologists declare he struck no blows himself, he is depicted in the Bayeux Tapestry waving a mace and encouraging 'the boys' to further bloodletting. His later life, too, shows more inclination towards that of a robber baron rather than a prince of the Church.

The suggestion in relation to the younger William seems to be borne out by the fact that his education was entrusted, at an early age, to Lanfranc, at the time first abbot of St Stephen's Abbey – the Abbaye aux Hommes – in Caen, and later to become the Archbishop of Canterbury. Lanfranc, an Italian by birth, was one of the outstanding teachers of theology, logic and rhetoric of his time, but his rule was said to be severe and it is likely William showed little enthusiasm for learning. Indeed, in his later life William of Malmesbury declares 'he had neither inclination nor leisure to attend to learning.' It is more than possible that his time spent with Lanfranc gave him a lifelong distaste for the clergy, and a fierce jealousy of his older brother Robert, whose own upbringing would have been far more to his liking.

We can only speculate as to what, if anything, was originally intended for Henry, since family plans were likely to have been changed shortly after his birth by the death of his brother Richard. There are different accounts of how this came about and even the date is not certain. At the earliest it would have been in 1069, since that is the last year when he appears as witness to a charter. The latest is around 1075. Since Vitalis describes him as a youth 'who had not yet received the honour of knighthood' the earlier date is often preferred. He would at that time have been about fourteen years old, while the later date would put him at nearly twenty and far more likely to have been knighted by his father.

All accounts declare that Richard met his death in the New Forest, an area that was to prove singularly unlucky for the family of William the Conqueror. By the twelfth century, writers were declaring that this was God's revenge on William for destroying thirty-six parish churches and laying waste large areas of agricultural land to establish his hunting ground. This description, though, is highly misleading. We get a mental image of bullying Normans turning peasants off their land in order to plant a forest. In fact there may have been some farmsteads and a few small hamlets displaced, but, given the character of the soil in the area and the fact that England in general was more wooded than in later times, the change was mainly legal.

Declaring an area a 'royal forest' meant that the character of the existing wood and heathland could not be changed by agricultural development. No new holdings could be established, nor could boundaries around existing holdings be fenced. Those people who did live there now came under the 'forest law' designed to preserve the animals that, from that time on, could only be hunted and killed by the king and his friends. The animals included deer of various species, wild boar, hares, wolves and martens. The human inhabitants could have no weapons that might be used for hunting and, although they were allowed to keep watchdogs, these had to have their front two claws removed so they could not harm the protected animals.

This, no doubt, caused considerable hardship to people who had previously been able to supplement their poor farming by taking and eating deer and other animals. It was not, however, quite the same as being turned off the land wholesale. In the

Domesday Book relating to Hampshire, many entries record that 'the woodland of this manor is in the King's forest,' or that land was 'assessed at five hides; now at two hides because three hides are in the forest,' sometimes adding, 'The king put it there.' In a lot of cases, meadowland was excepted, which seems to indicate that the better grazing land was left outside the forest domain. In general, the taking of land into the forest brought about a reduction in the assessment of the land for tax, and there is even one entry where other land was given in exchange. In any case, the proclamation of the royal forest was not made until 1079, so it can hardly have had any bearing on the death of the king's son, Richard, which took place up to ten years earlier.

According to Vitalis, Richard was 'hunting in the new forest, not far from Winchester, and running down a stag at full speed.' He then, 'sustained a violent blow on the pommel of the saddle from a stout hazel bough and was mortally injured.' It is unlikely the monk was much of a horseman but what he describes most probably involved a misjudgement of the height of a low branch when riding at full pelt under a tree. Another version has the boy struck by a falling tree, which seems less likely, although more in accordance with the supposed wrath of God mentioned above.

William of Malmesbury, in an altogether different account, says Richard 'contracted a disorder from a stream of affected air'. However, this can be squared with the others if it is seen as some infection, or even pneumonia, brought on by the previous injury. Vitalis indicates that the death followed up to a week after the injury, giving ample time for 'confession of sins, absolution and the administration of the last sacraments.'

This death, in whatever way it was caused, raised William up to second in line to his father's dominions and would at once have put an end to any thought of a clerical career. Whether that was now the path laid out for young Henry is a matter for speculation but, if so, it may account for the more extensive education that came his way.

It was only in the 14th century that Henry was referred to as *Beauclerc* or 'fine scholar', a nickname that many feel overstates the matter. Nevertheless it is clear that he was better educated than his predecessors, and possibly placed a higher value on this accomplishment. According to William of Malmesbury, 'The early years of instruction he passed in liberal arts, and so thoroughly imbibed the sweets of learning that no warlike commotions, no pressure of business could ever erase them from his noble mind.' Vitalis confirms that, 'From his childhood his parents had devoted him to the study of letters.' A Victorian translation declares, 'He became admirably imbued with the knowledge of both moral and natural philosophy,' suggesting a study of the scientific speculations of the classical writers, as well as the more usual histories and philosophy.

We can, of course, only guess at the depth of his learning. He could certainly read and probably write Latin, and maybe French as well. At the time, English was the language of a conquered people, and it is very unlikely he would have read any of the many splendid Anglo-Saxon works that existed before the Conquest. He may, however, have picked up a smattering of the language, in the same way that English officers in the British Empire picked up a smattering of the Indian and African languages of the people they ruled.

There is a suggestion that Henry became boastful about his accomplishments. William of Malmesbury has a story of him declaring within the hearing of his father that, 'An illiterate king is a crowned ass.' If he did so before that famously illiterate and bad-tempered king, it argues a considerable degree of daring – or else complete confidence in a father's indulgence towards his youngest child. Very likely the story is made up, though a declaration from the same author that later, 'he neither read much openly nor displayed his attainments except sparingly,' suggests that at some point he had been firmly put in his place.

Where Henry acquired his education is not entirely clear. He would, of course, have spent his early years in Normandy with his mother's household, but later it is strongly suggested that he was attached to the household of Osmund, Bishop of Salisbury. They are certainly found together as charter witnesses over a period of some half a dozen years from 1080 onwards. This suggests Henry would have spent a great deal more time in England than either of his brothers, and would have had access to one of the finest minds, and one of the finest libraries, available at the time.

Osmund came from a noble Norman family. Some accounts claim he was related to the Conqueror himself, and he was certainly a trusted advisor, accompanying him on his expedition to England. He was Chancellor of England from 1070 until 1078, when he became Bishop of Salisbury. This was one of the newly created Norman bishoprics and at the time Osmund became bishop, a new cathedral was being built, alongside the new Norman castle, on the hill at Old Sarum, outside present-day Salisbury. The bishop seems to have been a man relatively free of personal ambition, devoted to God and king, not always in that order, and also to the love of learning. As well as supervising the building of the cathedral, which was consecrated in 1092, he also put together liturgies and rituals for the various sacraments of the Church, known as 'Sarum use', which were followed until the Reformation. Not only did he collect books but he copied, illuminated and bound them himself, behaviour which was noted as eccentric by a fifteenth-century writer, though it may have been less so at the time.

If young Henry had any degree of intelligence and curiosity at all, and later events suggest that he did, it is easy to see how exposure to this environment at a young age might have encouraged in him an appreciation of learning and a willingness to acquire such skills for himself. That he did so is evidenced not only by the later written accounts mentioned above, but also by the fact that he was acknowledged at the time as being better educated than his fellows.

In fact, he is an early example of a change that would soon spread throughout Western Europe. The so-called Dark Ages were at an end and the twelfth century would see a revival in learning and in the arts that was almost a mini-Renaissance. Soon the sons of even the highest nobles would be expected to acquire some gentler skills of learning, along with the military training of their youth, and the courts of Europe would become the patrons of writers, poets, historians and artists in a new flowering of early Medieval culture.

How much actual contact Henry had with his older brothers is debateable. By the time of his birth only Adela would have been left in the ducal nursery, which might explain the bond between those two, which lasted for life and was certainly not shared with any of the other siblings. William was at least eight years older and had already been dispatched to Lanfranc, while Robert, at up to seventeen years older, was practically grown up.

Robert, in fact, had already passed some significant milestones in the adult world. As part of his father's expansionist policy towards the County of Maine, he had been betrothed when about eight years old to Margaret, sister of the exiled Count Herbert whose cause William was pursuing. Margaret was some half-a-dozen years older. When the count died in 1062, William declared he had been promised the succession for Robert and his future wife and, in fact, the couple took part in a ceremony performing homage and swearing fealty to Geoffrey of Anjou for it. When Margaret died the following year William held on to the county and from 1063 onwards, Robert was, in theory at least, Count of Maine.

Again, in 1066, before he departed on his expedition to England, William had assembled all the Norman magnates and, in a traditional Norman ceremony, had them acknowledge Robert as his heir, perform homage and swear fealty to the boy who was, by then, in his mid-teens. At the time Robert took no part in the regency council that governed Normandy while his father was away – that role fell to his mother – but in 1068, when Matilda joined her husband in England, the chronicler William of Jumièges says that Normandy was committed to Robert as regent.

It seems likely, then, that there was very little interaction between the brothers and few opportunities to create real friendship. Nor did their father help in this respect. As is often the case with fathers and eldest sons, it seems that for some reason Robert fell short of his father's expectations. It was the Conqueror himself who bestowed on him the nickname that has stuck down through the centuries. Usually given as 'Curthose', the Latin equivalent in the chronicles is rendered *Curta ocrea*, literally 'cut off greave' or 'Short boots'. Since William is estimated to have been about 5 feet 10 inches tall, we can only assume that Robert disappointed his father by failing to achieve that height. It is not a kind nickname, however, and the fact that it was in general use – Vitalis refers to it as a 'surname' – seems to indicate that the Conqueror was indifferent to any disrespect shown to his son and heir. The other nickname given, though less commonly used, is *Gambaron*, possibly translated as 'Fat-legs', which again suggests the relationship between father and son was one of casual dominance and repeated humiliation. It is notable that neither of the other sons seem to have been treated in this way.

By the time Robert was in his early twenties, the Conqueror had another cause for concern about his eldest son. According to Vitalis, 'A set of factious young men took advantage of the inexperience of the king's son Robert by continually flattering him and urging him to fruitless enterprises.' These were, by and large, the sons of those magnates who had profited by their loyalty to the Conqueror. Among them Vitalis names Robert de Bellème, son of Roger of Montgomery, 1st Earl of Shrewsbury; William de Breteuil, son of William FitzOsbern the close friend and counsellor of the Conqueror; and Robert de Mowbray, nephew of Geoffrey, Bishop of Coutances. Ambitious and thrusting as their fathers had been, these young men expected from Robert the same benefits their fathers had received from his father. Of course, Vitalis was not there at the time, and the conversations he later records are imaginary, but he certainly had access to at least one impeccable source who *was* at court at that time, and it is likely he is correct in indicating the essential frustration of this younger generation at being kept from what they saw to be their due – and the equal reluctance of their parents to indulge their perceived extravagances. No doubt Robert himself was chaffing at the restraints put on him by his father, and by the fact that he was not allowed any real responsibility despite being nominally Count of Maine and heir-designate of Normandy. The demands of his flattering followers, however, cannot have helped the situation. 'Alas,' Vitalis has them say at one point, 'your great liberality is miserably curtailed by the poverty to which your father's parsimony restricts you,' while Robert is reported as 'listening like a raw youth.' Again, the confrontations with his father, as reported by Vitalis, are not verbatim accounts, but something very similar must have occurred. Robert is said to have demanded his own establishment, and even suggested that, while William had England, he might rule

Normandy, 'subject to fealty to you.' The reply was that such a suggestion was 'quite preposterous'. 'I will never suffer my native land of Normandy to pass out of my hands as long as I live,' declared the Conqueror, and advised his son to wait patiently for what was coming to him in due course, and to get rid of those followers who were urging him to make such demands. Robert, it is said, 'left his father's presence in great anger.'

There were no doubt a number of scenes like this and since by that time the younger William was almost certainly present at his father's court, he would have been well aware of what was going on. We are told that this William was his father's favourite, though why is not clear. His nickname, Rufus, came a lot later and is thought to refer to either the colour of his hair or beard, or to a ruddy complexion. Nor does it carry the insulting overtones implicit in that of his brother.

It is fairly clear that through his teens William Rufus was happy to play the role of dutiful son, making a marked contrast with his rebellious older brother. Quite possibly he was equally happy to take advantage of any situation that might make the split between William and Robert even wider. That certainly seems to be the explanation for an incident at L'Aigle in 1077, which involved all three brothers.

There, says Vitalis, 'a diabolical quarrel arose between the king's sons, from which sprung afterwards endless contentions and crimes.' Although Henry was involved, he was only eight or nine years old at the time, and almost certainly the dupe of William Rufus in what had the appearance of a childish prank but was, in fact, rather more sinister. The king and his three sons were together in Normandy, billeted in various houses in the town of L'Aigle. According to Vitalis, William Rufus and Henry went to the house where Robert was staying and, climbing to the gallery above the room where Robert was entertaining his friends, began a noisy game of dice. As if this was not annoyance enough, they then 'threw water on the heads of Robert and his hangers-on who were underneath'. This 'water' is clearly a euphemism, for later Vitalis has one of Robert's friends declare that the brothers 'shower their filth upon you and us in contempt.' Furthermore, they said, if he failed to punish them suitably then, 'You are a lost man and can never lift up your head again.' Robert immediately went to 'chastise' his younger brothers, and the row that followed drew the Conqueror himself from his nearby lodging to put an end to the quarrel. In doing this, he seems to have come down heavily on the side of his younger sons rather than the eldest and this reaction appears to have been the final straw as far as Robert was concerned. The very next night he rode away with a group of his followers and tried to attack his father's castle at Rouen. If his father would not give him Normandy, no doubt in the heat of the moment he felt justified in trying to take it for himself.

Needless to say, Robert failed to take the castle, and perhaps realising too late what they had done, he and his supporters fled, first to the castle of Robert de Bellème's brother-in-law at Chateauneuf-Thimerais and, when that came under attack from the furious Conqueror, further afield. Vitalis says that Robert went to his uncle, Robert of Flanders, but he then seems to mix this up with a later occasion, describing years of wandering when, in fact, this episode lasted little more than a year. He does, however, say that wherever Robert went, 'he stated his grievances, in which he often mixed falsehood with truth,' which may well be correct.

Wherever he went, he ended up with Philip of France, who, always happy to undermine William, set him up in a castle at Gerberoy on the border between France and Normandy. This was 'a very strong fortress, both from its site and its walls and other defences', and there Robert gathered around him a band of followers and their forces drawn from both France and Normandy, 'promising them … in return for their assistance, more than he could ever perform.'

Indeed he seems to have been continually short of money and received subsidies from a most unexpected source, his mother Queen Matilda. When William discovered this, he was not only furious but probably deeply hurt. 'My own wife, whom I love as my very soul,' he declares, 'succours my enemies who are plotting against my life, enriches them with my wealth, carefully supplies them with arms to attack me and abets and strengthens them in every way.' Matilda's response was to justify her actions by her 'tender affection for my first-born son'. If he were dead and buried seven feet under the ground, she declared, and she could bring him back to life at the expense of her own blood, she would shed it for his sake.

Although we usually take the grand speeches of Vitalis with a pinch of salt, we have an unusually good authority for this exchange, since William's next action is to fly into a rage and demand that the messenger who had carried the money to Robert, a Breton called Samson, be blinded for his part in the affair. Samson, however, was warned in time and fled to a monastery where he became a monk and remained for the next twenty-six years. The monastery was the one where Vitalis lived, arriving there as a ten-year-old some half-a-dozen years after Samson, so he must have known the man well.

Perhaps a little less reliable is the prediction of a hermit, which Vitalis claims Matilda obtained at this time. The hermit described a vision he had seen of a beautiful meadow clothed with grass and flowers, where a fierce horse lived. All round the meadow were herds of cattle yearning to come and eat the grass, but the high-bred horse kept them away. Then one day the horse disappeared and a 'lascivious heifer' became the guardian of the meadow. At once the herds of cattle barged in, ate the grass, trampled it underfoot and destroyed its beauty with their dung. When asked to explain this vision, the hermit declared that the meadow was Normandy, the grass and flowers its people and its churches. The high-bred horse was, of course, William the Conqueror, and the herds of cattle, the people of neighbouring lands who envied Normandy and wanted to plunder its riches. When William died, Robert, the 'lascivious heifer', would abandon himself to lust and sloth, and be treated with contempt by the enemies of Normandy, who would invade and despoil her territories. Whether or not this was written with hindsight, it would almost certainly not be what a doting mother wanted to hear, and the only consolation offered by the hermit was that Matilda would be dead and gone before any of this happened.

Robert's raids into Normandy, along with the betrayal by his wife, eventually persuaded William to take serious action against his son. At first he had laughed off Robert's exploits, saying, 'This little Robin Short-Boots will be a brave fellow,' but it had become more than a laughing matter. As a result, in January 1079, he set out to besiege Gerberoy with great vigour. With him, surprisingly, were not only his favourite son William Rufus, but also Philip of France, who must have undergone a change of heart since he had set Robert up in the castle.

The siege was clearly a lively one, with constant outbreaks of fighting when defenders sallied out to challenge their attackers. In one such outbreak, William and Robert unknowingly came face to face in combat and it was William that came off the worst. In fact according to one account, with a wound in his hand and his horse killed under him, the Conqueror was on the point of losing his life to his son when Robert recognised his voice. Horror-struck, he immediately gave him a horse and told him to ride away, which advice William was no doubt happy to accept.

In fact it was the shock of this incident which led to a patching up of relations between father and son. William himself took some persuading. Both he and William Rufus had been injured in the siege, and his pride, too, was hurt. The cooler counsels of some leading nobles – Roger of Shrewsbury, Hugh de Gournay, Hugh Grandmesnil and Roger de Beaumont among them – together with envoys from France and the Queen herself, eventually prevailed, however. Judging by later events, it was probably the Queen who had the greatest influence in persuading her son to confess himself at fault and be reconciled with his father.

In the end Robert was formally pardoned, along with his followers, and was reinstated in his position as heir designate. Again, William had the nobles pay homage to him, possibly the third time they had done this if Vitalis is to be believed, since he declares that on an earlier occasion when the king was ill the ceremony had already been repeated.

Although Robert's reconciliation may have been done largely to please his mother, the Conqueror appeared to accept his son's change of heart as genuine, and it may even be that his daring and prowess during the time of this estrangement had raised him a little in his father's estimation. Certainly in 1080, William trusted him enough to send him to the north of England to deal with an incursion by the Scottish king, Malcolm, who had broken the terms of an earlier peace treaty. Not only did Robert deal with the matter most efficiently, but in re-establishing the peace treaty he became friendly with Malcolm and is said to have stood as godfather to his daughter, Edith, born about this time.

Now is the time, too, when Henry seems to have spent some half-a-dozen years in England in the household of Osmund, Bishop of Salisbury, getting his education. We have no certain knowledge as to the whereabouts of William Rufus during this period, but the chances are that he remained with his father, as, too, did Robert. After 1081, however, neither is likely to have spent much time in England.

Fulk of Anjou, taking advantage of the Conqueror's absence in his English kingdom, was once again attacking Maine. Raising an army, which Vitalis estimates at 60,000 men (probably a significant exaggeration), William and his eldest son marched together, for the last time, to recover the county. Before the rival armies could clash, however, an intervention by monks led to a negotiated peace. Once again the suzerainty of Anjou over Maine was recognised, and again Robert performed homage for the county and was confirmed as count. This confirmation of his title should have made a difference – he was, after all, an adult now, not an under-aged youth – but, again, it did not. William carried on ruling Maine as before, adding another spark to the fire of rebellion that was probably already burning again in the breast of his son.

Late in 1083 Queen Matilda died and shortly afterwards, Robert quietly left his father's court, never to return. There seems to have been no final row this time, just an incompatibility that could not be overcome. Vitalis says Robert was 'too proud to attend or obey his father,' while William 'loaded him in public with accusations and reproaches for his disobedience.' It was at this time that the wandering described by Vitalis probably took place. Over a period of years Robert is said to have visited Lorraine, Germany, Aquitaine and Gascony. William of Malmesbury says he also visited Italy and wanted to marry Countess Matilda of Tuscany. Unsurprisingly, she turned him down. Young princes did not make matches for themselves and, in any case, the indigent Robert would not have held much appeal for the famously wealthy countess.

In the meantime, Henry's childhood was coming to an end. On 24 May 1086 he was dubbed a knight by his father at Westminster Abbey and the young prince would now be expected to play a full part in his father's court. There is evidence that on Queen Matilda's death the estates she held in England were left to her youngest son. This was not unknown at the time, the estates being intended to provide for a son who might otherwise have no practical means of support. Henry, however, was too young to take possession of this property. Twenty-one was the age at which a person could legally hold land. In the meantime, the king, as overlord, would legitimately hold it and take the profits from it, but the failure to hand it over later would become a source of friction between Henry and his brothers.

Both Henry and William Rufus would have been present at Old Sarum on 1 August of 1086, when the Conqueror called together 'all the landowners in England, whose vassals soever they were,' and required from each a personal oath that 'they would be faithful to him against all others.' This unprecedented oath was clearly intended to supersede any previously sworn to an intermediate overlord, and put the final stamp on the king's authority over all other landholders in England. It was not England, however, but Normandy that would present the Conqueror with the final crisis of his life.

After a period of travelling the courts of Europe, Robert had again arrived at that of his father's long-time enemy, Philip of France, and was again raiding Normandy itself with encouragement from that king. In the autumn of 1086, the Conqueror crossed into Normandy, certainly accompanied by William Rufus and probably by Henry, his intention no doubt being to deal once and for all with this ongoing threat to his lands and people.

There is evidence that the king was ill in the early part of 1087, a rare occurrence if the chronicles are to be believed. William of Malmesbury tells of Philip taunting him for keeping to his bed, 'like a woman after her delivery', a jibe that may also refer to the fact that the aging Conqueror now bore a belly like a pregnant woman. By the end of July, however, he had recovered enough to lead an army into the Vexin. This had long been disputed territory between Normandy and France, and there is no real evidence that Robert was directly involved in the trouble that had erupted there. William of Malmesbury even suggests it was Philip's taunt that drove William's determination to press home his claim to the land and, in particular, to launch an attack on the town of Mantes.

What happened then depends on which account is to be believed. Henry of Huntingdon, following the Anglo-Saxon Chronicle, declares that William burnt Mantes, destroying all the churches in the town and killing many people, including two holy hermits who were burnt alive there. 'Wherefore God in his anger visited him on his return with sickness, and afterwards with death.' Orderic Vitalis and William of Malmesbury make the link more specific. Vitalis says William was overcome by the heat of the burning town, while Malmesbury reports that 'some say' William was mortally injured when his horse leapt a ditch and the pommel of his saddle was driven into his stomach. Whichever is true, this was to be the king's final illness.

It is not certain whether any of his sons were present at Mantes but by the time William had returned to Rouen, both William Rufus and Henry, along with a large crowd of bishops and magnates, were to be found at his bedside. Vitalis emphasises that throughout William was in excruciating pain but nevertheless puts into his mouth an extended speech, reviewing his career and admitting to every crime the Anglo-Norman monk could throw at him. The final dispositions of the king, though greatly elaborated by Vitalis, are, however, corroborated in essence by other writers, and by events as they fell out.

Robert, of course, was not there, but he was nevertheless granted the Dukedom of Normandy, 'reluctantly and by compulsion,' Malmesbury says. Vitalis is a little more generous. Robert must inherit because he was the eldest and because the barons had already paid homage to him as heir as long ago as 1066. 'The grant thus made I cannot annul,' he has William say, and then, probably with the benefit of hindsight, 'But I know for certain that the country which is subject to his dominion will be truly wretched. He is a proud and silly prodigal.'

As far as England is concerned, Vitalis once again has the Conqueror in full confessional mode, admitting, 'I have persecuted its native inhabitants beyond all reason,' before declaring, 'Having made my way to the throne of that kingdom by so many crimes, I dare not leave it to anyone but God alone ...' This noble sentiment does not last long, however, since immediately afterwards, the king is offering the Almighty a large hint as to who should be favoured with the crown. 'I trust,' he says, 'that my son, William, who from his earliest years has always attached himself to me and been dutiful under all trials, ... may live long and prosperous ... and should it be the divine will that he succeed to the throne, his reign may be illustrious.' Then the king addressed a letter to Lanfranc, the Archbishop of Canterbury, on the appointment of a successor to the throne, sealed it with his seal, and gave it to William commanding him to embark for England without delay. The object of this is confirmed when, after kissing his son and bestowing a blessing, the king then tells him specifically to 'hasten his departure and cross the sea to secure the crown.' John of Worcester, writing about the same time as Vitalis, cuts through all this to give the view that was probably the English interpretation. The Conqueror, he says, 'made over the kingdom of England to his son William'.

As for Henry, in the account of Vitalis he initially cuts a rather pathetic figure. 'Henry, his youngest son, hearing that no provision was made for him out of the royal wealth, said sorrowfully to the king, "And what, my father, do you give to me?"' No doubt he felt he had been just as loyal and dutiful as William, and just as deserving of some reward – or possibly, at about eighteen years of age, he was beginning to wonder what future might await a landless, penniless younger son. He need not have worried. 'I bequeath you five thousand pounds of silver from my treasury,' came the answer. A generous gift, but possibly not what the boy had hoped for. 'What shall I do with this money, having no corner of earth which I can call my own?' he next asked, and now, with a gift of foresight that would have done credit to an Old Testament prophet, Vitalis has the king tell his son, 'Be contented with your lot and trust in the Lord ... you also, in your turn will succeed to all the dominions which belong to me and you will surpass your brothers in wealth and power.'

Once again these conversations are imaginary. Vitalis would have been about twelve years old at the time and newly arrived at the Abbey of St Evroult in Normandy, but it is likely he picked up the gist of what happened at the deathbed of the great King William from others who were there. Robert, of course, had already exhibited his prodigality, and William had clearly been the dutiful son for years, no doubt in the hope of reward. Malmesbury declares he was 'always exerting himself in (his father's) sight in battle, ever at his side in peace.' Henry, too, he suggests, had 'trained his early years to the hope of a kingdom,' and been encouraged in this by his father.

To a great extent, though, hindsight, and particularly the later characters of the actors, would have coloured the imagination of Vitalis. What is clear from his writing, however, is that there was little harmony and no trust between any of the brothers, even at this early date. William rode straight off to claim a kingdom that some would say he had no right to at all, while Henry was equally prompt in securing his money. 'He had it carefully weighed, that there might be no deficiency, and, summoning his friends in whom he could confide, sought a place of safety in which to deposit his treasure.' A careful man, Henry, even at the age of eighteen!

So when the Conqueror finally breathed his last on 9 September 1087 there was no member of his family present to lead the prayers for his soul, to organise his funeral, or even to take charge of the body. And with no controlling authority in place to do these things, it seems chaos ensued. The magnates disappeared to their estates, the bishops to secure their own lands, and even the servants were seized with a kind of madness, stripping the royal apartments of anything of value and, by some accounts, leaving the body of the king lying naked on the floor. For those, Vitalis among them, looking for a moral involving the downfall of the mighty, this could not be bettered, though he assures his readers it is 'not a well-feigned tragedy ... but a true narrative.'

Nor did matters improve when at last the clergy of the nearby church of St Gervase returned to say the prayers for the dead. The Archbishop of Rouen decided that William's body should be transported to Caen and buried in the Abbey of St Stephen, which the Conqueror himself had founded. Once again, though, no family member could be found to take charge of the body. William Rufus was already crossing the Channel and Henry, no doubt, was busy at the treasury. In the end a 'country knight' that Vitalis names as Herluin, arranged for the body to be prepared and transferred by water and by land to Caen, a journey itself fraught with complications.

By the time of the funeral, in the still unfinished Abbey Church of St Stephen, Henry had returned to pay proper respect to his father's body. Again drawing a moral from the Conqueror's end, the Anglo-Saxon Chronicle comments that, 'He who had been a powerful king and the lord of many territories, possessed not then, of all his lands, more than seven feet of ground.' In fact William did not possess even as much as that. In the middle of his funeral, as the presiding cleric, Gilbert of Evreux, concluded his oration by asking those who in any way William had offended to forgive him, a loud interruption was made by one Ascelin. He declared that the abbey church itself had been built on land belonging to his father and no proper compensation had been paid. Some rapid haggling then took place and it was Henry who agreed to pay the considerable sum the man demanded, thereby allowing the funeral to proceed.

As a final indignity, Vitalis records that the grave, under the lantern tower, had been made too small – much less than the 'seven feet of ground' recorded in the Chronicle. When they tried to force the body into it, he says, the stomach burst and the stench that resulted brought a rapid end to the funeral of the mighty Conqueror. It has been claimed, however, that this was simply a malicious rumour, put about later. When in 1522 the tomb was opened, apparently the embalmed body was revealed as still intact.

Some time after the funeral William Rufus gave gold, silver and precious stones for a suitably magnificent monument to be erected over the place where his father lay, and later still an effigy was added. Nothing of this remains, however. In 1562 a Protestant mob invaded the church and destroyed, among other things, the Conqueror's tomb. All the remains were lost except one thigh bone, which now lies under the plain tombstone found in front of the high altar.

The King of England was dead, but very shortly a new King of England would be consecrated and crowned in Westminster Abbey. The Duke of Normandy was dead, and affairs in Normandy were about to suffer 'a great revolution.' Meanwhile Henry would have to adjust from being a loved and favoured son, to being just an unregarded younger brother.

2

King, Duke and Count
(1087–1100)

No man can serve two masters, so the Bible tells us, but that is exactly what most of the Anglo-Norman nobles were asked to do after the death of William the Conqueror. He had never intended that situation to arise, never intended to divide up his possessions, but circumstances had forced his hand. Robert must have Normandy, but he would not be rewarded for his treachery with the gift of England as well. William could have England, but the Norman nobles would not accept any usurpation of his elder brother's rights. And Henry – Henry must shift as well as he could between the two, with the money his father had left him.

We have pen portraits of all three brothers provided by the various chroniclers. Vitalis tells us that Robert was 'very bold and valiant and a strong and sure archer; his voice was loud and clear; his tongue fluent; his features dull and heavy, his body stout, his stature short; whence he commonly received the surname Gambaron or Curthose.' As far as character went, however, he was 'inconsiderate in conducting his affairs, profuse in spending and liberal in his promises, while no dependence could be placed on them'. Later the words sloth and indulgence would be most commonly applied as descriptions of his behaviour.

The adult William Rufus is described by Malmesbury as 'well set; his complexion florid, his hair yellow; of open countenance; different-coloured eyes, varying with certain glittering specks; of astonishing strength, though not very tall and his belly rather projecting; of no eloquence, but remarkable for a hesitation of speech, especially when angry.' Whether it was the severity of Lanfranc or the dominance of his father that produced his stammer is impossible to say, but it no doubt increased his jealousy of his eloquent brother. In character William Rufus was 'imperious, daring and warlike ... distinguished for his valour and secular magnificence', but 'a young man of loose and debauched morals,' 'prone to pride, lust and other vices,' and with 'scanty zeal for the worship of God.'

Physically, when fully grown, Henry seemed to resemble his brothers, except as regards hair. He was 'of middle stature, exceeding the diminutive but exceeded by the very tall; his hair was black, but scanty near the forehead; his eyes mildly bright; his chest brawny; his body fleshy.' In disposition, though, he seems altogether a different creature. Malmesbury tells us that 'He was plain in his diet, rather satisfying the calls of hunger than surfeiting himself by variety of delicacies. He never drank but to allay thirst; execrating the least departure from temperance in himself and in those about him.' Furthermore, he adds, he was a heavy sleeper and snored.

None of the brothers was married, although by then Robert was in his mid-thirties and William his late twenties. Since his short-lived engagement as a child to the sister of the Count of Maine, no other arrangement had been made for the Conqueror's eldest son. It is almost certain, though, that by this time he had three illegitimate children. One of these, a daughter, would be married to a minor lord, Helias of Saint-Saens, thus securing his loyalty to Robert and his cause for life. We know nothing of her mother, or of the mother of his illegitimate sons, Richard and William, except that the latter is described as being the handsome concubine of an elderly priest who lived on the borders with France. It is most likely that Robert's liaison there took place during the time when he was in revolt against his father, and it is possible that the boys may have been twins. What seems apparent from the story is that the affair did not last long and that Robert was not initially aware that he was a father. Nor can his affection for the woman have been very strong, since, when she later appeared at his court with the boys, he denied any involvement. Only when she had 'publicly carried red-hot iron and received no injury,' in other words, proved her case by trial by ordeal, did he accept that the boys were his and arrange for their upbringing.

No marriage had been arranged for William Rufus, either. The monk chroniclers of the day, in fact, hinted in the strongest manner that he was homosexual, a practice that, at the time, was regarded as one of the gravest sins. It is generally claimed that he never produced any children, however in the 17th century a compiler of the history of English kings, one Richard Baker, claimed that William had an illegitimate son called Bertrann, for whom he arranged a suitable marriage. Where this information came from is a complete mystery, particularly as, at the time, Baker was in Fleet Prison for debt. His writings are most commonly labelled 'unreliable'.

Within a very few weeks of the Conqueror's death, each of the new rulers had moved to claim his title. Robert returned to Rouen, the ancient capital of Normandy, and with no sign of opposition, became, as Vitalis puts it 'in name at least, duke of Normandy and lord of Maine'. In the meantime the letter William presented to Lanfranc helped smooth his way to the throne of England. It has been suggested the archbishop felt some qualms about the nomination of the new king but eventually accepted it, and what Lanfranc accepted, the country accepted. The old Anglo-Saxon method of electing a new king had died at the time of the Conquest and no formal machinery had yet replaced it. So on Michaelmas Day, 29 September 1087, William Rufus was crowned at Westminster Abbey as William II of England.

Neither of the new rulers had any experience of governing. The Conqueror's policy of keeping all power in his own hands, one of Robert's loudest complaints, meant that, while they may have *watched* a strong ruler at work, neither had ever had the chance to practise what they had seen. Their reaction to their father's deathbed wishes, however, is instructive. He had ordered that all the prisoners he still held should be freed, albeit with reservations about his half-brother Odo, Bishop of Bayeux. Robert duly freed those he found in his duchy, including Duncan, the son of his friend

King Malcolm of Scotland. William took with him to England two notable Anglo-Saxon prisoners, Morcar, a former Earl of Northumbria, and Wulfnoth, youngest son of Earl Godwin. Both had been imprisoned for a considerable number of years. Far from freeing them, though, in accordance with his father's wishes, when they reached England they found they had merely exchanged one prison for another. It seems clear William was not going to take the slightest risk of any challenge to his own authority by setting free a potential focus for Saxon discontent.

While William's accession and first few months in England passed off peacefully, the lifting of the strong hand of government in Normandy brought about very different results. It seems that the land-holding nobles on each side of the Channel had had ample opportunity to size up the characters of those now set over them, and they acted accordingly. Even as the Conqueror lay dying his magnates were taking matters into their own hands, deserting his bedside and riding to take control of their own estates. Robert de Bellème never even made it to the bedside. This son of Roger of Montgomery had inherited his mother's extensive lands in southern Normandy some years before but until this time, all his many castles had been garrisoned by the Duke's men. Now he instantly threw out these garrisons and replaced them with his own, as did most of his fellows across the land, 'so that everyone might be able to prosecute with impunity his infernal feuds against his neighbours.' As Vitalis, who lived in the midst of the worst of these feuds, tells us, 'the unarmed population shuddered with alarm, while the powerful gave full vent to their towering ambition without any check.'

Henry, too, would have weighed up the characters of his brothers and decided where his best interests lay. With money but no land, his position was weak. Money was a diminishing asset, whereas land gave not only revenue but power. Nor could he rely on the generosity of his brother William, now King of England. William had benefitted by being the good son who remained true to his father when Robert rebelled – but Henry, too, had taken his father's side, and had, no doubt, been viewed as a rival for his favour. By all accounts Robert had the more forgiving nature, and though they had recently been on opposing sides, it was to Robert, therefore, that Henry went in search of advancement.

A number of charters issued by Robert in the autumn of 1087 and early 1088 were witnessed by 'Henry, my brother.' Some sources even suggest the nineteen year old became a trusted counsellor to the new duke. By March 1088, however, the designation had changed, and Henry had become 'Count Henry'. Events were moving in Normandy and England and with a shrewdness beyond his years, the boy had been quick to obtain an advantage.

We don't know if Robert had anticipated being King of England. Nor do we know his reaction when that title went to his younger brother. He seems, however, to have accepted the situation and made no move to change it until roused to do so by another player in the game, his uncle, Odo of Bayeux.

That noble bishop had once been the most powerful man in England, after his half-brother the Conqueror, but a swift fall from grace had found him a prisoner at Rouen at the time of William's death. According to Vitalis, the traditional deathbed pardoning of prisoners had expressly excluded him, and it was only the pleading of their brother, Robert of Mortain, that eventually secured Odo's release. Even then Vitalis, no doubt with the benefit of hindsight, has the Conqueror declaring, 'I wonder that your penetration has not discovered the character of the man... It is against my own judgement that I permit my brother to be liberated ... for be assured he will cause the death or the grievous injury of many persons.' Less than six months later this warning proved correct.

Once freed, Odo had quickly established himself as the chief counsellor to his nephew Duke Robert. He had also visited England and been restored to his extensive estates there, though, according to William of Malmesbury, he quickly found his influence in England had been overtaken by that of Lanfranc, and by William's preferred adviser the Bishop of Durham, William of St Calais. We could be generous and suppose that Odo really felt Robert had suffered an injustice in losing the throne of England. It is much more likely, however, that he believed the overthrow of William Rufus, and especially his enemy Lanfranc, would restore his own power and influence over both England and Normandy when the weak Robert Curthose was nominal ruler of both.

Certainly all accounts agree that it was Odo who first began whispering treachery into the ears of the Anglo-Norman nobles, and his whispers fell on fertile ground. The nobles' position was neatly summed up by Vitalis. 'If we do our duty to Robert ... we shall offend his brother, William. It will follow that we will forfeit our great revenues and high powers in England. On the other hand, if we keep our fealty to King William, Duke Robert will take from us our patrimonial estates in Normandy.' Had the brothers been friendly there would have been no problem, but how could they serve 'two lords so different and so remote from each other'. Nor did it take long for Odo to persuade them which they should choose. William was 'youngest and most arrogant, and we owe him nothing.' Robert was the 'elder brother, and of a more pliable temper and to whom we have already sworn fealty.'

The whispering probably began at Christmas 1087 when all would have been gathered at the court of William Rufus for a show of magnificence designed to impress those who had been absent from his hurried coronation. The Anglo Saxon Chronicle says that the king thought highly of Odo, but that the bishop 'purposed to do by him as Judas Iscariot did by Our Lord'. At this stage Robert was not involved. Only later, when their plans were maturing, did they announce their intentions to him. 'The principal Frenchmen' in England are accused by the Chronicle, and certainly Odo seems to have spread his net widely. Among those supporting the rebellion were the Earl of Shrewsbury, Roger of Montgomery, and his sons, with extensive lands in Shropshire and Sussex; the Earl of Northumberland, Robert Mowbray, and his uncle, Bishop Geoffrey of Coutances; Odo's brother Robert of Mortain, with lands in Cornwall and Somerset; William of Eu in the west of England; Robert of Rhuddlan in north Wales; Roger de Lacy and Bernard de Neufmarché along the Welsh Marches; Gilbert of Clare in Suffolk and Kent; Hugh de Grandmesnil in Leicester, and Roger Bigod in East Anglia.

'The plan was concerted during Lent,' says the Chronicle, 'And as soon as Easter came (16 April) they marched forth and plundered and burned and laid waste the lands of the Crown.' The lands around Bristol and Bath were laid waste by Robert Mowbray and his uncle, those around Leicester and Northampton by Hugh de Grandmesnil, while Roger Bigod plundered around Norwich and William of Eu devastated the royal estates around Berkeley. Roger de Lacy sacked Hereford, and he and Bernard de Neufmarché led a force to attack Worcester. Meanwhile in the south-east Robert of Mortain, Gilbert of Clare and Odo himself fortified their castles at Pevensey, Tonbridge and Rochester respectively, and rode out to plunder all those estates around that showed support for William, giving particular attention to the estates of Lanfranc. William must have wondered what had hit him.

Though a latecomer to the scheme, Robert in Normandy was enthusiastic and had he moved quickly with Norman forces behind him, he might have achieved complete success. He did, indeed, dispatch Eustace the Younger of Boulogne and Robert de Bellème with their retainers as an advance force, and set about raising an army to support them, but this required money and vigour, two commodities always in short supply for Robert.

Although he had inherited great wealth in the ducal treasury at Rouen, he had been generous in disposing of this to the Church and to his followers in the short months of his rule. Indeed, Henry had been well advised to quickly count and remove his inheritance before Robert arrived. It was, in fact, to Henry that Robert now turned in his need. A loan was refused – the younger brother could drive a much harder bargain than that – and eventually it was agreed that Henry should receive lands in western Normandy in exchange for £3,000 in silver.

The lands in question comprised the Cotentin peninsular, with all the Norman lands of Hugh d'Avranches, Earl of Chester. The title of Count of the Cotentin went with this, making Henry overlord of the Cotentin, Coutances, Avranches, Mont St Michel, and, some have suggested, even parts of the Bessin in the direction of Bayeux and Caen. Together this comprised something like a third of the lands and revenues of Normandy, and represented a considerable return for his money.

It has been claimed that Robert intended this grant to last only until he repaid the money, but the title of count suggests something more permanent, while Vitalis makes clear that 'the duke ... was ready to *sell* him part of his territories.' The majority of the barons with lands in the area seemed happy enough with their new overlord, who, far from rushing to join the rebellion in England, was content to take possession of his new lands and govern them quietly. In return, many of those he now ruled became his supporters for life.

Meanwhile in England, William – who Malmesbury describes as 'deficient neither in prudence nor in good fortune' – was keeping his head whereas a lesser man might have surrendered in the face of overwhelming odds. It was a heavy blow when his trusted advisor William of St Calais quietly detached himself from the court and returned to his own lands in the north. On the other hand, the attack on Worcester was thwarted by the prayers of the venerable Bishop Wulfstan, then in his eighties, and the efforts of the local garrison and citizens, who marched out against the odds and defeated their attackers amidst fields of burning crops.

By his usual methods of bribery, smooth talking and promises, William Rufus began to fight back. He persuaded Roger of Montgomery to abandon the rebel cause by dint of reminding him that, 'the same person made him king, who made them earls,' and that their powers could be removed as easily as his own if that authority was overturned. Then, with his fellow Normans against him, he appealed to his English subjects. He promised them the best laws they had ever had, an end to unjust taxes and the relaxation of the hated forest laws. It worked. The bishops, by and large, supported him, Lanfranc supported him, the English supported him, and even some Normans and other 'Frenchmen', such as Alan the Red of Brittany, supported him. With their help he set out to break the heart of the rebellion in the south-east of England.

Robert was still in Normandy, and an advance party of troops he had sent to aid Eustace and Robert de Bellème had been attacked and defeated in the Channel by English sailors, who, the Chronicle tells us, 'slew and drowned more than anyone can number.'

Odo was, therefore, the key, and it was to Odo's territory of Kent that William directed his forces.

Tonbridge surrendered in a matter of days and the royal army prepared to besiege the strong fortress at Rochester, where Odo was believed to be. Receiving news, however, that he had escaped to his brother's castle at Pevensey, they diverted there, setting up a siege around the mighty Roman walls that lasted six weeks. It took that long for the inmates to be starved into submission, but then with Odo and Robert of Mortain as prisoners, it seemed the rebellion was collapsing. The end should have been swift, especially as Odo agreed to persuade those holding Rochester to surrender to the king. There was, however, to be a sting in the tail. Sent ahead of the main force with a small escort, Odo arrived at the castle only to be 'captured', willingly or not, by a sortie from inside, who then became themselves besieged by the bulk of William's forces.

It was by now high summer and the castle was packed with men, not only the usual garrison but those who had rallied to them, including Eustace and Robert de Bellème and all their retainers. As time passed hunger and thirst were not the only problems. Vitalis writes of a Biblical plague of flies, 'like the plague of the Egyptians', that infested the place. Bred on the dung and the corpses of the besieged that could not be disposed of, they swarmed so thickly that men could not eat without first driving away a cloud of flies from their food.

By the end of June it was clear that Robert's promise of a large force to support the rebellion, and a personal appearance at their head, was as unreliable as most of his promises. According to the chroniclers he had frittered away his money on expensive mercenary soldiers, and his time in idleness, and seeing the reverses suffered by his supporters in England, had given it up as a bad job. On a charter dated 7 July 1088 he rather wistfully notes that it was 'the day I should have set off for England.'

Some time before that Odo and his fellows had begun to sue for peace with William, rather boldly suggesting that they should be reinstated in their lands and would then serve him faithfully. Incensed by the idea, he declared he would hang them all, but was dissuaded from this. Many of those inside the castle had relatives outside who had not joined the rebellion. In particular Roger of Montgomery, a precious and fragile convert to William's cause, had three sons among the besieged, Robert de Bellême being the eldest. Vitalis devotes several pages of noble speeches to the argument, the gist of which has William declaring that if he lets them go they will rebel again, while the nobles reply that the rebels have learnt their lesson and, if he shows them mercy, 'He who is your enemy now, may be your useful friend another time.'

In the end they were permitted to leave with their horses and arms, much to the annoyance of the English who yelled, 'Halters! Bring halters and hang this traitor bishop and his accomplices,' as they rode through the crowd of besiegers. Odo was banished for life and never set foot in England again. Of the rest, probably guided by Lanfranc, William pardoned and reinstated some of the more important, such as William of Eu and Robert Mowbray, while others lost their lands. Even some of these regained them later, when they had worked their way back into the king's favour.

It took some time for William to lay hands on William of St Calais, who only agreed to appear before his court when granted a safe conduct. There he ran rings around those attempting to try him for treason and, much to the fury of Lanfranc, tried to claim instead that he had been mistreated by the king and his officers. Furthermore, he declared he could only be tried by canon law – that is, the law of the Church – and he demanded to be allowed to go to Rome and put his case to the pope. In the end William seized his lands and expelled him from the country, but only after taking possession of Durham Castle, and with the proviso that the ships that carried him and his retinue to Normandy must be sent straight back and not detained for the use of Robert.

In Normandy, Robert was already regretting the bargain he had made with Henry. Left now with neither money nor land, he was probably also jealous of the good order in the part of the duchy ruled by his brother, which showed up the chaos in the part under his own weak rule. There, Vitalis tells us, 'fire, robbery and homicide were matters of daily occurrence,' while 'strong places were everywhere constructed without lawful authority, where the sons of robbers were nourished like wolves' whelps to mangle sheep.'

When Robert demanded his land back, Henry merely set about strengthening the defences on his castles, and felt secure enough in the late summer of that year to travel to England. He had got what he could from Robert. Now he would try to see if his other brother would hand over to him the lands he should have inherited from his mother. At first all seemed well. 'King William received him graciously, as became a brother,' says Vitalis, 'And granted him fraternally all that it was in his power to bestow.' This rather strange way of putting it may hint that he had already granted the lands to someone else. Certainly, despite the king's fine words and promises, they never came to Henry. In fact the lands were included in a grant made to Robert Fitzhamon, one of the few Normans to support William Rufus throughout the rebellion earlier that year. This reward, which also comprised the feudal Barony of Gloucester, brought him to prominence as a landholder in England, while his lands in the Bayeux area of Normandy came under Henry's overlordship as Count of the Cotentin. Strangely, there seemed to be no animosity between the two as a result of the land grant. In fact they later became staunch allies and close friends.

No doubt Henry soon came to realise he would get nothing more out of his brother in England, but they seem to have parted on good terms. So far he had managed the balancing act well. He had taken no sides in the contest between Robert and William, and had even succeeded in coming out ahead of the game with his lands in Normandy. Now, however, he was to find just how precarious his position really was.

He sailed back to Normandy on the same ship as Robert de Bellême, newly released and expelled from England after his part in the rebellion. Robert was some ten years older than Henry, and already establishing the reputation for cruelty that would follow him through the years. He had been an early supporter of Robert Curthose even back to the days of their youthful revolt against the Conqueror, and his lands in Normandy bordered those of Henry. Given these attributes it is hard to see what they might have had in common, nor is it known what, if any, communication they shared during the voyage. Their presence together, however, was enough for an inspired schemer to work on, and according to Vitalis that schemer was Odo of Bayeux.

Already expelled from England, Odo had rapidly resumed his place as chief advisor to his nephew, Robert, but Vitalis declares that '... finding Duke Robert sunk in slothful ease (he) set himself to acquire the mastery over the whole of Normandy'. Odo's power in England had been checked, first by the Conqueror and now by his son. He could foresee no such check in Normandy at the hands of its easy-going duke. The only challenge was likely to come from the more powerful and forceful barons within the land, Robert de Bellème, for instance, who was also friend and advisor to Curthose. Similarly, something like a third of the territory was at present being ruled by the young Count of the Cotentin, and this arrangement, too, should be ended. It was to Odo's advantage, therefore, that both Robert and Henry should be removed and, if possible, all their lands brought into the hands of the duke, who would then, of course, be ruled by Odo.

Thus, 'malevolent sowers of discord who mix falsehood with truth' whispered to Duke Robert that his brother, Henry, and his friend, Robert de Bellème, had not only made peace with William Rufus in England, but had also taken an oath to support William against the duke. As a result, even as these two landed from their ship they were 'seized and fettered' and given over to Odo to imprison. Henry was held at Bayeux and Robert at Rouen.

No-one interceded on behalf of Henry, but Robert's father, Roger of Montgomery, with encouragement, no doubt, from William Rufus, crossed the channel to demand his son's release. Now Odo stirred the duke into action, declaring that with a little effort and resolution he could rid himself of the entire family and take all their strongholds in western Normandy for his own. Indeed, Odo volunteered to lead an army himself. He was certainly at the head of the forces that took the castle at Ballon in Maine from those reluctant to acknowledge their Norman count, then joined with Duke Robert to besiege an almost impregnable fortress at Saint Céneri. When this was starved into submission, the unusual savagery of Robert in blinding the castellan and mutilating many others may also be down to the influence of

Bishop Odo. It had an effect, however, in that those holding other fortresses of the Montgomery family at Alençon, Bellème and other places were prepared to surrender to the duke as soon as he requested it. He never did.

With much more characteristic loss of interest, Robert abruptly called off his campaign and returned to Rouen, disbanding his army on the way. Envoys were sent from Roger of Montgomery, 'fair-speaking', and 'demanding peace and his son's release with many empty promises.' No doubt the promises concerned the future loyalty and good behaviour of his son, both of which would be highly questionable. Curthose, though, 'imprudent and fickle, and easy to be persuaded,' agreed to the release, which he must have regretted almost at once. Vitalis declares that as soon as Robert de Bellème regained his liberty he became, 'more insolent than ever, paid little attention to the orders or threats of the duke, and ... took a long and multiplied vengeance for his wrongs.'

No mention is made of Henry but it appears that he was released about the same time, having spent some six months in custody. Again, his feelings towards his brother are not recorded and he seems to have been allowed to return to his lands in the Cotentin, but no doubt he was now fully on his guard and prepared for further attempts to undermine his position. There is no evidence, though, that Robert's ill-treatment made him transfer his support to William. As before, he seems to have kept himself out of his brothers' quarrels.

These quarrels were about to enter a new phase. William was not one to forgive and forget the rebellion that might have cost his throne, nor the fact that it was undertaken in Robert's name. As early as 1089 he was sounding out his nobles on the subject of sending an army to Normandy, but initially his 'invasion' was of a more insidious kind. By persuasion and bribes he began to tempt those with holdings in the north-east of Normandy to transfer their allegiance, and with it their useful lands and fortresses, to him. Stephen of Aumale on the River Bresle was one of the first, followed by Gerard of Gournay a little to the south. Robert of Eu at the mouth of the Bresle soon joined them, with Reginald of St Valery at the mouth of the Somme, Walter Giffard further west on the River Scie, Ralph of Mortemer and Ralph de Tosny, the last two being close to the River Seine, south of Rouen. Slowly but surely William was ringing his brother with a chain of potential enemies to the north and east of the Seine, and it was probably as an attempt to counter this that Robert married his illegitimate daughter to Helias of Saint-Saens, whose lands were right in the middle of this area, and who was also given castles at Arques and Bures. Helias would become Robert's most faithful supporter.

For a time, too, Robert was supported by his overlord, Philip of France, who took action to restore at least one castle to the duke. His assistance, however, was short-lived, for, as the Anglo-Saxon Chronicle records, 'For love of William or for his great bribes,' he soon decided to return to France. As with the others, it was more likely the money rather than the love that brought about the change of attitude, and by this time this was costing England dear. It is again the Chronicle that notes, 'During all these transactions, England was greatly oppressed by unlawful taxes and many other grievances.'

By 1090 it seemed that William's bribes might secure him the very heart of Normandy, Rouen itself, the capital and seat of the dukes. Some of his agents had infiltrated the city, stirring up discontent among citizens already suffering from the state of near anarchy that existed throughout the land, and which their duke seemed unwilling or unable to control. A leader was needed, sympathetic to William and ready to act as a focus for this discontent, and it was found in the person of Conan, a wealthy burgher whose large household of dependants and retainers was almost a private army. More than happy to accept William's money and promises, Conan agreed a plan to hand over the city to the king's men. When all was ready a message was sent in October 1090 to William's supporters waiting in their castles to the east, appointing a day when the gates of Rouen would be thrown open to them. Unfortunately for Conan, Robert got wind of this plot and immediately began calling up his own followers to come and defend the city. Surprisingly, among those called were Henry and Robert de Bellème – and, perhaps even more surprisingly, they came.

Henry, indeed, came so quickly that he had already brought his reinforcements to join his brother in the castle at Rouen before the action began on 3 November. On that day, Reginald of Warenne led 300 of William's men to the west gate expecting an easy admission to the city. At the same time, however, Gilbert of L'Aigle arrived at the south gate with a troop of horsemen in Duke Robert's service. While some of the citizens rushed to open the gates to Reginald, others endeavoured to prevent the entry of Gilbert, and others again, not of Conan's faction, did their best to attack their fellow citizens at each gate on behalf of the duke.

In the midst of this chaos Robert Curthose and Henry, together with their followers, came charging out of the castle, but whereas Henry immediately pitched into the fray, Robert kept charging on. Out of the east gate, he went, into a boat and across the Seine to take refuge in the church of Notre Dame du Pré on the other side. Even without him, however, his side was winning the contest. Gilbert and his men had forced their way in to join Henry, and battle raged in the streets with the citizens and the king's men, who also had got into the city. Vitalis gives a stark account of the struggle. 'The city,' he says, 'resounded with cries of grief and terror … The innocent and guilty alike were everywhere butchered, or captured or driven to flight.'

It was William's men that were fleeing, though, finding the confused situation and sturdy resistance not at all what they had expected. Those that had not been captured or killed managed to escape the city and hide themselves in a nearby wood until, under cover of darkness, they crept away, back to their castles in the east.

Meanwhile the fighting in the city was over. Robert returned, victorious but with his prestige severely damaged. He claimed that it was his advisors who had hustled him out of the action lest, in the confusion, he might be accidentally slain. No-one really doubted his courage, but once more he had acted in a way that no Duke of Normandy should act. Nor did his proposal to pardon the wrong-doers go down well. Instead the victors, who now included Robert de Bellème, took charge of the captives, and any that had money or rich connections were carried away to imprisonment until they could raise a ransom for themselves.

By contrast Henry came out of the action a hero, and he claimed the right to dispose of the leader of the insurgents, Conan himself, who had been captured alive. It was not, however, a ransom that Henry was after, though Conan offered him all the wealth that he and his family possessed. Instead he took the terrified prisoner to the top of the castle tower and, according to Vitalis, tormented him for some time with invitations to admire the beautiful view over the rich city and parkland beyond. Then, finally, 'seizing him with both hands (he) dashed him backwards from the tower window,' the corpse being afterwards dragged behind a horse through the city streets as a lesson to all would-be traitors.

This act of cold-blooded murder, clearly carried out personally by Henry, passes without comment by the monk-chronicler. It was a 'deed of vengeance' by a man 'impatient to avenge his brother's wrongs'. Indeed, he adds without a trace of censure that the place where Conan fell 'is called to this day "Conan's Leap"'.

There is a tendency to see Henry, especially at this time, as the innocent younger brother, tossed about and beset by the whims of his elders. Clearly, though, there was a strong streak of his father's ruthlessness in the young man's make-up, and also a strong conviction as to what was due to people of his class and upbringing. Conan was a citizen – a burgher and a wealthy man, but still a citizen. For the likes of him to challenge a duke was treachery of the highest order and should be punished accordingly. Nor did any of the writers of the time condemn him for such thoughts and actions. It was the accepted order of things – though it is tempting to suggest that, in his place, William Rufus might just have taken the money.

If Henry had thought his support for his brother might have secured his affection, or at least his approval, he was soon disillusioned. Instead it appeared that Robert grudged him his success, particularly in view of his own perceived failure. There was still the matter of Henry's lands between them, as well, and it was to those lands that Henry now returned.

For the time being, however, Robert had his hands full elsewhere. He had already visited Maine in 1088 and received homage from almost all its lords, and an incipient rebellion there had been put

down in 1089 by Fulk of Anjou in exchange for Robert obtaining
for him his latest wife, Bertrada, the niece of William of Evreux.
The castle-swapping involved in this, however, led to a rash of
private wars across Normandy that needed firm action from the
duke, though, of course no such action was taken. There was a
danger, however, that if Robert gave no assistance to his warring
nobles, they would seek it elsewhere, and this is exactly what
happened when Ralph de Tosny was attacked by William of
Evreux. Failing to win support from the duke, he invited William
Rufus to help him, in return pledging his allegiance to the English
king, and thereby giving him a first foothold in Normandy west
of the Seine.

The worst of the warmongers, however, was Robert de Bellême to
whom Vitalis devotes an entire page of damning eloquence. He was
'of a subtle genius, deceitful and wily ... intrepid and formidable in
war ... but desperately cruel: his avarice and lust were insatiable.'
He 'displayed great skill in constructing buildings and machines
... and inexorable cruelty in tormenting his enemies.' Bellême's
ambition knew no bounds. 'He used his utmost efforts to reduce
to subjection the lords of his neighbourhood,' and succeeded by
'insupportable hostilities'. Lands were ravaged, castles attacked
and burnt and their inmates maimed or blinded.

Such was the state of the land when William Rufus decided
the time was right for him to make a personal appearance in
Normandy. The excuse he gave was the devastation being wrought
on the Norman Church by the daily violence and robberies going
on around it. 'And now our holy church addresses to me her
lamentable complaints,' he declares, for, 'without a just patron
and protector she finds herself among her malignant enemies like
a sheep in the midst of wolves.' This was the sheerest hypocrisy
from a man engaged in getting into his own hands as much of the
wealth of the English Church as he could. Nevertheless it clothed
his arrival in Eu in north-east Normandy with some measure of
decency – as did his own sumptuous state and the generous bribes
he was prepared to hand out to those who supported him.

Within a very short time it became apparent to Robert that he
would have to come to terms with his brother or lose everything,

and the two met in February 1091, at Rouen, to hammer out an agreement. Whether or not they were truly reconciled is doubtful, but the one thing they clearly agreed about was that Henry must at all costs be excluded. The final deal declared that William would keep all the lands and castles he had obtained in Normandy, with the addition of the Abbey of Fécamp and its lands and, according to the Anglo Saxon Chronicle, the seaport of Cherbourg in Henry's Cotentin Peninsular. In return Robert would receive some unspecified lands in England, and William would assist him to secure Maine and all other areas of Normandy which had been ruled by their father, another possible reference to the lands now held by their younger brother. Even more pointedly, it was agreed that if either of them was to die without a legitimate heir, all his lands and titles would pass to the other.

The agreement was sealed with the oaths of twelve barons on each side, and almost at once William and Robert began gathering forces. It might be that the original intention was to march on Maine, where Helias of La Flèche, grandson of a former count, Herbert Wake-Dog, had claimed the county and seized the key castle at Ballon. Their mutual animosity towards Henry, however, soon overrode that idea. For his part Henry was prepared to defend what he had bought, but he soon found his support falling away. It was the old problem of men with lands in both Normandy and England. Even those such as Hugh of Chester and Robert Fitzhamon, who had been happy until now with Henry's overlordship, weighed up the odds and decided they had too much to lose by going against the will of William Rufus. With castle after castle handed over to the English king, Henry gathered what men he could from Normandy and Brittany and retreated to Mont St Michel.

Wace declares it was Hugh himself who recommended Henry to base his defiance there, fortifying the church and sending his mercenary men out to harry and wage war on the Normans. He declared it to be impregnable, surrounded as it was by the tide twice a day, and he may well have been right. What it was not fit for, though, was a prolonged siege, having no adequate supplies of drinking water.

Around the middle of March Robert and William arrived with their armies to cut off access to supplies, and though Wace gives a highly romantic view of knights riding out daily from the mount in search of jousts, it is far more likely they were simply in search of water. In one of these daily skirmishes, William of Malmesbury describes the English king being unhorsed by one of Henry's soldiers, who, failing to recognise him, was about to kill him when he identified himself. Killing kings was, of course, just not playing the game in those days, and William Rufus was swiftly helped up and provided with another horse, whereupon he suitably rewarded the soldier for his prowess. 'Nobly done, magnanimous king,' declares Malmesbury. Wace has a similar story, though in his the king is rescued by a troop of his own men.

Both, however, tell of Henry appealing to Robert for water. According to Malmesbury, Robert then told his men to turn a blind eye while Henry's men came to gather supplies. Wace goes one step further and has Robert deliver to him a tun of best wine. Both agree that, when he found out, William Rufus was furious, and Malmesbury suggests that this put an end to Rufus's part in the siege.

In fact it is likely that Vitalis has the true ending of the episode. After holding out for fifteen days, he says, 'The prudent young prince, seeing himself thus pressed by his brothers ... weighed in his own mind the state of affairs, and ... determined on abandoning his rash enterprise and reserving himself for better times.' A truce was negotiated and Henry was allowed to march out honourably with his men and arms. After that, however, and after paying off his men, he had to keep on marching.

Left now with neither land nor money, Henry's fortunes were at their lowest ebb. For a while he disappears from the record, though Vitalis declares he travelled through Brittany and France, living in obscurity with only five companions. One of these, a clerk, may well have been Roger le Poer, a priest from Avranches, who became a close companion of Henry's and whose fortunes would later rise accordingly. It was said that Henry favoured him because of the speed with which he could get through the ritual of the Mass. Ever happy to draw lessons from the events he describes, Vitalis says of this time, 'Thus a king's son learnt in exile how to endure poverty ... and having himself experienced the lot of the humble, might kindly sympathise with them.'

Having adequately disposed of their younger brother, Robert and William Rufus managed to remain on friendly terms for the rest of the year, but the expedition to Maine was seemingly forgotten, despite appeals from the Bishop of Le Mans for their help. A new claimant, Hugh of Este, had appeared and Helias had given him his backing, but the bishop still held out for his Norman master. When threatened by the proposed expedition of William and Robert, Hugh had quickly sold all his interest in Maine to Helias, and at that point, thoroughly exasperated, the bishop finally recognised Helias as Count of Maine, as did Fulk of Anjou. With typical apathy Robert Curthose seems not to have given the matter another thought.

In July 1091 Robert and William Rufus made a joint enquiry into the rights traditionally enjoyed by Norman dukes. No doubt William, if not Robert, was determined to get all he could from his new position in Normandy. Then in early August they made their way to England. One account has Henry travelling with them and witnessing a charter with both his brothers. It is now generally accepted, however, that the charter was a forgery, and by this time Henry was probably in France.

There was a pressing need for William to be in England since both the Welsh and the Scots were preparing to challenge the Norman rule in his absence. In the case of the Scots, this was partly due to the terms of the treaty between William and Robert which had once again dispossessed the unfortunate Edgar Atheling.

Edgar, now approaching his forties, had spent most of his life being shifted from one place to another at the whim of English kings, having held that title himself for a matter of weeks in the autumn of 1066. He was one of the last descendants of King Edgar of England, his grandfather Edmund Ironside being the half-brother of Edward the Confessor. Edgar himself had been born in Hungary after his family fled there for protection at the time when the Danish King Cnut had conquered England. Then in 1057 his father, known as Edward the Exile, had been invited back to

England, together with his wife Agatha and three small children, to be heir to Edward the Confessor. Edward the Exile had died almost immediately, but the children had been taken into the royal court and raised by the Confessor and his wife, with Edgar being given the title 'Atheling' or 'throne-worthy', as designated heir to his foster father. At the time of the Confessor's death, however, Edgar was a boy of fourteen, and with England threatened by both Danes and Normans, the crown had gone instead to Harold Godwinson. This was the choice of the Witanagemot, the body of nobles and church leaders whose job it was to choose a king from among several possible candidates. At the time the idea of automatic hereditary rights was still some way in the future.

Soon after the Conquest, Edgar had fled with his sisters to the court of King Malcolm of Scotland, and his sister Margaret had, rather reluctantly, married Malcolm. For a time Edgar was the figurehead for every rebellion against the Conqueror, but eventually he had become reconciled with him, and latterly had been living in Normandy as a valued advisor to Robert Curthose. For reasons known only to himself, William Rufus had insisted that Edgar now be expelled from Normandy, with the result that he immediately returned to his sister in Scotland, raising complaints about his treatment by the English king.

Needing little encouragement, Malcolm then assembled an army and prepared to march into England, while William Rufus and Robert brought an English army north to resist. In fact they were so slow in doing this that it was late in the year before the army got as far as Durham, and the English fleet sent to support it was wrecked in autumnal storms. There was a brief standoff, probably in the area of the Firth of Forth, and then Robert, with no doubt a strong sense of déja vu, was sent to negotiate on one side, with Malcolm and Edgar Atheling on the other. Although Malcolm declared he had done homage to Robert as heir to the Conqueror, it seems Robert had little stomach to pursue that claim further. Circumstances had changed, he told Malcolm, and a treaty was swiftly agreed whereby the Scottish king would give the same homage to William Rufus as he had to his father. There is a suggestion that William, with his usual reliance on the power of money, offered Malcolm a pension in return.

This was all very satisfactory for the English king, but then Robert waited in vain for any sign of the lands William had promised him in England. By Christmas he had given up and returned to Normandy, having once more learnt the lesson that promises for William were a means to an end, and fell far short of any definite obligation. As William himself is said to have remarked to Lanfranc, 'Who is there who can fulfil all the promises he makes?'

Though some accounts have Henry spending several years in impoverished exile, in fact his wanderings lasted only about fifteen months. It is most probably in July of 1092 that he was offered the castle and town of Domfront, which he took over in what appears to have been an entirely bloodless coup.

The original fortification at Domfront was built by the great-grandfather of Robert de Bellème, high on a promontory in a strategic location on the southern borders of Normandy. It had been a key stronghold of the Bellème family, and as such came into the hands of the Conqueror's great friend and supporter Roger of Montgomery when he married the heiress Mabel de Bellème. If the chronicles are to be believed, Mabel was a woman renowned for her cruelty – a trait her son Robert seemed to inherit – but she got her comeuppance, being beheaded while sleeping by a group of her enemies. That was in 1077, and Robert then came into his mother's property – but it was not he that handed Domfront over to Henry.

The initiative came from the inhabitants, in particular a 'noble and rich' inhabitant, variously named as Harecherius, Haschier, or Archard (no doubt variations on the same name), who found Henry in Paris and offered him Domfront complete. In order to do this he must have wielded considerable power, not only in the town but with the castle garrison too, and the likelihood is that he was the castellan, possibly from a family who had held that post as an inheritance over many years. We have no information as to why Henry was chosen, though Vitalis says he obtained Domfront, 'by God's help and the support of his friends,' and later Henry seems to refer to Archard as 'my teacher'. The motive, however, is clear. Again it is Vitalis who tells us the inhabitants, 'threw off the yoke of Robert de Bellême, by whom they had been long grievously oppressed, and declared Henry their lord.'

Robert de Bellême's response is not recorded, but Henry seems to have had no difficulty in holding on to what he had been given, and immediately commenced the building of a massive rectangular stone keep. This would eventually measure some 26 metres by 22 metres, with walls 3 metres thick and 28 metres high – an impregnable fortress if ever there was one, and one which he would hold for forty-three years. It was from this base in Domfront that he began 'reprisals for his own banishment,' attacking his brother's lands, pillaging and burning, and extending his power northwards until he had recovered effective control over all the lands he had previously held. This was not accomplished in a day, but over a period of time his former enemies fell away. Robert of Mortain died and his heir was too young to oppose Henry. Bishop Geoffrey of Coutances also died, and his nephew Robert Mowbray was concerned with affairs in England. It helped that William Rufus was also detained in England, suffering a severe illness in 1093, thus leaving Henry's former friends in the Cotentin, such as Hugh of Chester, a free hand to support him there. It may also be that William was happy to encourage anyone who would attack Robert, since their treaty of Rouen was now well and truly broken.

At Christmas in 1093 when William's court was assembled at Gloucester, Robert sent a formal defiance to his brother declaring that since William was perjured and faithless, he too would abandon the terms of the treaty unless immediately granted all that had been promised. William's response was to gather as much money as he and his chancellor Ranulf Flambard could squeeze out of England, and set off once more to make a bid for Normandy.

Initially, as Robert had demanded, they met at Rouen with all those barons who had sworn to the treaty three years before. As soon as the barons had solemnly decreed that William was guilty as charged, however, the brothers separated, and again made ready to attack each other.

As before, William spent his money on bribes and mercenaries, while Robert enlisted the help of Philip of France. Helias of Saint-Saens, supporting his father-in-law in Upper Normandy, lost a castle to William, but Robert and Philip together were so successful in taking castles from William's supporters further south and west that the English king was forced to look for reinforcements. In England 20,000 men were called up to serve their king, but in a most bizarre twist, according to the Anglo-Saxon Chronicle, 'when they reached the sea they were desired to return, and to give to the king's treasury the money they had received.' This would have been the money which according to tradition each had brought with him for his maintenance while in the king's service. The Chronicle declares it was 'half a pound for each man,' a considerable sum, and presumably valued more highly by William as a weapon of war than the services of 20,000 men.

It may be that it was this money that once again bought off Philip of France, who advanced northward with Robert as far as Longueville on the River Scie – presumably close to William at Eu – and then abruptly left the conflict. Some of it may also have made its way to Henry at Domfront, or it may be simply that William's tacit consent to his re-occupation of the Cotentin prompted him to answer his brother's call for help when it came in the autumn of 1094.

It is a measure of the predicament that William had got into that Henry was not able to cross Normandy directly to go to his aid. Robert's supporters in between were clearly too strong. Instead William sent ships for him, and apparently there was a change of plan, since, rather than joining William in Eu, Henry arrived in England.

Once again there was trouble in Wales. Robert of Rhuddlan who, with his cousin Hugh of Chester, had subdued all of north Wales, had been killed the year before, and now Gruffydd ap Cynan, king of Gwynedd, had escaped from his long captivity at Chester and was leading a major uprising. William could not fight Gruffydd in Wales at the same time as Robert in Normandy, so four days after Christmas 1094, he returned to England to negotiate with Henry.

The outcome of this was that in the spring of 1095 Henry, now clearly the king's man, was dispatched across the channel once more, as the Anglo-Saxon Chronicle relates, 'with much treasure to be employed in the king's service against their brother Robert.' This he accomplished with rather more success than William achieved in his campaign in Wales so that by the year's end, it was Robert who was now beleaguered, his power on the wane everywhere, and almost surrounded by enemies. By that time, however, something had happened that would affect almost every country in western Europe.

In November 1095 Pope Urban called a council of the bishops of France and Spain, held at Clermont in France. There he announced what has become known as the First Crusade. The Holy Land, he said, Jerusalem itself, had been occupied by a race utterly opposed to the Christian religion and he detailed all manner of torment and defilement, which he said was currently taking place there. He praised the Frankish people for their courage and glory at arms and their staunch defence of the faith, and he called upon them now to hurry to the aid of their fellow Christians in the East. It is interesting that, in the various accounts of his sermon written up later, there is a strong emphasis on the evils to be found within the Frankish lands, the private wars, the violence and robbery that was carried on, not only by the lower classes but by the nobles themselves. Going on crusade was clearly to be an act of penance that would gain forgiveness for such sins, and further, reading between the lines, the violence that they seemed to love could be practised without guilt in the cause he had laid before them.

It would be unfair, however, to attribute such cynical reasoning to those who now flocked to join the crusade as word spread steadily around Europe. It was the following Easter before the Anglo-Saxon Chronicle mentions it, declaring, 'there was a very great stir in this country and in many others ... and an innumerable multitude of men, with their wives and children, departed to go and conquer the heathen nations.' The stir in England, however, did not reach the highest levels. Neither William nor, more surprisingly, Henry, showed any inclination to join the crusade. Across the Channel, though, it was a different matter. Among those recruited to the cause were Robert, Count of Flanders; Eustace of Boulogne and his brother Baldwin, later to become King of Jerusalem; and Raymond, Count of Toulouse. And Robert, Duke of Normandy, determined that he, too, would join the crusade. Vitalis records, 'The king of England heard this determination with sincere pleasure,' and no doubt even more pleasure when he heard of Robert's proposal to raise the money he needed for the expedition. Normandy was to be mortgaged to William in exchange for £10,000, redeemable when – if – Robert returned, a date speculatively fixed for three to five years in the future.

Yet again William and Ranulf Flambard between them squeezed the money out of England and, in September 1096, William personally delivered it to his brother at Rouen. After all he had spent in the past five years to obtain the duchy, this must have seemed a small price to pay. The fact that William was taking charge may also have been decisive in persuading Odo of Bayeux that he too should join the crusade, and a few weeks later William Rufus was no doubt delighted to bid goodbye to the pair of them. Odo, in fact, never reached Jeruselem, dying and being buried in Palermo in Norman Sicily.

So at last, after years of striving, William had got what he wanted, and one of his first acts was to reinstate Henry as Count of the Cotentin with a wide authority over western Normandy. The Norman barons soon learnt that their days of lax government were over, but the following years kept William very busy, holding on to what he had got and even seeking to extend it.

In England the year before, a sudden rebellion led by Robert Mowbray and William of Eu had tried to give the throne to Rufus's cousin, Stephen of Aumale. The speed of the king's response, besieging the leaders in Bamburgh Castle, led to a falling away of support, and both ringleaders were captured. Mowbray was imprisoned for life, and William of Eu, undergoing trial by battle for treason, was defeated, blinded and mutilated, and died soon after.

There was trouble in Scotland, too, following the assassination of King Malcolm in 1093. This rumbled on for some time but, in 1097, William successfully supported his own candidate, Edgar, to the throne. That same year William was involved in north Wales, attempting and failing to drive back the resurgent Welsh king of Gwynedd, Gruffydd ap Cynan, from the lands he had retaken from the Normans. There was more success the next year when, in the absence of the English king, Gruffydd was forced back as far as Anglesey, though at the cost of the life of the new young Earl of Shrewsbury, Hugh of Montgomery. Hugh had only inherited his title on the death of his father Roger in 1094, and soon after this his brother, Robert de Bellême, who had been reconciled with William, would pay the sum of £3,000 to the English king in return for inheriting both the lands and the title.

These actions were mere sideshows, however, to William's driving ambitions across the Channel. Late in 1097 he launched an attack on the Vexin, intending to accomplish the conquest of that area which he and his father had failed to do ten years earlier. With Robert de Bellême as one of his main commanders, he was aiming to take three major objectives, Chaumont, Pontoise and Mantes, but had probably not got much further than Gisors, where Bellême began engineering a mighty fortress, when this enterprise was interrupted.

It was, in fact, Robert de Bellême who dragged William reluctantly away to Maine. There Helias of La Flèche was trying to extend his influence close to the Norman border by building a new castle at Danguel, between Le Mans and Bellême's castle at Alençon. An unexpected attack in February 1098 was thought likely to be successful, but in fact got bogged down by the guerrilla tactics employed by Helias. William returned to Rouen, but the situation changed soon after when Helias was captured. This prompted Fulk of Anjou, whose son Geoffrey was betrothed to the daughter of Helias, to intervene and occupy Le Mans.

In June William collected an army, which one account estimated at 50,000 men. As they advanced into Maine, the castle at Ballon, held for Helias, was quickly surrendered and given to Bellême. A siege of Le Mans was begun but soon had to be abandoned, as Vitalis says, 'because it was the season between the old and new crops,' and there was not enough food around to sustain the men and beasts trying to maintain it. As soon as William withdrew, however, Fulk marched north to besiege Ballon. The beggars of that place must have favoured the Normans, as the story goes that they tipped off those in the castle that the besiegers were most vulnerable at breakfast. Thereupon a sudden raid from within succeeded in capturing a large number of knights and their leaders. This seems to have unnerved Fulk, for when William returned and relieved Ballon, he was prepared to open negotiations. In the agreement that followed, Helias was to be released in exchange for the city of Le Mans, and all the castles which had previously been held by the Conqueror were to be handed over to William Rufus. In August 1098 William made a solemn triumphal entry into Le Mans, and then, within a matter of a few weeks, was to be found once again pursuing his war in the Vexin.

Between September 1098 and the spring of 1099, attacking towards Paris, he had taken Pontoise from its castellan Walter Tirel, and besieged Chaumont. The latter, however, did not surrender, and he never came near to taking Mantes. By Easter 1099, William was forced to negotiate a truce before returning home to England.

His stay there was not long. Already Helias was stirring up more trouble in Maine. Several accounts relate that, on his release, he had offered to serve William faithfully and thereby earn his right to Maine, but William had been advised not to accept this offer. Helias had then declared that he would not rest until he had recovered the county, to which William's reply is usually rendered along the lines of 'Go on, then, and do your damnedest! I don't care.' That 'damnedest' was exactly what Helias was doing, and by June 1099 he had already retaken Le Mans. At this point Robert de Bellême sent to William for help, prompting one of the most famous responses in that king's reign.

Receiving the letter from Bellême while out riding, so the story goes, the king immediately put spurs to his horse and rode to the coast. There, despite the stormy weather, he forced a ship's captain to take him across the Channel, declaring that he had never heard of a king who was shipwrecked. When his few followers suggested he gather an army before proceeding, his reply was that the army would flock to him as he went, though he did pause at Bonneville for a while to gather forces.

As he advanced, so Helias withdrew, but employing scorched earth tactics to delay his pursuers. When finally he was besieged in a strong castle at Mayet, he was able to resist all attempts to take him. As the Normans filled the moat with branches to enable them to cross and attack at close quarters, so the defenders set fire to them, thereby repelling the assault, and while William stood nearby assessing his next move, a stone flung from the castle narrowly missed him and killed the man standing beside him. By September it had become obvious that Mayet would not be taken, and William's return to Le Mans this time was less than triumphal.

There are very few details as to the whereabouts of William's brother Henry during this time. His name appears as one of the commanders of the army in the Vexin, but since Henry and Robert de Bellème had been bitter enemies for years, it is unlikely they would have served comfortably together. It is likely that initially he spent his time either in Western Normandy or with the king. His name appears from time to time on English charters, so it is clear he visited the country on occasion. In May 1099 he was certainly at William's court in Westminster, the first time this had been held in the vast new Westminster Hall William had had constructed on the site of Edward the Confessor's old palace.

And, most opportunely, he was also in England the following summer when William Rufus decided to go hunting in the New Forest.

3

An Arrow in the Forest
(August–December 1100)

On the morning of 1 August 1100, Abbot Fulchered of Shrewsbury was visiting the abbey of St Peter in Gloucester and was invited to give the sermon. He thereupon let rip with a blistering attack on the sinful state of the country and the greed and 'dissolute lust' of its rulers. However, he declared, a change was at hand. 'The bow of divine vengeance is bent upon the reprobate, and the swift arrow taken from the quiver is ready to wound. The blow will soon be struck.'

No doubt others were saying much the same thing in other places and at other times – 'Repent sinner for your end is nigh,' is a fairly common refrain throughout history – but Fulchered's timing was impeccable. The very next day, as recorded by the Anglo-Saxon Chronicle, 'King William was shot with an arrow by his own men as he was hunting.'

The bare facts of the matter are very simple, but the various writers who later recorded the events give a number of different versions of how the king met his death, who was with him at the time, and how they reacted to the situation. The Chronicle does not name the man who fired the arrow, but everyone else is unanimous that it was Walter Tirel, described as a wealthy French knight, whose castle at Pontoise had been surrendered to William the previous year. Henry of Huntingdon simply declares, 'Walter Tirel unintentionally shot the king with an arrow aimed at a stag', while John of Worcester is equally concise, merely saying William Rufus was killed by an arrow carelessly aimed by a Frenchman. William of Malmesbury, however, gives a much fuller account. He, along with others, places the action in the afternoon, when William had gone with some companions into the New Forest to hunt deer. The only one he names is Walter Tirel, and he says the king was alone with Tirel as the others had spread themselves out through the forest, no doubt to have the best chance of killing a deer as the animals were driven in their direction. Presumably they had been there some time, since he says the sun was then declining when William shot at and slightly wounded a stag. Shielding his eyes against the sun, he was following the animal's progress when Tirel shot at another stag that passed near him and, 'without power to prevent it' struck the king in the breast. Without uttering a word, William broke off the end of the arrow, fell forward thereby driving it further into his chest, and expired. Why the king would break off the arrow is a mystery, but a possible explanation is that he was trying to remove it. It may equally be that the story passed on by those finding the body was that the arrow was found broken on the ground and it may simply have snapped off when the king fell on it. Either way, Walter Tirel was not there to explain since Malmesbury says he instantly fled the scene when he found the king was dead.

Orderic Vitalis names two other companions of the king that day, namely his brother Henry, and William of Breteuil, the eldest son of the Conqueror's friend William FitzOsbern, who had inherited his father's extensive estates in Normandy. His version of events, which may be fitted with Malmesbury's, is that a stag ran between the king and Tirel. For some reason the king had moved from his post so that when Tirel shot at the stag and his arrow glanced off its back, the king was in range of the arrow, which struck and killed him. Vitalis, too, has a rather ironic prequel to the story. Before setting out on the hunt, William was brought six new arrows, two of which he gave to Tirel since he was the best shot, and 'knows best how to inflict mortal wounds with them.'

Approximately a decade after Vitalis and Malmesbury, Geoffrey Gaimar wrote an account of William's death for a member of the de Clare family. Tirel himself was married into that family, and though initially Gaimar says it was Tirel who killed the king, later on he contradicts himself and says he doesn't know who fired the arrow. In his version, William lived long enough to cry out for a consecrated host before he died but, being in the middle of a forest, of course, none was available. Instead, Gaimar records a huntsman feeding the king a handful of grass and flowers. This rather bizarre action may have the same origin as the tradition recorded at the Battle of Agincourt, whereby immediately before going into action each soldier knelt and kissed the ground, and took a morsel of soil into his mouth in remembrance of the holy sacrament received in church. Gaimar certainly seems to suggest it was a token of the forgiveness of the king's sins.

Later again, in the 1160s, Wace is blunt as usual about his lack of precise knowledge. He doesn't know, he says, who fired the arrow that killed the king, but he gives us all the stories he has heard about it. Thus, people said it was Tirel that fired the arrow, and some said he stumbled and got caught up in his cloak and that was why the arrow went amiss. Others, however, said that the arrow glanced against a tree and so was diverted into the king.

Most people, especially the clergy of the time, seemed to care very little about whose hand had fired the arrow since it was abundantly clear to them that it had been guided by a higher power. God had killed William Rufus, exactly as Fulchered had predicted, as an act of divine vengeance for all his wrongdoings. Furthermore, they had the omens to prove it.

Omens, of course, are fairly easy to find, especially with the benefit of hindsight, but the death of William Rufus seems to have attracted a particularly heavy crop of them. William of Malmesbury has almost every year of his reign blighted by floods, famines, comets and lightning strikes, but the last year especially saw fountains flowing with blood and the devil himself appearing to people in wooded places and actually speaking to them. More specifically he declares that the night before his death William dreamed he was being bled by a surgeon and the stream of blood shot high into the sky, blotting out the light. Although he had only just recorded that William scoffed at dreams and omens, the monk nevertheless says that the king was so frightened by this dream that he called for lights and servants and for the rest of the night would not be alone in the dark.

That same morning Robert Fitzhamon, no less, reported to the king a dream recounted to him by 'a certain foreign monk'. This time William was in a church gnawing on the arms and legs of Christ on a crucifix, until the figure gave him a mighty kick that threw him backwards. Then, as he lay open-mouthed, flames shot from his mouth, again reaching up to the sky. By now the king must have recovered his courage, for he apparently laughed this off, as usual, though Malmesbury says he nonetheless put off going hunting that morning as he had intended, instead 'dispelling the uneasiness of his unregulated mind by serious business.' Furthermore, before going hunting in the afternoon he drank 'a more than usual quantity of wine'.

Vitalis, too, has a story of dreams. Indeed he suggests that 'terrible visions' concerning the king were widespread among the clergy in cathedrals and abbeys, so much so that they became 'the common talk of the vulgar in the market places and churchyards.' Specifically he recounts the dream of a monk at Gloucester, again supposedly just before the king's death. In a vision of heaven the monk saw the Virgin Mary begging the Lord to 'look with an eye of compassion on thy people which now groans under the yoke of William,' and urging vengeance on the king. The Lord then replied that vengeance would not be long in coming. Whether it was the telling of this dream that inspired Fulchered in his prophecy the next day, we don't know. We are told that the abbot, Serlo, took it so seriously that he wrote to warn the king, though when the letter was received, apparently when William was just about to leave on the hunt, once more he laughs it off. Why, he asks, does Serlo bother him with 'the dreams of his snoring monks? "Does he think that I follow the example of the English who will defer their journey or their business on account of the dreams of a parcel of wheezing old women?"' If all these things really did happen on that day, it shows a determined opposition to such matters by the king in that he went hunting at all. Indeed, Malmesbury says his friends tried to dissuade him, saying he 'should not suffer the truth of the dreams to be tried at his personal risk.' Of course he went, and a few hours later was dead.

The writers of the time, then, were content to put William's death down to an accident, possibly aided by divine intervention. Good riddance, seems to have been the general response and, after all, then as now, accidents did happen. Hadn't William lost another brother in the same place, in the same activity, soon after his younger brother Henry was born? History, however, has not been so generous.

The actions of two of the members of that hunting party have raised suspicions that this accident was not all it appeared to be. Malmesbury tells us that as soon as he realised the king was dead Tirel 'leapt swiftly upon his horse and escaped by spurring him to his utmost speed.' Nor did he ever return. Some, we are told, pitied him and some 'connived at his flight'. These last were likely to be members of the de Clare family, major landowners in Kent. Tirel's wife was a daughter of Richard FitzGilbert, 1st Lord of Clare and Tonbridge. Her brother Gilbert, now Lord of Clare, was one of the hunting party on that afternoon, and he and his family would certainly have done all they could to protect their kinsman. Even if the death was accidental, this would have been a sensible precaution. Vitalis says the mercenary soldiers of William Rufus went searching for Tirel, threatening to tear him to pieces. And if it was not an accident ...

Tirel himself would seem to have little to gain from the death of a king who, we are told, was his intimate friend. If we are looking for someone who *would* benefit we don't have to look far, and Henry's behaviour on that afternoon could also be regarded as suspect.

There was clearly little love lost between any of the brothers, and Malmesbury describes Henry as 'assisting or opposing each of them as they merited.' His recent support for William was no doubt more strategic than sentimental. On the other hand, he was keen on upholding the distinctions of rank, as Conan could probably witness. He may have been ambiguous about how he felt about his brother but William was also a king, and it might have been expected that Henry would have remained with his body, or at least set about arranging suitably impressive transport to an appropriate place where the king could lie in state before his funeral. Instead, the first thing Henry did, according to Vitalis, was to seize a horse and gallop away to Winchester to demand that the castle and royal treasury be turned over to him as heir to the Crown.

He did not get it just for the asking. Although the writers describe the other members of the hunting party going off to secure their own estates – an echo of the death of the Conqueror himself – a number of them must have either accompanied or followed Henry on his journey of some 20 miles to Winchester. By then it must have been early evening and it is unlikely any word of the king's death had been received before they arrived. Of course the castellan would have known Henry, and he might have immediately granted his request, if it had been unchallenged. However, at least one of the other nobles at once disputed Henry's claim to be the rightful heir.

Vitalis names him as William de Breteuil, who 'arrived at the same instant with breathless haste, for he anticipated Henry's deep policy and resolved to oppose it.' He would have been much of an age with Robert Curthose, was one of his earliest friends and supporters, and spoke up for him now. In the words of Vitalis he tells Henry, 'We ought to have loyal regard for the fealty we have sworn to your brother Robert. He is undoubtedly the eldest son, and both I and you, my lord Henry, have paid him homage.' There was also, of course, the small matter of William Rufus declaring Robert should be his heir in the Treaty of Rouen, to which William of Breteuil may well have been a witness.

Neither point carried any weight with Henry. The Treaty of Rouen was long gone and his fealty to each of his brothers had been rewarded by treachery. The strong temptation to see Henry as the dutiful little brother caught in the backlash of his brothers' disputes might have been true at the time of his father's death when he was eighteen, but he was now in his early thirties and had had a few hard knocks in between. Now Henry knew what he wanted and intended to get it.

A 'sharp contention' followed, says Vitalis. Crowds gathered and things might have turned very ugly had it not been for the intervention of the Beaumont brothers, Robert de Meulan and his younger brother Henry, Earl of Warwick, who were long-time supporters of Henry, and whose age and experience carried some weight. Gradually things turned in his favour and, as Vitalis shrewdly notes, 'the influence of an heir present in person to claim his rights began to prevail'. Henry's opinion of his brother Robert was perhaps revealed as never before, however, when at one point in the argument he drew his sword and declared that 'no foreigner should, on frivolous pretences, lay hands on his father's sceptre.' At last he got his way and castle and treasury were duly handed over. More than that, it seems clear that after these 'trifling dissensions,' as Malmesbury calls them, it was now generally accepted that Henry was to be king of England.

So where was Henry when his brother was killed? Beyond saying he was one of the hunting party, none of the earliest writers give any clue. Only Wace, writing some sixty years later for Henry's grandson, seems to go out of his way to give Henry an alibi. According to Wace, soon after entering the forest with the rest of the party, the bowstring on Henry's bow had failed. Thereupon he withdrew to a peasant's holding, obtained some suitable materials and set about mending it. While he was there an old peasant woman with clairvoyant powers predicted that he would soon be king. Then, as he set out again for the forest, Henry met men coming back who told him of his brother's death. Hearing this, in fear and sorrow, Henry quickly went to find the body and wept over it before 'they', implying Henry was one of the party, took the body to Winchester for burial.

This, no doubt, is what Wace felt Henry should have done, but the story is completely at variance with all those earlier accounts, which show the new king in a more discreditable light. It may be that by the 1160s whispers had already begun that there was something more than an accident involved in William's death, and Wace was, either voluntarily or not, taking pains to scotch them.

The story itself is thin. If Henry's bowstring was broken it is inconceivable that there would not have been another bow available for him to use, and the clairvoyant peasant is pure fantasy. Nor does the account of him weeping over his brother's body and accompanying it to Winchester stand up against the earlier accounts. Both Vitalis and William of Malmesbury declare that the king's body was brought back from the forest on a cart, either by some servants or 'a few countrymen'. Malmesbury adds the lurid detail that it was dripping blood all the way, which rather contradicts his earlier statement that William died instantly. Local legend goes further and names the owner of the cart as one Purkis, though this seems to date from a claim by a local charcoal burner called Purkis in the early 19th century, that he was a direct descendant of the man with the cart. Furthermore he claimed he was in possession of the king's bridle *and* a wheel from the very cart!

Malmesbury wrote his account for a son of Henry's, Robert of Gloucester, and it might be thought that if Henry was involved in paying due respect to his brother's body, he might have mentioned it. Gaimar was writing for a member of the de Clare family, and he goes some way towards Wace's tale, describing members of the nobility weeping over the body, arranging a suitable bier and covering the body with costly cloaks as they accompanied it to Winchester. Those he names, however, were two members of the de Clare family, Gilbert and Robert FitzRichard, together with Robert Fitzhamon. Again, if Henry was involved he might have been expected to say so.

So, if we discount Wace's convenient alibi, it seems from all these accounts that Henry's whereabouts at the time the arrow was fired was unknown. Yet he seems to have been one of the first to know of the death, and certainly the sharpest to react. Clearly, at the very least he was quick to see his opportunity and equally quick to grasp it.

And it was an opportunity unlikely to be repeated, for, accident or not, William's death came at an exceptionally convenient time for Henry. In the first place, they were in England, within striking distance of the royal treasury at Winchester, always the first target for anyone aiming to secure the crown. Nor were they likely to be there long, for we are told William was taking the opportunity of some relaxation while men and ships were being gathered on the south coast, ready for an expedition to Normandy and beyond.

Given the past history of William Rufus it is unlikely that he ever meant to hand back the duchy of Normandy to his brother Robert, so these forces, though likely gathered with the Vexin in mind, may also have been intended to repel the rightful duke. Robert, meantime, was on his way home from the Crusade, covered in glory, and with a new wife he had married in southern Italy, the daughter of Geoffrey, Count of Conversano. Her substantial dowry would enable him to repay the loan from William and redeem his duchy, though it seems he would probably have had a fight on his hands in order to do so.

There would be renewed wars in Normandy, then. Robert would very likely produce a legitimate heir, and even William Rufus, whatever his inclinations, might be prevailed upon to marry and get an heir of his own for England. If Henry ever had ambitions to be more than just a younger brother, tossed about by the whims of his elders, this was the time when everything hung in the balance. He might have backed himself to win in conflict with the idle Robert, but William, with the might of England behind him, was a different proposition.

Convenient, then, that they were in a place where accidents were likely to happen, even to members of the royal family. The death of his brother Richard in the New Forest may not have made much impression on Henry who was a baby at the time, but a more recent death would certainly have registered.

Robert's illegitimate son Richard was at the time being brought up at the court of his uncle William. Whether he was any kind of hostage for his father's good behaviour we don't know, but he was certainly free to enjoy the privileges of rank, among them the opportunity to hunt in the New Forest. In May 1100 while out with a hunting party, 'this illustrious young prince,' as Vitalis calls him, was struck and killed by an arrow badly aimed at a deer. Quite clearly what had happened once could easily happen again.

Means, motive and opportunity – the classic trio beloved of detective fiction. Henry certainly had the means, he may well have had the motive, and opportunity would not be lacking if the descriptions given of the hunt were in any way accurate. Of course, Walter Tirel fired the arrow, as proved by his running away afterwards, so everyone said. Everyone, that is, except Tirel himself. Years later, comfortably at home in France, he became friendly with Abbot Suger, the biographer of the French king, Louis. Suger declares, 'I have often heard him assert on his solemn oath, at a time when he had nothing either to fear or to hope, that on that day he was neither in the part of the forest where the king was hunting, nor saw him at all while he was in the wood.'

If that was true, why would Tirel be blamed for the death even when it was clearly put down as an accident? Here we enter the territory of the conspiracy theorists. Two members at least of the de Clare family were present in the wood that day and almost certainly aided Tirel's escape. It was an escape so complete that William's mercenaries never caught him, though they must have set off soon afterwards. While traffic across the channel was fairly brisk, it was not a regular ferry service, which implies there may have been some pre-planning in arranging a boat for Tirel so quickly. He was certainly never pursued by Henry, and the de Clare family seemed to enjoy the favour of the new king, though not, perhaps, to the extent one might expect if they had been involved in a conspiracy to put him on the throne.

One possibility, then, is that William was deliberately killed and the blame diverted onto Walter Tirel, whether or not he fired the arrow, with the connivance of the FitzRichard brothers. It is worth noting that Gilbert FitzRichard had previously been involved in the rebellion against William in 1088, being wounded and captured in the taking of his castle at Tonbridge. Although later pardoned, he was not likely to have had any great love for that king, and while the earlier rebellion was in favour of Robert, he may in the meantime have decided that Henry was a better proposition. Against this idea is the fact that Tirel was the FitzRichards' brother-in-law, and such a plot would put him in a certain amount of personal danger, even if they had an escape plan ready.

A startling alternative proposes that William was killed not for Henry's benefit but for that of the French. Walter Tirel's lands at Pontoise were in the Vexin, the borderland between France and Normandy. Though he had come to England, probably in 1099, and become friendly with William, he was equally friendly with the French king, Philip, and his more active son, Prince Louis, and Gaimar at least seems to regard him as something of a double agent. At the time of William's death, the English king was planning a major expansion on the Continent. The Count of Poitou, who had fought beside William in the recent war in the Vexin, now proposed to join the crusaders in the Holy Land. In order to equip a large force to take with him, he intended to make the same arrangement with William as Robert had made, pledging either Poitou or, by some accounts, all of his lands including Aquitaine, in exchange for cash. Even to hold this area for a few years would make William a major power in France. If he could hold on to it, together with Normandy and Maine, he would be a threat not merely to neighbours such as Anjou, but to the king of France himself. The scale of the expedition he was preparing seemed to suggest he intended to do just that, and in fact, when asked where he planned to spend Christmas 1100, he declared it would be spent in Poitiers in Aquitaine. Some rumours declared he had his eye on the French throne itself.

Gaimar includes in his account a purported conversation between Tirel and William Rufus where Tirel seems to do his best to find out about William's plans for the coming expedition. Add to this Tirel's rapid acceptance back at the French court and his continued position as lord of highly strategic castles, and it gives some weight to those who claim he was acting throughout on behalf of King Philip of France. Whether this would be with the knowledge or approval of Henry it is impossible to say, but the death of William certainly put paid to the planned expedition and expansion of English influence in France, and thus achieved the immediate aim of the French king. We could just add that one of the earliest visitors to the court of King Henry was Prince Louis of France, though the purpose of the visit is unknown.

Alternatively, Henry himself may have fired the fatal arrow and contrived to put the blame on Tirel. We know he was capable of cold-blooded murder, though in vastly different circumstances, and he had spent some time in the rough and tumble of Norman feuding, being described by some as simply a robber baron. To kill a brother and steal a crown, however, would require a far higher level of ruthlessness and daring. He would need to be sure, for example, of transferring any blame to someone else, or it might have been he that was pursued by William's mercenary soldiers and torn to pieces. He would also need to be sure he had enough backing to make good his claim to be the rightful heir. As it transpired, it was touch and go, and he was lucky (or possibly clever enough) to have his own backers near at hand, while some of the leading magnates such as Hugh of Chester and Robert de Bellème had already crossed to Normandy to be ready to greet the return of Robert.

Henry also seemed to be remarkably well prepared for an event that appeared to be an accident. Not only did he secure the treasury within hours, but in three days he had the crown on his head, in a fortnight he had disposed of William's chief advisor, and within weeks he was married and ready to secure his own dynasty. If there was no pre-planning in that, he showed a supreme talent for quick thought and even quicker action. In all of it, of course, he had the very important advantage that he was there on the spot while his rival was still slowly returning homeward from Italy and, given the dangers inherent in travelling at that time, there was still a chance he might never arrive at all.

An accident? Walter Tirel on behalf of Henry, or the French king? Or Henry himself, either pre-planned or seizing a once-in-a-lifetime opportunity? We can never know for sure. The evidence is purely circumstantial and an equally plausible case can be made out for each of the theories. Indisputably William was killed by an arrow in the New Forest. The rest is one of history's unsolved mysteries.

Before we leave Walter Tirel, however, we can just point out that he was not the only member of that family involved in such a mystery. Some four centuries later another Tirel – this time spelt Tyrell – was allegedly involved in a plot to kill a king. In 1483 Sir James Tyrell is said to have entered the Tower of London and murdered the two Princes, one of whom had already been proclaimed Edward V. Twelve generations separate the two, and Sir James was not as lucky as his ancestor. Walter lived out his life in peace until he died while undertaking a journey to the Holy Land, around the year 1131. Sir James, however, was arrested and hanged for a later treason, some twenty years after his alleged crime, though the confession he is said to have made at that time concerning the murder of the Princes has never been produced.

As for William Rufus, Gaimar declares he had a mighty funeral such as no king was likely to have again, and unprecedented quantities of alms were given to the poor. This is again at odds with the other chroniclers, who briefly state that he was buried in the new cathedral at Winchester on the day after his death, which would give little time for the preparation of a lavish funeral. Vitalis names only clergy, monks and poor citizens as attending the body and says in some churches the bells did not toll at his passing. He also says no alms were given to the poor. Malmesbury, perhaps more accurately, says the body was 'attended by many of the nobility, though lamented by few.' No-one mentions whether or not Henry attended the funeral, though perhaps it would have been noted if he did not. In a final touch, Malmesbury adds that the tower under which William was buried collapsed a few years afterwards, though he is generous enough to concede that it 'might have fallen through imperfect construction, even though he had never been buried there,' an opinion clearly running counter to the common assumption at the time.

The reign of William Rufus is frequently seen as a brief interlude between those of his more illustrious father and brother. It lasted nearly thirteen years, however, and if the summaries at the time are to be believed, contributed significantly to what followed, if only by easing Henry's passage to the throne as a replacement for a thoroughly unpopular king. Even before telling of William's death, Malmesbury apparently quotes a 'wise man' as declaring, 'England would be fortunate if Henry could reign,' though he gives no explanation of who this daring 'wise man' might be. It is also hard to estimate the truth of William's unpopularity since almost all who wrote about him were his bitter enemies. Even his apologists, however, concede that he said and did some things that were outrageous for their times, the more outrageous statements generally being passed off as 'jokes'.

The Anglo-Saxon Chronicle declares, 'all that was abominable to God and oppressive to man was common in this island in William's time: and therefore he was hated by almost all his people, and abhorred by God as his end showeth ...' It then spends less than two lines on his death and burial. The monk Eadmer, close friend of Archbishop Anselm who he felt had been particularly badly treated by the king, is even more forthright in his condemnation. As 'those who ... were present ... bear witness,' he says, 'He never got up in the morning or went to bed at night without being every time a worse man than when he last went to bed or last got up.' Furthermore, he sums up the clerical opinion of the day when he declares, 'Sufficient to know that by the just judgement of God he was stricken down and slain.' It should be borne in mind that Eadmer was an eye-witness of the events he writes about, albeit an extremely biased one.

If we examine in more detail the misdeeds of William, as seen by his contemporary Englishmen, we will see how these contributed to Henry's quick and complete success, not only in seizing the crown, but in successfully holding on to it.

For the clerics, William's worst offences were against the church. 'He trampled on the church of God,' says the Anglo-Saxon Chronicle, keeping offices vacant when bishops and abbots died so he could divert the revenues from their lands into his own treasury. When Lanfranc died, for instance, the office of Archbishop of Canterbury was kept unfilled for more than three years until William himself thought he was dying. Then he hurriedly appointed Anselm as the new archbishop, subsequently quarrelling violently with him and driving him into exile, where he remained at the time of William's death.

Equally the king's behaviour and that of his followers was condemned by the chroniclers. He 'abandoned himself without restraint to lewdness and debauchery,' says Vitalis, 'Setting his subjects a fatal example of gross lasciviousness,' while Malmesbury deplored the 'flowing hair and extravagant dress' that became the court fashion. The rewards he offered to anyone who could boast feats of arms attracted to his court large numbers of military-minded men 'out of every province on this side of the mountains,' leading Vitalis to write that he was generous to foreigners while oppressing his own people.

These men were not subjected to any kind of control. Anyone with the king's favour could do more or less what he liked with impunity. Thus Malmesbury records, 'The courtiers preyed upon the property of the country people ... taking the very meat from the mouths of these wretched creatures ... assailers of other's chastity, prodigal of their own.' On one occasion the Chronicle declares that William's retinue, 'did as much injury in the country in which they were detained as ... even an army could have committed in a peaceable land.' Of course it was customary for invading armies to plunder all they wanted from the surrounding land – witness the dismay of Robert's crusaders overwintering in southern Italy that they could not steal what they wanted from the friendly countryside – but plundering one's own people was another matter and well worthy of condemnation.

Perhaps the greatest complaint of the English against William Rufus, however, was his constant demand for money. 'He was ever vexing the people with armies and with cruel taxes,' says the Anglo-Saxon Chronicle at the time of his death, while earlier years record 'unlawful taxes', and 'manifold oppressive taxes', and how, even in years of near famine, 'the people had, nevertheless, no respite from unjust taxes.' Nor was it only taxes. Justice itself could be bought and sold to the highest bidder. 'The halter was loosened from the robber's neck if he could promise any emolument to the sovereign,' writes Malmesbury, and 'Men of the meanest condition, or guilty of whatever crime, were listened to if they could suggest any thing likely to be advantageous to the king.'

In all these exactions William was ably assisted by the man variously described as his chaplain, his treasurer and his justiciar, Ranulf Flambard. Ranulf was the son of a priest of Bayeux. How he picked up the nickname Flambard is not at all clear, but none of the explanations is complimentary. Some said it was due to his incendiary personality, others to the way he burned through men's possessions like a devouring flame in obtaining money for the king. Anselm declared it was his flame-like cruelty that earned him the name. He began in the service of Odo of

Bayeux, moved to that of the Conqueror, and soon after his death appeared as chief fundraiser for William Rufus, a job for which he showed both flair and imagination. According to some accounts it was he who pointed out to William the profits to be obtained by leaving vacant bishoprics and abbacies. He is again credited with the ploy of calling up the levies and then taking from them their maintenance money and, of course, as justiciar or chief judge there were all manner of ways of extracting money from wrongdoers, even if some wrongs had to be invented in the first place.

Of course, William's policy of bribing his way to success in Normandy needed constant supplies of money, as did his takeover of that duchy in return for a substantial loan. Rewards to favourites and payment for mercenaries also needed regular cash, but particular anger seemed to be felt against what might be called William's vanity projects, a high wall around the Tower of London, and especially his new hall at Westminster, completed only the year before his death. This mighty structure, the largest of its kind in Europe at the time, was designed to show off the king's magnificence, but was hugely resented, not only by those who had to pay for it, but also by those many local men owing service to the Crown who had to build it. No doubt if they had heard the king's remark when it was finished, that it was not half big enough, they would have been even less happy.

These, then, were the perceived wrongs that Henry could turn to his advantage at the beginning of his reign, and his initial actions show that he was fully aware of just how to do this. Again, we can probably discount Wace's story that Henry was reluctant to take the crown and had to be persuaded to it by an assembly of bishops and barons. There is no record of any such assembly, nor do Henry's movements suggest any kind of reluctance. Indeed, he seems very well prepared for such an unexpected eventuality.

William Rufus died late on a Thursday afternoon. The following Sunday, 5 August 1100, Henry was anointed and crowned as King of England in Westminster Abbey. Traditionally a coronation was carried out by the Archbishop of Canterbury, but Anselm was still in exile in France, and the Archbishop of York was ill at Ripon. Henry could wait for neither, so the required ritual was performed by Maurice, Bishop of London, the most senior clergyman available.

Immediately afterwards Henry showed his determination to distance himself from his brother's reign by issuing his Coronation Charter, sometimes referred to as the Charter of Liberties. For some considerable time, part of the coronation ceremony had involved the swearing of an oath by the new king that he would uphold the Church, maintain peace in the kingdom and dispense justice to all people. Henry's charter, however, went considerably further than this, containing fourteen detailed clauses aimed at putting right the perceived wrongs countenanced by William Rufus. Further, it was committed to writing, witnessed by a number of bishops and nobles and a copy sent to every shire in the land.

It was quite clearly a bid for popular support, and the very salutation set the tone. Henry addressed his greeting to bishops, sheriffs, barons and all his other vassals *both French and English*. Apart from his presence on the spot in England, there were two factors that gave him a slight edge over his brother in claiming the English crown. Firstly, he was the son of a king of England, whereas when Robert was born his father was only Duke of Normandy. Secondly and perhaps more importantly, Henry had been born in England and could thus claim some affinity with the land he aspired to rule. The reference to his brother as a foreigner during the confrontation in Winchester shows he was well aware of this advantage, and though the first factor might carry some weight with his Norman magnates, the second would have had far more appeal to great swell of the population below that level. In 1088 William had called on the English to support him, and quite clearly from the very beginning Henry intended to do the same.

The Charter itself contained an assortment of promises, some for each of the groups he needed to win over. For the clerics there was the promise that in future the church in England would be free of the unjust demands William Rufus had imposed on it. With a nod to the reformers, he promised he would not sell Church offices, nor prolong vacancies so as to take the revenues intended for its support.

For the magnates there were promises that heirs should only pay lawful and reasonable reliefs to enter into their inheritances, not the extortionate sums his brother had demanded, such as the £3,000 paid by Robert de Bellème. When his chief men wanted to marry off their daughters or sisters they must ask the king's permission, but he would not unreasonably refuse it or charge them for it. Widows would not be married off without their consent, and as long as they remained free of affairs, should have their own money and even custody of lands and children until the children came of age. These benefits, he commanded, should be passed on by his magnates to their men in turn. Furthermore, those knights who held their land in return for military service would hold that land free of land tax and other labours, so they could devote their time and money to preparing themselves fully to serve the king and defend the realm.

For the English the major promise was a return to the laws of King Edward the Confessor, subject only to amendments made to these by the Conqueror in agreement with his barons. Together with a promise that magnates would no longer be able to buy their way out of justice but would have to pay compensation according to the law, this seemed to promise a return to a more stable legal landscape in place of the arbitrary justice practised by William Rufus and his justiciar. Murderers, too, would be dealt with according to the law, except that Henry specifically pardoned all murders committed before the day of his coronation. It is tempting to wonder if he had a particular murder in mind. One thing, however, that Henry did not give up, which might have pleased the English, was his right to the royal forests. He declared he would hold them just as his father had held them before him.

Then in one simple clause the king set his firm peace over the whole realm and commanded that it be kept. This concept of the 'King's peace' was not a new idea – indeed many of the ideas in the charter were not new, some dating back as far as King Cnut some eighty years before. At that time, however, the 'King's peace', his authority to keep order, was personal to the king and died with him. The re-establishment of a new 'King's peace' was a firm statement that England had a new king now, and one, furthermore, who intended to maintain his authority throughout the entire realm. To underline the point, the last clause in his Charter recognised that between William's 'Peace' and his own there may have been deeds done and advantage taken of that time without authority, however brief it had been. If, then, in that time, anyone had taken anything from the royal properties, or indeed anyone else's properties, they were to restore it freely at once or face the consequences.

These clauses, therefore, can be linked to the first in the Charter, where Henry declared that 'by the mercy of God and with the common counsel of the barons of the realm of England, I have been crowned king of that realm.' The message is clear. I am the king, crowned and anointed. I am here to stay.

There were eleven witnesses to the Charter, a rather miscellaneous bunch and clearly an example of Henry making the best of what was available. Maurice, Bishop of London was the most senior cleric to sign, his name being followed by that of William, Bishop-elect of Winchester. Winchester was, of course, a major bishopric, but William Giffard had been bishop-elect for a matter of two or three days, the first appointment made by Henry after his brother's death. William had been chancellor to William Rufus, so his support was important to Henry, as was that of his elder brother Walter Giffard who also appears as a witness. Walter had inherited large estates in Buckinghamshire and in Normandy, and witnessed without the title of earl, though shortly after he appears as 1st Earl of Buckingham.

The other earls listed as witnesses have a very second-class appearance. True, Earl Henry de Beaumont was 1st Earl of Warwick and younger brother of Robert, Count of Meulan. Simon de Senlis, however, was Earl of Huntingdon and Northampton only by virtue of his marriage to Maud, the daughter of Waltheof, the last Anglo-Saxon Earl of Northumbria. Possibly his presence as witness was a further attempt to tie Henry in with the older English aristocracy, though the link is rather tenuous.

Some of the other signatories show continuity with the previous reign such as the Giffard brothers, Robert de Montfort and Eudo Dapifer, who had served as steward to both Henry's brother and father. Roger Bigod and Robert Malet had both lost lands under William, while Robert Fitzhamon had held lands under Henry in the Cotentin and was a long-time friend and supporter.

While the list appears relatively weak, it must be remembered that some of the major earls, of Chester and Shrewsbury for example, were away in Normandy at the time. There is no knowing whether or not Henry would have won their support had they been present, but clearly that was a chance he was not prepared to take. The Earl of Shrewsbury, Robert de Bellème, was more likely to oppose him on principle, but it was a great deal more difficult to overthrow a crowned and anointed king than a mere claimant to the throne.

Crowned and anointed he was, with his manifesto clearly set out, but there was more yet that he could do to consolidate his position and he wasted no time in doing it. On 15 August the hated Ranulf Flambard was arrested and imprisoned in the Tower of London, reputedly the first prisoner ever held there. There was a certain irony in this since, until very recently, Flambard had been overseeing the building of the strong wall around the outside of the famous keep. In most men's minds, though, he was chiefly associated with the constant raising of money for William by legitimate and illegitimate means, and his arrest would have been a popular move.

Similarly popular would be Henry's invitation to Archbishop Anselm to return to England to resume his role as head of the English Church. According to Eadmer, Anselm had been surprisingly upset at the death of William, but was ready and willing to return when first urged to do so by messengers from Canterbury. These were backed up by a letter from the new king himself, urging Anselm to hurry back to England and promising that he would submit himself and his kingdom to the advice and direction of the archbishop.

Anselm and his party arrived in England on 23 September to general rejoicing. A few days later he met with the king at Salisbury. The meeting was amicable on both sides, Henry in particular going out of his way to express his joy at Anselm's return, and to apologise for not waiting for the archbishop to consecrate him at his coronation. It soon appeared, however, that the religious sticking point that had led to Anselm's exile would not be so easily dissolved. There were principles at stake on both sides.

Eadmer, who was probably present at the meeting, shrewdly points out that, when Anselm declared himself ready to return at once to exile, the king was presented with a considerable problem. He could not give in to the archbishop's demands, but nor could he let him immediately sail away again. Compromise was called for and Henry produced one. Both sides of the problem should be submitted to the pope before the following Easter. In the meantime, Anselm would remain in England with all his estates and duties restored to him. Rather reluctantly the archbishop agreed to this truce and the two parted in peace.

As it happened, very shortly after this Henry found himself in need of his archbishop's help, the matter concerned being his proposed marriage. In a move that was more pleasing to his English subjects than to the Norman magnates, the king declared his intention to marry Edith, the daughter of King Malcolm of Scotland and his wife Margaret. On her mother's side, Edith was descended from Edmund Ironside, half-brother of Edward the Confessor, and one of the long line of Anglo-Saxon kings that ruled before the Normans came. Edgar Atheling was her uncle. If Henry's aim was to unite the still firmly divided population of England behind a single line of royal stock, he could not have picked a better bride. He may even have heard the story of Edward the Confessor's death-bed prophecy. In this Edward is said to have described a vision of a green tree split in half down its trunk. One part was then carried away to a distance of three furlongs before later being rejoined to the other part, whereupon the tree became whole again and produced leaves and fruit. Only when this had been fulfilled, he declared, would the troubles he foresaw for England be at an end.

For those interpreting this prophecy its message was clear. The tree was England and its trunk the royal line of kings, split by the coming of the Normans. Only when the old royal line was united to the new, would England find peace and prosperity. This reunion was exactly what Henry was proposing, but he had a few problems to overcome first.

Edith had been born in 1080, her English name reflecting her mother's royal descent, though her godfather was Robert Curthose and the Conqueror's wife, Queen Matilda, may have been her godmother. Quite early in life Edith, with her younger sister Mary, had been sent south to the care of her aunt Christina, abbess of Romsey Abbey, to receive a suitable education. Around 1093 Christina died and the girls transferred to Wilton Abbey, long favoured by the English royal family. In the same year she was visited by her father who was apparently disgusted to find her wearing the veil of a nun. He was at the time in dispute with William Rufus, and intended to remove his daughters back to Scotland to find them suitable husbands – William Rufus himself has been mentioned as a possible suitor. Before this happened, however, Malcolm and his son Edward were killed, and Queen Margaret herself died a few days later.

What happened to the girls after this is not entirely clear. There is a reasonable chance they may have remained at Wilton, or moved to another convent, but equally they may have found shelter somewhere else. Nothing more is heard of Edith until Henry chose her for his wife, though both Malmesbury and Vitalis say Henry had known her for some time before this and 'been attracted by her many graces and virtues.' At some point she had also changed the English 'Edith' into the more acceptably Norman 'Matilda'. The question now arose, however, whether having lived so long among nuns and having been seen on at least one or two occasions veiled like a nun, she might in fact have been given into the convent life by her parents with the intention that she herself would become a nun. She might even have taken vows, in which case there would be no question of her marrying anyone, not even the new king of England.

The lady herself declared she had never taken vows and never intended to become a nun. She had worn the veil on occasion – she called it a little black hood – at the insistence of her aunt to protect her from 'the lust of the Normans'. Whenever she was out of sight of her aunt, however, she confessed she had childishly torn the thing off and trampled it underfoot as she hated it so much.

We have these details from Eadmer who declares he was present when Matilda came to Anselm to submit her case to him and obtain his advice. Anselm summoned a meeting of bishops, abbots and nobles at Lambeth Palace, at which the story was corroborated by witnesses, and Matilda herself offered to prove the truth of it by any oath they might require her to swear. The verdict of everyone was that she was free to marry.

Once again, at the very church door, Anselm challenged the assembled crowd that if anyone there knew anything that disproved their verdict, or any reason why the marriage should not go ahead, he should say so at once. Nobody did, and Matilda was duly married to Henry on 11 November 1100, and crowned as Queen by Anselm immediately afterwards.

In personal terms there is no reason to believe it was anything other than a happy marriage. Henry was 32 years old and his bride some 10 years younger. Eadmer, who would have seen both of them, gives as a fact that the king was in love, and that both parties desired the marriage. Similarly, both Vitalis and Malmesbury, looking back on it, believed there was a real attraction and affection there. Clearly it was as successful as such a marriage was likely to be at the time. As a royal marriage it worked equally well. In due course either three or four children were produced, although only two survived to adulthood. As a political marriage, however, it was the greatest success. Though for a while at least some of the Norman lords referred to the couple sarcastically by the Saxon names Godric and Goda, Henry's English subjects were delighted at the union, as he must have intended.

By the time he held his Christmas court at Westminster, Henry had done all he could to establish himself securely on the throne of England. All the greatest magnates had returned and done him homage for their English lands. He had rewarded his friends, disposed of his enemies and obtained the wife he wanted. The next move now would have to come from someone else.

4

Robert the Hero
(1101–1103)

The return of Robert Curthose to Normandy in September 1100 was probably the high point of his life. He had fulfilled the oath he made when taking the cross more than four years earlier. He had made his pilgrimage, played his part in defeating the Turks and capturing Jerusalem and, as one of the earlier returners, was able to receive in full measure the glory that resulted from those deeds.

Unlike many who had undertaken that First Crusade, Robert had had no ulterior motive in accepting Pope Urban's challenge to Christendom to retake the Holy Places. Indeed, even the pope himself might be accused of mixed motives since his call to arms did much to secure his own position on the papal throne, and bore little resemblance to the appeal for help that had been made to him by the Byzantine Emperor, Alexius Comnenus.

The emperor had succeeded some fourteen years before to an empire besieged on all sides and divided within. It must have taken some effort for him to appeal to the leader of the Western Church barely fifty years after the decisive split between Greek and Roman Christianity. He had hoped for some military assistance to drive back the Seljuk Turks who had overrun the whole of Anatolia (modern day Turkey), which had previously formed an important part of his empire. Urban's call for the West to reclaim Jerusalem was a wholly different matter, though, and from the start it was not clear whether this was intended to return these lands to the

Byzantine Empire or to carve out a sphere of influence in the East for the pope himself.

Nor was Alexius anticipating the mass of crusaders who now descended on Constantinople on their way to the Holy Land. Indeed it seems Urban himself had no real plan further than the mobilisation of the Franks of Western Europe. He never entered Normandy itself, contenting himself with touring the southern and western French lands, and appears to have anticipated the gathering of a single army, led by the papal legate, Adhemar, Bishop of Le Puy, and by Raymond, Count of Toulouse.

In fact in addition to this, three other separate armies made their way to the east, each with its own leaders. Robert Curthose joined with his relatives Robert, Count of Flanders, and Stephen, Count of Blois, along with Hugh, brother of King Philip of France, to lead a force from the northern lands. Another group from the Franco-German borders was led by Godfrey de Bouillon and his brothers, Eustace, Count of Boulogne, and Baldwin. This perhaps shows the breadth of the appeal of the call to arms, since Godfrey had long been a supporter of the Holy Roman Emperor in his conflicts with the pope. Last, but by no means least, was the army led from the Norman states of southern Italy by Bohemond of Taranto and his nephew Tancred.

It is clear Robert Curthose was not in the first rank of leaders of the crusade. Bohemond, Raymond of Toulouse and Godfrey de Bouillon are usually credited with that honour, all of whom obtained significant territories in the east. Nor is he mentioned as an outstanding general. Instead he appears to have remained utterly true to his previous character – brave and fearless in battle, often acting the peacemaker between his quarrelsome fellow leaders and, whenever possible in between, relaxing and seeking whatever ease might be found in the largely inhospitable lands through which they passed.

The journey south through Italy, for example, took so long that, unlike some, Robert and his forces had to overwinter in the southern Italian states. There he and his fellows enjoyed a comfortable time as guests of Roger of Apulia, who regarded the Duke of Normandy as his rightful overlord. The following Easter they went on again, crossing the

Adriatic and proceeding to Constantinople where they received further hospitality from a rather wary Emperor Alexius. The passage of these hordes of crusaders through his land had already led to conflict and he was not at all sure of their motives. Some, Bohemond for example, had recently been his bitter enemies, attacking the Byzantine Empire itself and trying to carve off chunks for themselves.

To try to regain some measure of control, Alexius had devised an oath of homage and fealty to himself, which he required all the leaders to take in return for a promise of support from the empire. Perhaps surprisingly Bohemond took the oath without argument, as did all the others with the exception of Raymond of Toulouse, who would only swear to undertake no enterprise against the life of Alexius or against his State. Robert, one of the late arrivals, took the oath without any argument.

The siege of Nicea had been underway for some time before Robert arrived, but he shared in the triumph when it fell, and also, no doubt, in the rewards handed out by Alexius. Soon after, however, came one of the episodes that boosted the legend of Robert's crusade. The army had marched south in two separate but parallel divisions. Vitalis suggests this was because they were unsure of the way to their next objective, the city of Antioch, while William of Malmesbury's idea is that they were spreading out in that desert land, the better to forage for their needs. It may well be, though, that splits in the leadership were already becoming apparent, since Bohemond and his nephew headed the smaller division with Robert and Stephen of Blois, while Raymond of Toulouse and Godfrey de Bouillon led the other. Several other writers flatly state that they do not know why the army was split, or that it happened accidentally.

It was the smaller division, stated by some to be the vanguard, that suddenly found itself face to face with an enemy force led by Kilif Arslan. Vitalis describes their numbers as 'like the sand on the seashore', and Henry of Huntingdon and several others put the estimate at 360,000 men. Despite other wildly varying estimates, it is clear that the crusader force was well outnumbered.

Bohemond, however, determined to make a stand, sending messengers to the other division of the army to come to their aid, but Vitalis declares that these messengers were not at first believed, and that the action known as the Battle of Dorylaeum lasted at least six hours before any relief came. 'The Franks,' he says, 'bore the brunt of the attack without recoiling,' while the women followers 'rendered essential service to the combatants by running to them with pitchers of water when they were dying of thirst.' Henry of Huntingdon describes the horses of the crusaders becoming unnerved 'under the strange shouts of the Saracens and the braying of their trumpets,' and refusing to obey their riders, and it is when they seemed to be on the point of running away that he puts a stirring speech into the mouth of Robert Curthose (strongly reminiscent of that with which William the Conqueror rallied his men at Hastings) to rally them to fresh efforts. 'Why are you fleeing' Robert demands. 'The Turkish horses are swifter than ours; flight will not save you, it is better to die here; if you think as I do, follow me.' He then charged into the fight, striking at the chief of the enemy, and inspiring Bohemond, Tancred and the others to return to the action. Neither Vitalis nor Malmesbury mention this incident, so possibly the tale grew in the telling, particularly as the consequence of the action was the overrunning of the Turkish camp. This was found to be full of gold and silver and other riches as well as the more necessary supports of life, an abundance of food and drink. The crusaders left, so Vitalis tells us, 'laden with booty, in triumph and inexpressible joy.'

What is made clear, however, is the reduced state of the crusader army at that point. Malmesbury declares that they could not pursue the Turks further because their horses were exhausted and, 'scarce able to support life on the barren turf.' Nor were the soldiers and their camp followers any better off as they marched onward towards Antioch, being 'reduced to the last extremity of hunger and thirst.'

Antioch, the next great prize on the way to Jerusalem, was besieged from October 1097 to June 1098. Malmesbury describes the city as next in precedence after Rome, Constantinople and Alexandria, and here again the fortunes of Curthose display all parts of his character. Leading the vanguard in the approach to the city, and fully active in the early months of the siege, by December he had withdrawn to the port known as St Symeon, which was the closest to Antioch. This port had been taken from the Turks at the end of November, probably by a combined English and Byzantine fleet, and was now able to support the crusaders with supplies imported from Cyprus. However, the Turks had tried to retake the port and to attack the inland supply route, and accounts describe an appeal to Robert to come to their aid, which he was more than willing to do. No doubt he gave sterling service protecting the port and the supply routes, but his position was certainly more comfortable among the plentiful supplies in St Symeon than it would have been sitting outside the walls of Antioch. Indeed, it is recorded that he had to be ordered back to the siege and went only on the third summons, under threat of excommunication for abandoning his crusader's oath.

Nevertheless he did return, and once again fought bravely, preventing a break out from the city at a time when the rest of the crusading force was engaged with a relieving army nearby. He was there, too, when the siege finally ended at the beginning of June, not by some mighty onslaught, but by Bohemond successfully bribing Firouz, one of the commanders within the city, to open the gates and let them in. Even then, however, they failed to take the citadel, and within days the arrival of another relieving army outside the walls turned the besiegers into the besieged.

Morale was at its lowest. Henry of Huntingdon describes them eating the leaves of the trees and softened horse hides. 'Hope,' he says, 'increased on the side of the Infidels, and famine on that of the Christians.' Some tried to slip away over the walls by night, and it is recorded that Stephen of Blois, who had been ill and was rejoining the army at Antioch, saw the size of the army camped outside, and instead deserted his friends and fled away home. Even worse, Huntingdon says he met the emperor coming to the aid of the crusaders, and 'induced him to retire by telling him with tears that all the Franks had perished.'

Robert and his fellows left in Antioch, however, had in fact taken an oath that they would fight on to the death. A miracle was needed to save them – and a miracle duly arrived. Peter Abraham, a Provencal clerk, had a vision in which St Andrew appeared to him and told him where to find the 'Holy Lance', the spear that had pierced the side of Christ on the cross. It took some time before he could finally persuade others to believe him, but then, after a whole day searching in the church that had been indicated in the vision, the spear was duly found. 'It was lifted from the spot among general acclamations, crowds of people running to see it and covering it with kisses of devotion. Their joy was so great ... they forgot their griefs, and from that moment took courage to think of war.'

Nor was that their only miracle. It was decided to face the besiegers in open battle, and they marched forth in seven divisions. Some accounts put Robert Curthose in the first and some in the third, with 15,000 men from Normandy, Maine, Anjou, Brittany and England. Vitalis reports a gentle refreshing rain fell as they left the city, and then, as the attack began, 'there was seen to issue forth from the heart of the mountains, a countless host mounted on white horses and carrying banners.' They were led by three holy martyrs. St George, St Demetrius and St Mercury had decided to join the fight. Vitalis concedes they were not seen by all, 'but it is attested by many who were eye-witnesses.' Needless to say, their attackers fled, those in the citadel surrendered and Antioch was secured.

They had still a long way to go to reach their main objective, Jerusalem, and now the divisions in the army threatened to destroy them. Baldwin had already turned aside to become Count of Edessa. Now Bohemond declared that Alexius had forfeited his right to Antioch by failing to come to their aid during the siege, and he claimed the city for himself. Raymond of Toulouse reminded him of the oath he had sworn to Alexius, and Robert Curthose was called on to mediate between them, but to no effect.

In the end after a rest of some months, Raymond set off for Jerusalem accompanied by Robert Curthose, Godfrey of Bouillon, Tancred and Robert of Flanders, while Bohemond remained in Antioch. Jerusalem in turn was put under siege at the beginning of June 1099 and the siege lasted until the middle of July. At that point a wooden siege tower constructed by the crusaders was brought close enough to a weaker, part of the walls to allow a party of the invaders to force their way across, and to open the gates for their fellows. What followed, however, was by far the most shameful episode in a campaign that was not short of horrors, as the Muslim and Jewish inhabitants of the city were massacred almost to a man. 'No-one knows,' says Vitalis, 'The number of the slain, but the floor of the temple was knee-deep in blood, and great heaps of corpses were piled up in all quarters of the city, as the victors spared neither age, sex, rank nor condition of any kind.'

Although once part of the Byzantine Empire, Jerusalem had long been in the hands of the Egyptian Fatimid Caliphate (who had allowed free access to both Christian and Jewish pilgrims) before the arrival of the Seljuk Turks. There was no question, then, of handing it over to Alexius. Instead it would become a Christian kingdom. William of Malmesbury declares that Robert Curthose was invited to become its king, but turned it down, 'not through awe of its dignity, but through the fear of endless labour.' All his later misfortunes, Malmesbury declares, arose from this refusal, 'which tarnished his glory with an indelible stain.' Other writers suggest the title was offered to a number of other leaders of the crusade before eventually Godfrey of Bouillon agreed to be, not 'king', for he said there can only be one King of Jerusalem, but 'Defender of the Holy Sepulchre'. He would very soon have some defending to do.

In the years immediately before the arrival of the crusaders, the Fatimids of Egypt had succeeded in driving the Seljuk Turks out of Jerusalem, and it was the Fatimids that had defended the city. Now their leader, Al-Afdal Shahanshah, brought up an enormous army of many nations to try once again to recover it. The Battle of Ascalon followed, where again the crusader army was heavily outnumbered – Vitalis says by ten to one – and again Robert Curthose's display of heroism on the field of battle proved inspirational. He held the middle of the battle line, along with Tancred, Eustace of Boulogne, and Robert of Flanders, while Godfrey led the left wing and Raymond of Toulouse the right. The story is told that as they charged forward to engage the enemy, Robert Curthose targeted the battle standard of the Fatimid leader, the rallying point for the whole army. Cutting down the standard-bearer, he seized the standard, a silver lance topped with a golden sphere, and carried it off, so inspiring his fellows that they smashed right through the centre of the army, causing their opponents to panic and flee. 'The field flowed with blood,' says Vitalis, 'and was covered with the corpses of the pagans.'

For Robert the fighting was now over. Though divisions among the leaders meant that the city of Ascalon itself was not conquered, he had fulfilled his oath as a crusader and could now return home. With other retiring leaders, we are told, he bathed in the River Jordan and gathered palms from Jericho before setting out on his return journey, by sea this time, first to Constantinople to receive thanks and rewards from the emperor, then on to Italy. His honour was intact, his reputation greatly advanced and, unlike some, he had made no enemies during the whole long crusade.

In Italy, too, he acquired a wife. Sybilla, daughter of Geoffrey, Count of Conversano, was an excellent match in every way. Not only did she bring him a substantial dowry with which to redeem his mortgaged duchy, but all the writers declare she was beautiful, virtuous and intelligent. Indeed, some suggest that in brains and application she outshone her husband and that during a brief period when she was regent of Normandy, she ruled far more effectively than he had.

It is likely that Robert heard the news of William Rufus's death while travelling home from Italy. He immediately began to call himself King of England, but typically seems to have done nothing whatever to actively assert his claim on this title. Arriving back in Normandy, he was no doubt delighted to recover his duchy without either paying or fighting for it; indeed, fighting seems to have been the furthest from his mind. He and his wife first made a pilgrimage to Mont St Michel to give thanks for a safe return, and then he seems to have visited his sister Cecilia, the abbess of La Trinité Abbey in Caen to present her with a banner captured during the crusade.

His state of mind at the time is well illustrated by an episode recorded by Vitalis. Helias of La Flèche had also heard of the death of William Rufus, and at once he again asserted his right to the county of Maine, and was joyfully admitted to the town, but not the citadel, of Le Mans. That fortress was still held by the garrison installed by William Rufus, and now, it appears, they became unsure as to whom they should be serving, either Robert or Henry, king of England. Good-natured banter is recorded between Helias and the garrison leaders, and eventually it was decided that they should send to both Robert and Henry to see on whose behalf they were now holding the fortress. According to Vitalis, Robert was found to be 'exhausted by the fatigues of his long pilgrimage,' and when asked the question replied, 'I am worn out with my protracted labours, and am contented with the duchy of Normandy.' He advised them to make peace with Helias. It is only fair to add that the messengers found Henry equally unwilling to claim their service. He 'wisely preferred devoting himself to the care of what was lawfully his,' and, thanking them for their good will, also sent them away. The fortress was duly handed over to Helias, who was then openly declared to be the lawful Count of Maine.

Robert's peaceful tendencies were not allowed to last for long, however, and this time the catalyst for action was Ranulf Flambard. That 'inveterate robber of his country' had been imprisoned for less than six months in the Tower of London when he made his spectacular escape, partly aided by the generosity of the new king. Henry had made Flambard an allowance of two shillings a day while he was in prison, in order to provide him with food and drink. This enabled the disgraced justiciar to dine sumptuously every day, to which feasts his gaolers were also invited. One day early in February 1101 Flambard's friends concealed a length of rope in a large flagon of wine provided for the evening meal. That evening Flambard was particularly generous in serving the wine, so that soon his gaolers were sound asleep. He then secured the rope to a mullion in the centre of the window and let himself down the tower wall. Vitalis adds the delightful, if possibly invented, details, that he remembered to take his pastoral staff with him but forgot his gloves, as a result of which his hands were torn to the bone on his descent. He also records that the rope was too short so that 'the portly bishop fell, and being much bruised, groaned piteously.' His friends were on hand, though, to pick him up and speed him on his way to Normandy. There he was welcomed by the duke and, much as Odo of Bayeux before him, quickly established himself at the centre of the government. His main aim, so Vitalis claims, was to 'rouse the duke to engage in hostilities with his brother, using all his efforts to exasperate him against the king.'

As usual Robert went along with what was demanded of him and began to make preparations to invade England. He should have had more than adequate resources for this, especially with Flambard, the master fund-raiser, at his side. Nevertheless, Malmesbury records that, 'he lavished so profusely on buffoons and worthless people that in a few days he was penniless.'

His major supporters were Robert de Bellême and his younger brother Roger, known as 'the Poitevin', William of Warenne and William of Mortain, all of whom were major landholders on both sides of the Channel, and all of whom had some personal reason for opposing Henry's kingship. Robert de Bellême had, of course, been a lifelong supporter of Robert Curthose, though his violent anarchy in Normandy must have strained the relationship. In addition, though, Henry had been gifted one of the major Bellême castles at Domfront, and his continued possession of it must have been a constant affront to Robert. Roger, with lands at Eye in Suffolk and in Lancashire and Cumberland, would, of course, have been supporting the family interests in England. William of Warenne, who had inherited the lands and title of Earl of Surrey in 1088, had apparently wanted to marry Edith/Matilda and been rejected. Jealousy may therefore have played a part in his opposition to the king. William of Mortain, on the other hand, had family connections on all sides, being the cousin of both Robert Curthose and Henry on his father's side, and the nephew of Robert de Bellème on his mother's. For some unspecified reason, it was declared that he had always hated Henry, and again it is possible that jealousy comes into it, since Malmesbury declares that he was a young man of 'shameless arrogance'.

All these men were currently in England, having recently sworn homage to Henry as the new king. He can have had little doubt of their disloyalty, however. William of Warenne in particular is recorded as the author of a number of sarcastic nicknames for the king. Wace declares that he called him 'Stag Foot', ridiculing Henry's scientific approach to the art of deer hunting. He says the name derives from a rather pointed joke that Henry could tell how many branches the antlers of a stag held by the print of its foot on the ground. Where he gets this tale from he doesn't say, but the nickname is likely to pre-date Henry's kingship. William of Warenne is also likely to be the originator of the nicknames 'Godric' and 'Goda', now given to the king and his new wife, and openly used among some of the Norman nobles. The Anglo-Saxon names would have been a clear insult on the part of the Normans, and also, maybe, a hint to others that Henry's inclination towards his English subjects might undermine their own prospects.

Henry, himself, was not slow to see the danger, and as early as March moved to cut off one potential ally for his brother. Long ago the Conqueror had made a treaty of friendship with the Count of Flanders under which neither would support the enemies of the other and, in return for a regular payment, the count would supply a certain number of knights when requested to do so for the Conqueror's aid. This had been renewed from time to time by the original parties and their successors, and in March 1101 it was renewed again. Since Robert of Flanders had so recently been a close companion of Curthose on the First Crusade it might have been thought he would support him again, but he seems to have been happy enough to sign a treaty with his brother instead. Under the terms of the treaty, Robert of Flanders agreed to provide 1,000 knights to serve Henry either in England or in Normandy, and to pay all their expenses himself except for transport. It was recognised that he owed obligations to Philip of France, who was the overlord of both himself and Curthose, but if Philip was to move to support Curthose by invading England, Robert agreed to try and talk him out of it, and if he failed, only to provide 20 knights for his service.

Witnessing the treaty for Henry were a number of high-ranking clergy, including Gerard, recently appointed Archbishop of York, and Robert Bloet, Bishop of Lincoln, who had been chancellor to William Rufus and who, after his death, had firmly transferred his allegiance to Henry. The lay witnesses included Robert, Count of Meulan, Robert Fitzhamon and Eudo Dapifer, a royal steward. Perhaps more interesting is the list of sureties, those prepared to guarantee the treaty with their own possessions. Here, among others, are Arnulf of Montgomery, brother of Robert de Bellème, whose loyalty was not at all certain, along with Gilbert FitzRichard, Miles Crispin, now castellan of Wallingford, and once again Robert Fitzhamon, who put up twice as much in surety as the others.

Through Lent and the Easter season an uneasy peace seems to have held, though no doubt everyone was aware of the activities in Normandy as a fleet and army were assembled. By Whitsun, late that year at the beginning of June, it was clear that an invasion was imminent. Once again Eadmer is an eye-witness as tensions rose at the English court. The king, he says, was suspicious of the nobles, and the nobles suspicious of the king, and in that atmosphere of mutual mistrust, Henry found that Anselm, that unshakeable rock of integrity, was the only man he could wholly rely on.

Of the nobles, some, he knew, would betray him. Some would probably stand firm, the Beaumont brothers, for example, Count of Meulan and Earl of Warwick respectively; Robert Fitzhamon; Richard of Redvers, another long-time friend; and Roger Bigod. The rest were likely to wait and see which way the wind blew. Eadmer suggests they held back from giving Henry their full support for fear he should turn into a tyrant. More likely they held back to be sure of being on the winning side. To try to reassure them Henry repeated the promises he had made at his coronation, putting his hand in Anselm's as representing the entire people. It is notable the nobles made no promise of loyalty in return.

An army was needed and an army was called for. Nobles and bishops alike were asked to produce the forces they had promised in return for their lands. The bishops responded in full, even Anselm, camping with his men alongside the king. The nobles responded in part, and even then their men could not be relied on. Eadmer records that Henry regularly brought one or other of his wavering barons to Anselm for a stiffening talk, and in the end Anselm himself called the whole body together and reminded them of their duty to an anointed king, and the eternal damnation that awaited any who broke that faith. Indeed, Eadmer declares, had it not been for Anselm's intervention, Henry would surely have lost his kingdom.

If Henry could not rely on his nobles, however, there was another more enthusiastic group he could rely on, the English. The long-existing Saxon arrangement known as the fyrd provided for each shire to produce a certain number of fighting men, fully equipped and with money for their own maintenance. These had been called on several times by William Rufus, most notoriously on the occasion when he had simply taken their money and dismissed them. Their loyalty was due solely to the king and to the defence of their country, and in Henry they seemed to have a king who could unite both enthusiasms against an unknown foreigner.

They were not knights trained to arms, however, nor used to fighting the Norman way with strong reliance on cavalry. When they were gathered together, therefore – at Pevensey rather than Hastings whose lord was suspect – Malmesbury describes how Henry himself, 'anxious for their safety,' took on the role of instructor and 'frequently went through the ranks, instructing them how to elude the ferocity of the cavalry … and how to return their strokes.'

The fyrd could provide sailors as well as soldiers, and we don't know whether the naval force sent out by Henry to patrol the seas and intercept an invasion was made up of English fyrd or Norman retainers. Quite possibly some of each were involved since, in the event, at least a portion of them did the very opposite of their duty. John of Worcester gives Ranulf Flambard the credit for 'tampering with their fidelity' by bribes, so that, instead of barring Robert's way, they became his 'pilots to England.' They would, of course, have known of the whereabouts of Henry's army, now apparently swelled to a mighty force, at least in number, so rather than guiding Robert to an anticipated landing at Hastings or Pevensey, he was led safely to anchorage at Portsmouth, arriving there on 21 July 1101.

A swift decisive move then could have utterly defeated Henry. By some accounts Robert had approximately 200 ships, with cavalry, archers and foot-soldiers. An attack on nearby Winchester could have taken the town and royal treasury, and convinced any waverers that the Duke of Normandy was determined to seize the crown from his upstart brother.

That may well have been the original plan laid down by Flambard, who had been all along the driving force behind the expedition. Characteristically, however, Robert did no such thing. Wace, with his usual eye to a romantic story, declares that the duke refused to attack Winchester since Queen Matilda, his god-daughter, was there and was in childbirth. Since her daughter was not born until the following February, this would have been the longest childbirth in history and, in fact, Matilda would barely have known she was pregnant at the time. As so often, then, we can discount Wace's version.

It seems more likely that Robert was waiting for his forces to be supplemented by the support he had been led to believe would be his as soon as he mounted his invasion. Some support he certainly received since Vitalis declares that barons disloyal to Henry supplied troops for Robert's army, and urged the duke to challenge his brother to a battle for the kingdom. On the other side, Henry was being given the same encouragement to fight, with, apparently, a large part of his army still intact and hurrying to intercept Robert on the way to London. Vitalis says, 'The people of England, to a man ... were firm in their loyalty to their native king and demanded to be led to battle for him.' Henry, though, was listening to older, wiser counsels.

Robert de Meulan was by now in his fifties, a seasoned campaigner who had fought with the Conqueror at Hastings. With lands in Normandy and England, he had a shrewd assessment of where the balance of power lay and had supported Henry throughout. He had already advised him how to keep his support together, telling him, 'Speak graciously to all your knights; caress them as a father does his children; sooth them with promises, granting their requests ... If they should even ask for London or York, do not hesitate to make magnificent promises ... It is better to give away a small portion of the kingdom, than ... to lose victory and life.' He gave the same counsel now, negotiate, give promises rather than battles, and Henry heeded this advice.

The armies approached each other near Alton in Hampshire. No fighting took place, but there are different versions of what did occur. Eadmer suggests Robert lost confidence in the disloyalty of the wavering barons and was quick to accept the idea of coming to terms, which suggests his support was not as great as he had anticipated. Vitalis, on the other hand, says 'turbulent traitors desired war instead of peace', and 'their wily emissaries perverted the words of the princes and promoted strife rather than concord between the brothers.' He suggests that peace was only achieved when Henry insisted on meeting his brother face to face. Then, he says, 'After a short conversation they embraced each other with loving kisses and were reconciled without reserve.' With uncharacteristic reticence he then adds, 'I cannot insert here the words used at this conference, not having been present at it,' something that had never deterred him on other occasions, particularly in the many pages of confession supposedly uttered by the Conqueror on his death-bed.

Other writers paint a rather different picture, suggesting the brothers were quite happy to fight for the kingdom and were only deterred by others. The Anglo-Saxon Chronicle declares it was the 'chief men' who 'interfered and made peace between them,' while John of Worcester says 'the wiser men on both sides … mediated a peace between the brothers.'

Whichever way it worked, the result was the Treaty of Alton, which in many respects reflected earlier treaties between the Conqueror's sons, and may in part have been lifted directly from the Treaty of Rouen. There are no existing copies of the actual treaty, so its terms must be reconstructed from the writers of the day, who agree on the major terms but disagree on some details. Robert renounced all claim to the English throne and released Henry from the homage he had already given him, presumably when he became Count of the Cotentin. This latter would have been purely a formality in the circumstances, but an important one in the eyes of the followers of each. It would not do to suggest such homage could be lightly discarded. In exchange Henry gave up all his lands in Normandy with the exception of Domfront, where he had sworn to the people he would be their lord. He would also pay Robert a pension of 3,000 marks a year, and help him recover all the lands their father had ruled in the Vexin and in Maine. Beyond this, some writers suggest there was an amnesty for all who had supported either side against the other, while Vitalis says there should be punishment for 'those who had infamously sown dissension between them'. Again, some include a clause that, in the absence of any legitimate issue, each should be the other's heir. At the time there was a fair chance this might be invoked since, although each had a new wife, neither yet had any legitimate child.

Whatever the terms of the treaty, and despite the swearing of an oath to keep it by twelve of the highest ranking men on each side, it seems Henry was no better than William Rufus in his intentions. 'These were mere words,' says Malmesbury, 'For the king had promised this without any design of fulfilling it.' By this time knowing his brother's character through and through, he had 'deluded his soft credibility.'

He had, however, achieved his aim. The armies were disbanded, peace reigned and England rejoiced. Robert stayed with his brother as an honoured guest for a further two months, apparently taking some share in advising the king, and no doubt expecting the first instalment of his promised pension which never came. During this time the Chronicle sourly notes, 'His men did much harm wherever they went,' no doubt treating England to the same rampant indiscipline as they showed in Normandy.

When they departed at Michaelmas, with them went the last real threat to Henry's kingship. Traditionally times of unrest in England were a trigger for some manner of rebellion in Scotland, Wales or both, but circumstances had played into Henry's hands, so that neither posed any imminent problem at this time.

Scottish affairs had become entwined with England long before Henry's marriage to Matilda. Some sixty years before, her father, then a boy of eight or nine years, had fled to the English court of Edward the Confessor when his father, Duncan, was killed by Macbeth. Any reader of Shakespeare will be familiar with the names, though the great playwright took liberties with the historical events. Duncan was killed in battle rather than being murdered in his bed, and Lady Macbeth appears not at all. Nor was Macbeth the tyrannical, haunted figure Shakespeare portrayed, being in fact a long-reigning and well-respected king. Nevertheless, by some accounts Duncan's wife was related to Siward, Earl of

Northumbria, and it was Siward who in 1054 advanced into Scotland with an army in support of Malcolm, by then a young man in his early twenties. It took several years of struggle before Macbeth was overcome, and before that both Siward and his immediate heirs were dead. In 1058, however, Malcolm was crowned King of Scotland and he would reign for 35 years. He was not universally popular, tending to favour the English ways he had been brought up in over the older Gaelic traditions of northern and western Scotland. His first marriage was to the widow of the Earl of Orkney, Ingibiorg, thus securing peace and friendship with the Scandinavian world, and from this came three children including his eldest son, Duncan.

Despite all this he seems to have remained neutral in the tumultuous events of 1066, though he gave shelter to Tostig Godwinson, and probably supplies to Harald Hardrada whose expedition to seize the English throne from King Harold included his step-sons, the joint earls of Orkney. After the Conquest, however, his sympathies clearly lay with the deposed Anglo-Saxons. Edgar Atheling took his mother and sisters to Malcolm's court to escape the Normans and, after the death of Ingibiorg, Malcolm insisted on marrying Edgar's sister, Margaret, though she declared she wanted only to become a nun. It was Margaret's influence that turned Malcolm from the bullying thug of his youth into the mature and civilised king he became. His nickname 'Canmore', differently interpreted, bridges the change; some declare it means 'Bighead' and relates to his swaggering youth, while others interpret it as 'Great Chief'.

The regular sanctuary he provided for rebellious Saxons eventually brought him into direct conflict with William the Conqueror and, under the resulting Treaty of Abernathy, Malcolm was forced to recognise William as overlord, at least for the southern parts of his kingdom. To ensure that the treaty was kept, his son, Duncan, was handed over to William as a hostage. Duncan, then aged about 12 years old, spent the next 15 years being brought up at William's court and supporting the king in England and in Normandy.

This did not entirely prevent further raiding across the border into Northumbria, nor did Malcolm abandon his brother in law,

Edgar Atheling, and in fact he may have been instrumental in finally negotiating a peace between Edgar and William. The death of the Conqueror in 1087, however, changed the relationship again. Duncan was released but seems to have opted to remain in England. Possibly he felt his step-mother and her brood of eight children, including five sons, had undermined his position in Scotland. There is also a suggestion he got on well with William Rufus, who was roughly the same age and would have shared the same upbringing at the Conqueror's court.

Despite this, in 1091 Malcolm and Edgar Atheling launched a joint invasion of Northumbria. This may have been in support of Robert Curthose, whom they had both acknowledged as the Conqueror's rightful heir, or simply an attempt by Malcolm to enlarge his borders while William Rufus was engaged in Normandy. In either case it failed and the terms of the Treaty of Abernathy were re-imposed after negotiations conducted by Robert Curthose and Edgar on behalf of the two kings. When, soon after, William Rufus began to annexe Cumbria and fill it with English colonists, however, Malcolm was moved to protest. He travelled south to a meeting with William Rufus, but the meeting never took place, either because William rebuffed the Scottish king, or because Malcolm refused to acknowledge the authority of William's court, depending on which account is believed. Returning north, Malcolm then made what Henry of Huntingdon describes as 'a predatory inroad into England', and was ambushed and killed by Robert Mowbray, Earl of Northumbria, along with his son and designated heir, Edward.

This sudden ending of a long and settled reign caused great confusion in Scotland, especially as the acknowledged heir was also removed. There were, of course, other sons of Malcolm and Margaret, as well as Duncan, at present residing in England. However, many of the leading Scottish nobles, particularly those from the highlands, had long been unhappy at Malcolm's preference for southern ways and the Roman Church, over the old ways and the Celtic tradition. They now seized the opportunity to change this policy, and handed the crown to Malcolm's brother, Donald, who had been brought up in Ireland and had lived in the Western Isles.

Donald Bane, or Donald the White, who was probably nearly sixty at the time, immediately set about expelling all the Normans and English who had been favoured by his brother, which, of course, did not please William Rufus who found himself losing all influence over his near neighbour.

An army was found to support Duncan, many of whom probably came from his father-in-law's former territory, Northumbria. Within six months Donald had been overcome and driven back to the highlands, but in order to placate the Scots, Duncan was forced to dismiss most of his 'foreign' supporters, and without them he was vulnerable to a renewed onslaught on behalf of Donald. This duly arrived six months later, and Duncan was killed in battle leaving Donald Bane once more as king of Scotland.

There is a strong suggestion that this time, probably in an attempt to unite his kingdom, Donald shared some of his power with his nephew Edmund, Malcolm's eldest surviving son. This arrangement lasted until Edmund's support for Robert Mowbray's rebellion against William Rufus again prompted that king to take a hand. Nominating Edmund's younger brother, Edgar, as King of Scotland, William raised an army which, over a period of two years, and with the support of Edgar Atheling, succeeded in deposing both Donald and Edmund, and placing Edgar on the throne. A charter of Durham from about this time describes Edgar as, 'king of the Scots by the gift of William, king of England,' which is probably a fairly accurate assessment. Certainly Edgar was not going to pose any challenge to William Rufus, or to his successor, Henry. He is supposed to have carried the Sword of State at William's last court, held in Westminster Hall, and some accounts say he attended Henry's coronation, though, in the circumstances, that seems unlikely. Nevertheless, the marriage of his sister to the new English king a few months later made him ever more attached to the new regime in England.

In Wales the situation was a little different. Infighting among Welsh factions had soon let the Normans infiltrate south Wales, and the death of Rhys ap Tewdwr in 1093 had effectively ended any real resistance there. For some time, though, Bleddyn ap Cynfyn had kept them out of the kingdom of Gwynedd in north Wales.

His death in 1075 had led to a civil war for the throne, allowing the Normans, Robert of Rhuddlan in particular, to gain territory on behalf of his cousin, Hugh of Chester.

In 1081 Gruffydd ap Cynan succeeded in defeating his rival for the throne, but he had barely achieved this before he was betrayed by one of his own men into the hands of the Normans, and spent the next thirteen or so years as a prisoner of Hugh of Chester. During this time his lands were taken over by Robert of Rhuddlan, who built castles at a number of sites including Bangor and Caernarfon.

Sometime in 1093 or 1094 Gruffydd escaped, and it may have been he who led the raiders by the Great Orme that literally caught Robert napping and killed him. There followed a great Welsh revolt in north Wales, led by Gruffydd with Irish and Danish support, which took back Anglesey and much of the kingdom of Gwynedd, despite the attempts of William Rufus in 1095 and 1097 to defeat them.

In 1098 a two-pronged attack led by Hugh of Chester and Hugh of Shrewsbury, succeeded in driving Gruffydd back as far as Anglesey. He might have been able to hold on there but for the defection of his Danish mercenary fleet who, presumably for a promise of reward, abruptly threw in their lot with the Normans. With Gruffydd fleeing once more to Ireland, and the Normans celebrating their success, the whole area was thrown open again by the sudden arrival of Magnus Barefoot, King of Norway.

This grandson of Harald Hardrada, having secured his position in Norway, had set out almost like the Vikings of old, to extend his power through Orkney and down the Irish Sea. He had already overthrown the earls of Orkney, extracted a treaty from Edgar of Scotland and taken over the Isle of Man, before arriving at the coast of north Wales. There, either on his own behalf or at the behest of Gruffydd, he fell upon the Norman forces in what became known as the Battle of Anglesey Sound. In fact this seems more of a skirmish than a full battle, but it resulted in the death of Hugh of Shrewsbury, shot in the eye by an arrow through the slit in his helmet. Most sources agree that it was Magnus himself who fired the arrow, and some suggest he regretted the action when he discovered who he had killed. Either way the Normans were defeated and withdrew, while Magnus himself, possibly regarding Anglesey as already conquered, sailed back to the Isle of Man. The following year Gruffydd returned to Anglesey, but neither he nor the Normans seemed to have any desire to renew hostilities, and while English eyes were turned elsewhere with the events of 1100 peace of a sort reigned throughout Wales.

By the end of 1101, then, Henry had ridden out the only challenge that was likely to unseat him from the throne of England. Now he could begin to feel secure and to look with some confidence towards the future.

5

Church and State
(1101–1107)

It might be thought that, with Henry by this time owing so much to the steadfast support of Anselm, the Archbishop would now have been suitably rewarded and all divisions between them forgotten. The point at issue, however, went far deeper than this, well beyond the power of personal friendship or regal debt to heal it. It struck at the very essence of kingship and the relations between monarch and church, and had its roots far back in the past.

In part the Holy Roman Empire was to blame, that institution which, as Voltaire pointedly remarked, was neither holy, nor Roman, nor an empire. From the very start the empire was so closely associated with the papacy that at times it was hard to know where one ended and the other began. In the mid-11th century Peter Damian, hermit, monk and papal legate, wrote of the emperor and the pope that they were joint heads of the world, and ideally it should be possible to see the emperor in the pope and the pope in the emperor.

The union of purpose even preceded the empire. Pepin the Short, father of Charlemagne, took over the Frankish kingdom in 751 by express permission of the pope, in return guaranteeing him the Papal States (the Donation of Pepin) and protection against his enemies. Charlemagne himself, at the height of his powers, was crowned as emperor by the pope in 800AD, and though it proved impossible to keep together his extensive conquests after his death, the German duchies of Saxony, Bavaria, Franconia, Swabia and Lotharingia were later cemented together by Otto the Great, forming the nucleus of an empire that claimed to be a continuation of Charlemagne's.

The system of government established by Otto relied heavily on the use of bishops, archbishops and abbots to act as his administrators. The idea was to limit the powers of dukes and counts and to prevent posts from becoming hereditary, but, to make the system work fully, the co-operation of the pope was needed. In 951 Otto asked the pope to crown him emperor, in the same way as Charlemagne had been crowned, and was perhaps surprised to be refused. By 962, however, Pope John XII needed protection from his enemies and was forced to turn to Otto to provide this. In return Otto duly received his coronation, shortly followed by a declaration that the emperor had formally become 'protector' of the Papal States.

This led to an immediate misunderstanding. By formally crowning the Emperor, Pope John may have felt he was conferring a privilege on him, whereas in Otto's eyes the pope was now his man. When Pope John discovered his mistake and sought alternative protectors, the emperor immediately had him deposed and replaced with a more compliant candidate, Leo VIII. As a further precaution, however, his renewed agreement contained a provision that any future pope must take an oath of loyalty to the emperor before his coronation.

Thereafter, for more than three-quarters of a century, although there might be fluctuations in the relationship, there was a general understanding that the emperor must be consulted and approve any candidate for election as pope, even though these were often nominated by the great Roman families who had traditionally carried out this role. A crisis occurred when the great families fell out.

In 1045 Pope Benedict IX, a young man with a reputedly scandalous lifestyle, found himself opposed by a rival, Silvester III. Matters became even more tangled when Benedict decided to step down in favour of his own (far more suitable) godfather, who became Gregory VI, and then changed his mind and tried to retain the papacy. Three popes, two of them elected without any consultation and approval, was more than the Emperor, Henry III, could stomach.

The irony is that the last of them, Gregory VI was infected with the reforming zeal then beginning to appear in the Western Church and would probably have found sympathy with the emperor in other circumstances. As it was, he was persuaded to stand down – confessing he had paid (or at least promised to pay) Benedict for the papacy, and was therefore unfit for the office. Silvester and Benedict were both deposed by a synod supervised by Henry himself, and his own confessor was duly elected as Pope Clement II. Immediately after, in time-honoured tradition, Henry was then crowned emperor by the new pope.

A succession of German popes followed, all given imperial approval, but some people were beginning to question whether it was right that the highest office in the church should be so closely tied to a lay authority. The wind of change was beginning to blow through the Western Church, as yet only a gentle breeze, but soon to build into something strong enough to rock an empire.

To a large extent it began with reform of the monasteries. The founding of the Abbey of Cluny early in the 10th century set a pattern of renewed piety and strict observance of the monastic rule of St Benedict. This pattern was followed in numerous offshoots of Cluny, all part of the same 'Cluniac' congregation, answerable to no authority but that of the Abbot of Cluny and, through him, to the pope. Their aim was a purer religion, closer to the practices of the early church, and their example led to increasing condemnation of the lax ways current among church leaders, even at the highest level.

Among those advocating reform one name stands out, that of Hildebrand. As a young man of humble origins, he studied under the man who became Pope Gregory VI, and when Gregory was deposed and exiled to Cologne, Hildebrand followed him. There he found the zeal for reform, and understanding of the operation of the empire, that would make him such an influential figure in the latter-half of the 11th century.

Among the various changes to liturgy and monastic practices, the reformers had three major issues that they wanted the church to deal with. The first was that of married priests. From the fourth century onwards, the rule in the Roman Church was that priests should be celibate, the thinking behind this again coming from the biblical statement, 'No man can serve two masters.' A priest was supposed to care for his community, while married priests would be tempted to put family matters and family promotion first. It was a rule, however, far more honoured in the breach than the observance. Many priests and even bishops openly lived with wives, usually known as concubines, and their sons, coyly referred to as 'nephews', frequently followed them into church offices.

The second issue was with simony, the practice of buying an office in the church. Again it was felt a man should become a prior, abbot or bishop because of his fitness for the job, rather than on the basis of the bribe he could pay to obtain it. When such jobs also offered secular power, however, as most of them did at this time, the temptation to pay for oneself or one's son or other relation to obtain the post could be overwhelming, and it quickly became a normal practice.

Of course, when someone was buying such a post, by implication someone else was selling it, and that someone was almost always a layman. The founding of churches and abbeys was something of a hobby among noblemen of the 11th century. Almost anyone who achieved a position in the upper levels of society was expected to signal that position by founding one or the other. Piety might be one reason, status another, but the most commonly listed reason for doing so was as penance for the violence committed in reaching that position. Indeed, after the Norman conquest of England, the founding of a church was one way laid down in the so-called 'Penitential Ordinance' of 1070 by which a person could redeem himself for the mass slaughter involved in that campaign. It would have seemed obvious to the founders of such institutions that they should have a right to appoint priests and abbots to 'their' church or abbey, and as these posts grew more important, it was a short step to accepting money for them.

Stepping up the scale again, bishops and archbishops were part of the fabric of the State, major landowners and powerful advisors of kings. It would have been inconceivable to a monarch of the time that he could not appoint whoever he chose to such important offices. The administration of the Holy Roman Empire was entirely based on such a system. Whether or not the king also took money for the post depended on the individual king, his own attitudes and his needs at the time. What he did demand, though, was an oath of loyalty to himself personally, and the recognition that the bishop was answerable to him for the discharge of his duties. To make this quite clear it had long been the tradition that it would be the king who 'invested' the bishop or archbishop, which meant that it was the king who handed over the bishop's symbols of authority, the ring and the crozier, when a new bishop was appointed. It was this 'lay investiture' that became the third target of the church reformers. The church, they said, should not be subject to lay control, and therefore this symbolic subservience must be ended.

It was clear to the reformers that in order to achieve these ends, the power and authority of the pope had to be increased. To some, and especially to Hildebrand, it was equally obvious that the power of the emperor had to be decreased. For him there could be no joint heads of the world. There could be only one leader of Christendom and that had to be the pope.

His first association with papal authority came with the election of Pope Leo IX in 1049. Hildebrand accompanied him to Rome, quickly rising in power and influence and later becoming his personal representative or papal legate in foreign matters. Pope Leo quickly showed himself to be a reformer. In his first synod in 1049 priestly marriage was condemned, though enforcing this decree was another matter. Leo was related to the Imperial royal family, as was his successor Victor II, appointed in 1055 after Hildebrand had led the delegation to the German court to ask the emperor for a nomination. Victor had been a trusted advisor of Emperor Henry III, and while pushing the reforms on clerical celibacy and simony, nevertheless remained close to the ideals of the empire. He was with Henry when he died and became guardian of his six-year-old son, Henry IV, but the death of the emperor and the regency that followed was the beginning of the end of the partnership between pope and empire.

When Victor died the Romans elected a new pope, Stephen IX, without any consultation with the regent. A reformer, he was approved by Hildebrand who journeyed to the imperial court to ask for retrospective consent to his election. He was then confirmed in office despite the fact that he was related to a man who had previously rebelled against the emperor.

The increasing power of Hildebrand is shown by the events following the death of Stephen in 1058. A new pope was quickly elected by the Romans, again without consultation with the regent, and in defiance of a decree of Stephen that no new pope should be elected before Hildebrand returned from the imperial court. When Hildebrand found out he opposed the new Pope Benedict X, gaining the regent's approval for his own nominee who became Pope Nicholas II. It was not an imperial army that drove out and defeated Benedict, however, but help from the Normans, now firmly established in southern Italy. The first act of Pope Nicholas was to decree that in future popes would be elected solely by a college of cardinals of the Church, a practice that remains to this day. Nor was the approval of the emperor sought for this change. Instead the leader of the Normans, Robert Guiscard, now given the title of duke, would guarantee the independence of such elections. The pope, it seemed, had got himself a new protector.

There was no pretence of consultation with the next pope, Alexander II, a strong reformer and friend of Hildebrand. He was elected by the cardinals alone, and as a result a rival, Honorius II, was nominated and elected by the German court. For some years this rivalry continued, though most of the Western world outside of the Holy Roman Empire had no doubt that Alexander was the true pope, a position eventually recognised by the imperial regency. By now it was clear that the papacy was getting stronger, taking advantage of the weakness of the empire while the young Emperor, Henry IV, was growing up. The real test of strength, however, was still to come.

There are some who claim that Hildebrand cared less about the reform of the church and more about his own personal power, a claim that might be borne out by his own election as Pope Gregory VII in 1073. Even by his own account it is clear he was elected neither by the college of cardinals, nor by the nomination and consent of the Holy Roman Emperor. According to him, during the funeral of Pope Alexander, '... a great tumult and shouting of the people arose and they rushed upon me like madmen ... and dragged me by force to the place of apostolic rule.' Had the same happened to anyone else, it is tempting to suggest Hildebrand himself would have been the first to condemn it as a return to the old Roman mob rule. Instead he accepted this election by acclamation, perhaps justifying it as allowing him to push through the reforms he had spent a lifetime advocating. The name he chose, Gregory VII, might have been a tribute to his old teacher, the deposed Gregory VI who had set him firmly on the path to reform.

Certainly reform was his watchword, both pushing the reforms on clerical celibacy and simony already set in motion by his predecessors, and also going further, much further, in his aim to make the pope the head of Christendom. For this purpose he gathered together the writings of the early church, which made clear the primary position once held by popes in earlier times. From there it was a short step to the document *Dictatus Papae*, dated 1075, which set out the claims now made for the papacy. Among other statements, it was declared that the pope was head of the Universal Church; that he was answerable to no-one and that he alone could make new laws for the church; that he alone could depose or reinstate bishops; that all princes should kiss his feet; and that he could depose kings and emperors who refused to obey his laws, and absolve their subjects from the fealty they owed to such earthly rulers.

In addition to this he insisted that no cleric should accept investiture with his symbols of office from the hand of any layman, and that his papal legate would be superior to any council of bishops. Furthermore, every archbishop must come to Rome to receive his pallium (the broad band of woollen cloth signifying his authority) from the pope himself. Soon after this, a declaration known as the *Libertas Ecclesiae* emphasised that the aim was for a church free from lay control, though the *Dictatus* seemed to go much further than that. The message, however, was clear. The pope was head of the church and all lower clergy must derive their authority from him and from no-one else. In this brave new world of church reform, there was no place for lay interference, and woe betide any ruler, however mighty his title, who might try to do so.

This was all very well but it went against centuries of practice. No king could give control over bishops and abbots to a foreign power, even if that power was the pope himself. He had to be able to nominate whom he chose to positions of such importance in his own country.

By this time the Holy Roman Emperor, Henry IV, was a young man of twenty-five, already in dispute with the church over the Archbishop of Milan, whose position was of some importance in the empire, guarding the Alpine passes between Italy and the German lands. When Henry deposed the existing archbishop and replaced him with a candidate of his own, Pope Gregory threatened him with excommunication. This was a most severe threat which, if carried out, would cut him off from the church and its sacraments and, under the thinking of the time, from all possibility of reaching heaven. Henry, however, realised that there was a serious danger he could lose control of the appointment of bishops and archbishops within his empire, upon which the whole system would fail and the empire itself might well be lost. He therefore summoned a council of German bishops and archbishops at which each signed a declaration that they would no longer recognise the improperly elected Hildebrand as pope, and would no longer submit to him or obey him. When this declaration was delivered to Gregory, with an instruction that he stand down immediately, his response was to excommunicate the emperor, to release his subjects from their oaths of fealty and to forbid anyone to serve him as king.

The world was stunned. This was not abstract theology. Lives would be lost over this excommunication, and everyone had the instant dilemma of whether to back the secular power of the empire, or the spiritual power of the church. One group found the choice to be no problem at all. The Duchy of Saxony, long feeling they had been oppressed by the actions of the emperor, had revolted once already and now did so again. Joining with disaffected magnates of Swabia and Bavaria, they quickly gained the upper hand and, at a council in October 1076, declared that unless Henry had become reconciled with the pope by the middle of February the next year, they would depose him. They then did all they could to make sure no such reconciliation could take place.

For Henry, the situation was critical. He was not yet strong enough to defeat the rebels and delay would lose him his crown. The only option was to reconcile, or at least appear to reconcile, with the pope. It was mid-winter, and with followers on both sides of the Alps the rebels were closely guarding all the usual routes that led from the imperial court to the Papal States. The pope had been invited to a council at Augsberg at which it was intended to depose the emperor, and had already set out from Rome. By late January 1077 he was at the Castle of Canossa awaiting an escort over the Alpine passes, when, on the twenty-fifth of that month Henry suddenly appeared outside the castle gate.

He had thwarted the best efforts of his opponents by travelling through Burgundy and crossing the Alps well to the west. Nor did he bring a great army. Instead the king stood barefoot and bare-headed in the snow, by some accounts wearing a hair shirt or possibly a monk's tunic. He had come, he said, to do penance and ask for forgiveness and re-admission to the Church of Christ – and as a tactic to outmanoeuvre his enemies it was masterly.

How could the pope refuse forgiveness to a penitent sinner? Yet if he withdrew his excommunication and confirmed Henry as the rightful king, he would be deserting all the rebels who had risen in his support. For three days Gregory held out, refusing to open the castle gates and possibly hoping Henry's resolve would crack. There is no doubt that he saw through the tactic and was completely unconvinced by the appearance of penitence. Others, though, saw it differently and pressure began to grow to accept the gesture and grant the forgiveness requested so humbly. On 28 January it was Gregory that gave way, opening the gates and signifying Henry's re-admittance to the church by sharing Holy Communion with him in the castle chapel.

Nothing was said at the time about the emperor's deposition or about lay investiture. As regards Henry's kingship, Gregory seemed at a loss as to what to do, at various times suggesting he had, and then that he had not, reinstated him on his throne.

Henry had no doubt. The declaration he signed at the time began, 'I Henry, king ...'

The rebels, of course, were furious. They immediately declared that kingship was not hereditary but by election and deposed Henry, electing Rudolph of Swabia in his place. Civil war followed, but Henry had bought himself the time he needed. Though Gregory backed Rudolph and his followers, by 1080, when Rudolph was fatally wounded in battle, it was clear that Henry had won. Excommunicated again, this time permanently, he nominated a new pope, Clement III, who had been the Imperial Chancellor in Italy and had supported Henry throughout. Then, marching on Rome, he caused Gregory to flee to the nearby Castel Sant'Angelo, while Clement was duly consecrated in St Peter's Basilica on 24 March 1084. Needless to say, a few days later, the new pope crowned Henry as Holy Roman Emperor in the tradition of his ancestors.

It was the Normans who rescued Pope Gregory, taking the opportunity to sack Rome as they did so, and carrying him away to their lands in the south. There he died the following year, having withdrawn all the excommunications he had issued with the sole exceptions of those of Henry IV and Clement.

While this was going on there was little attention to spare for the rest of the church, and other rulers managed fairly successfully to pick and choose the reforms they would put into practice. William the Conqueror, for example, was an enthusiastic supporter of monastic reform, taking a special interest in the abbeys of Fécamp and Bec, and encouraging the growth of learning in these places. When he founded his own abbey at Caen, however, he consulted no higher authority in appointing his friend Lanfranc as the abbot, nor a little later when he named him Archbishop of Canterbury. He obtained the backing of Pope Alexander II for his conquest of England, but when that pope tried to suggest he must do homage to him for the land, he was firmly told that the Conqueror would do no such thing. The rule on clerical celibacy was useful in allowing him to dispose of unwanted bishops and other clergy, but enforcement was patchy to say the least. Bishop Æthelmaer of Elmham was removed on the grounds that he was married, but then was replaced by a married Norman bishop. As for lay investiture,

William appointed and invested who he wanted without reprimand of any kind, and it was on his practice that his sons based their right to do the same.

It helped, of course, that the Conqueror and his archbishop were so much of the same mind. Lanfranc had the ear of the king, as Eadmer says, but also had an excellent reputation abroad as a learned and pious reforming cleric. This reputation clearly helped to maintain harmony between church and state. When the Bishop of Lincoln accompanied Lanfranc to Rome and surrendered his bishopric on the grounds of simony (he had obtained it as a reward for contributing substantially to William's campaign expenses) he received it straight back again at the hands of Pope Alexander, no doubt on Lanfranc's recommendation. The archbishop made no protest, however, at the clear lines laid down by the Conqueror, that no-one was allowed to recognise a pope without his approval, that any letter from a pope must first be submitted to the king, and that no reforming church ordinance could be approved at a church council unless the reform was acceptable to the king.

All this harmony disappeared, however, with the death of the Conqueror in 1087. Though William Rufus must have known the archbishop well, there was no easy friendship between them. Instead, while Rufus seemed in awe of the other, still he was determined to get every advantage he could from him. All manner of promises were made when he needed Lanfranc's support to obtain the crown, but none were kept. Eadmer, however, records that, after William's famous retort to Lanfranc, 'Who is there who could fulfil all that he promises,' the king could never afterwards look his archbishop in the face.

When Lanfranc died in 1089, no new archbishop was appointed for four years. In the meantime Rufus plundered the revenues of Canterbury, gave away its lands to his followers and kept the monks on a barely subsistence allowance for food and clothing – as indeed he did with other bishoprics and abbeys that fell vacant at the time. That situation might have been prolonged indefinitely if the king hadn't fallen gravely ill in the spring of 1093. Then, fearing he was in imminent danger of death, he began to listen to the urgings of the remaining bishops and nobility in England, who had already decided who they wanted as the new archbishop.

Anselm had followed his countryman, Lanfranc, to the Abbey of Bec, succeeding him as prior at the tender age of thirty, and later becoming abbot. An intellectual who loved the secluded monastic life and produced noted writings on theological matters, the last thing he wanted was to be Archbishop of Canterbury. While he might have welcomed the opportunity to further church reform in England, he well knew the administrative burden that went with the post, as well as the duty to advise a king who was clearly hostile. Even up to his illness Rufus had been declaring that the bishops could pray for what they liked, but he would have no archbishop but himself.

Although Anselm had visited England a few times in the past on monastic business, he had deliberately stayed away for some time now, possibly hoping that someone else might be appointed in the meantime. Late in 1092, however, his friend Hugh of Chester became seriously ill and implored him to come and attend his deathbed. Anselm could not refuse, and though Hugh recovered fairly quickly, monastic business kept him in England for some months. He was on hand, then, when William Rufus was at last prevailed upon to name him as archbishop.

Eadmer says that when Anselm was informed of this he stood aghast and turned deathly pale. Then, although they tried to carry him off to the king to be invested straight away, he resisted with all his might. He was too old, he said, being then in his sixtieth year. He was an abbot and could not abandon his post. He needed the permission of his own archbishop and of the Duke of Normandy, his lord. Above all, he had no inclination or talent for dealing with worldly affairs. William Rufus himself was reduced to begging him to accept the post, declaring he was dying and would be condemned to hell if he had not appointed an archbishop before he died. In the end the archbishop's staff was brought and forced into Anselm's clenched hand, the fingers being prised up in order to do so, and he was borne away in a crowd of rejoicing bishops and clergy.

Eadmer was, of course, an eye-witness to these events, and gives us these details as well as Anselm's further protests and vivid imagery of how he saw his position. He was, he claimed, an old and feeble sheep, and they had yoked him together in a plough team with a wild, untamed bull. The bull would drag him through thorns and briars, crush him and wear him out with all manner of wrongs, and none of those who had forced him into that position would dare to oppose the king, wherever his whims might take him. So it proved in practice.

The main issues between Rufus and Anselm, apart from the return of the property of Canterbury, concerned the recognition of the pope, for the problems of the papacy had not ended with the death of Pope Gregory in 1095. While Clement III, supported by the Holy Roman Emperor, still reigned in Rome, the Normans in southern Italy had elected a replacement for Gregory. Victor III, as he became, had been abbot of Monte Cassino, deep in Norman territory, and was as reluctant as Anselm to take up the post. Named pope in May 1086, it was a year later before he could be consecrated in St Peter's Basilica in Rome when Clement had been temporarily driven out. Even then he stayed only eight days in Rome before returning to Monte Cassino, where he died later that year.

Before he died he nominated as his successor, Odo, Bishop of Ostia, who duly became Pope Urban II, supported by the Normans in Italy and Normandy, and later by the French. As Clement had returned to Rome, Urban spent much of his time travelling, but, as Abbot of Bec, Anselm had already acknowledged him as rightful pope before he came to England. William Rufus had not.

Anselm set three conditions to his final acceptance of the nomination as archbishop. First he wanted all the property formerly belonging to Canterbury to be restored in full. Secondly he wanted William to accept his advice on all spiritual matters, and finally he wanted William to accept Urban II as the rightful pope. The promises given by William, however, had no more effect on him that those he had earlier given to Lanfranc. The lands of Canterbury were never restored in full. Indeed, he started as he meant to go on, serving notice of law suits over disputed ownership on the very day Anselm was enthroned as archbishop. Nor did he accept Anselm's advice on spiritual matters. He refused to allow him to hold church councils to enforce reforms, and told him the appointment of abbots was none of his business.

It was the issue of the pope, however, that caused the most trouble. William claimed to follow his father's rule that no-one could recognise a pope without his approval, and that Anselm could not maintain his allegiance to Urban without being in breach of the allegiance he owed to William. Anselm, though, may have been old and weak but he was also remarkably stubborn. Even when William told the English bishops they were to shun him and refuse to obey him, still he held firm, quietly arguing it was a matter of rendering to Caesar that which was Caesar's and to God that which was God's. Interestingly, it was the nobles rather than his fellow bishops that stood by Anselm.

William made no secret of his dislike of the man he had appointed and the clergy followed his lead. Part of the problem might have been Anselm's refusal to buy the king's friendship. Early on he had offered £500 as a reasonable contribution to the king's campaign in Normandy. When, however, this was contemptuously refused, instead of increasing the amount, he gave the money to the poor. 'Tell the archbishop,' said William, 'that yesterday I hated him with a great hatred, today I hate him with yet greater hatred, and he can be sure that tomorrow and every day after I will hate him with an ever fiercer hatred.'

According to custom Anselm asked the king's permission to go to Rome to receive his pallium from Urban, and was, of course, refused. Instead William secretly sent two of his chaplains to check out the situation in Rome and see where his best advantage lay. He had instructed them to bring back the archbishop's pallium so that, if he could find a way of deposing Anselm, he could immediately bestow it personally on someone else. William of St Calais, the Bishop of Durham who had once rebelled against the king and who had spent the years since buying his way back into his favour, seemed a likely successor.

In fact Urban sent his own representative back to England, accompanying the chaplains, and bringing back the pallium. This man succeeded so well in persuading William that Urban would let him do as he wished, that the king immediately recognised Pope Urban and instructed everyone else to do the same. When it then it appeared that Urban would not allow Anselm to be deposed, it was too late for William to retract his recognition. Nor would he be able to give the pallium to Anselm, since the archbishop flatly refused to take it from his hands. Instead the pope's representative laid it on the altar at Canterbury and Anselm took it from there himself.

It was not likely that after this the relationship between king and archbishop would improve – nor did it. A little later, despairing of ever bringing about any reform of either the church or the king's irreligious practices, Anselm requested to be allowed to visit the pope and ask for his advice. Of course he was refused, but persisted in his request until William furiously declared that he must choose either to leave the kingdom and never return, or, if he stayed, to swear an oath never to appeal to the pope again, and to pay such fines as the king's court would decide to make up for vexing him with such matters. For Anselm the choice was simple. He would go. Even then, however, as a parting shot, the king said he must leave behind every single thing he had received from him in England, and sent an official to search his bags as he was about to embark, to make sure he had done so.

Making his way to Rome, Anselm was received there with great honour and stayed more than a year. He was therefore present at the Council held by Pope Urban at Easter 1098, where he once again condemned in the strongest terms the practice of lay investiture. According to Eadmer, the pope sentenced to excommunication not only those laymen conferring investitures, but also those who received investitures at their hands, and all those who consecrated in office those who had received such investitures. Soon after this, Anselm left Rome and settled at Lyons and that was how the matter stood when the death of William Rufus brought Henry to the throne of England.

Eadmer could not understand why Anselm was upset to hear of the king's death, but reports that he wept bitterly at the news. Almost at once, they set out for England, for though Anselm had asked the pope to be allowed to step down as archbishop, this request had been denied, and he was now determined to return and take up his duties once more.

He soon found Henry to be a different proposition to his brother. Not only had the king written personally to Anselm, a letter full of prayers and entreaties for his swift return to England, but their first meeting was entirely amicable – until, of course, the question of investiture was raised. Henry wanted to bestow the archbishopric on Anselm afresh and receive from him the customary homage, and was taken aback when the archbishop said he could do neither. Eadmer, who was probably a shrewder politician than his master, suggests that Henry was afraid if he opposed Anselm in this matter, the archbishop would immediately sail away again. If he did so, of course, he might offer his services to the more pliable Robert, thereby boosting his chances of taking the crown from Henry. On the other hand, he says, to give in to Anselm would seem to Henry like losing half his sovereignty.

When Henry produced his compromise of putting the matter once more before the pope, Eadmer declares that Anselm agreed to this despite believing it was a futile exercise and would do no good in the long term. Henry, however, had some grounds for optimism.

In the first place there was a new pope. Urban II had died the year before – fourteen days after the crusaders captured Jerusalem but before the news of their success reached the West. More importantly, before then he had, in gratitude for the constancy of Norman support, granted the right of lay investiture to Roger of Sicily. What had been granted to one might possibly be granted to another.

The new pope, Paschal II a former Cluniac monk, was, however, a firm supporter of the Gregorian reforms, and particularly the ban on lay investitures so recently affirmed at Urban's Easter Council. When his answer was received by Henry in the late summer of 1101 it suggested no compromise. Ask anything in accordance with the will of God and you shall have it, Paschal told Henry, but creating bishops and abbots was the right of the church and could not be made a royal prerogative.

At the time Henry was entertaining his brother Robert, having recently obtained his agreement to the Treaty of Alton.

Eadmer suggests it was Robert and his supporters that now urged Henry to stand up for his rights, perhaps to spite Anselm whom they might have blamed for the loss of a kingdom. In spite of this and of the bishops who, as usual, supported the king against the pope, Henry still looked for some compromise. A second delegation was sent, more eminent than the first. Three bishops were sent by Henry and two monks by Anselm, but their return caused fresh controversy.

The pope's letter to Henry was conciliatory in tone, congratulating him on a good start to his reign in reversing his brother's oppression of the church. Nevertheless it forbade him from continuing with lay investitures. Henry refused to publish the contents of the letter but demanded that Anselm now concede to him the rights his father had enjoyed. Meanwhile, however, Anselm had received his own letter from the pope, which told him to stand firm. Then, muddying the waters further, the three bishops declared that Paschal had privately told them Henry would be allowed to continue lay investitures provided he lived a virtuous life. The pope had not wanted to put this in writing, they claimed, because it might then be seized on as a precedent by other princes. The two monks immediately disputed this, and hard words were exchanged on both sides.

Whether Henry actually believed the bishops is not clear, but it certainly gave more power to his demands that Anselm consecrate the bishops he had previously appointed, and the two he now nominated. Anselm's response was that he would send to the pope himself to clear up the matter.

In the meantime, it is a measure of the relationship between king and archbishop that Henry now approved the holding of a general council of the church, presided over by Anselm, at which the main points of the Gregorian reforms were formally instituted in England. In particular, simony was prohibited and a number of abbots removed from office for this offence. Clerical dress was regulated and priests forbidden to marry or to attend 'drinking parties'. Rules on secret marriages were laid down, the trading of slaves was forbidden and rules were even set out about men's hair length (part of the ears must be visible and the eyes uncovered). All of this was done with Henry's consent, yet still the issue of appointment and investiture of bishops remained between them.

The king even tried to have his bishops consecrated by the Archbishop of York, but at the last moment one of the candidates, William of Winchester, withdrew from the ceremony, while the newly appointed Bishop of Hereford sent back his ring and crozier rather than participate.

Eventually Henry persuaded Anselm himself to travel to Rome and try to obtain a satisfactory solution. He set out in April 1103, then being some seventy years of age, with the king's envoy William Warelast, who had made the same journey several times before. William, arriving sooner than Anselm, attempted to win over the Romans, but in presenting his case to Paschal made some serious mistakes. First, he hinted that generous contributions made by England for the upkeep of the pope – notably an annual donation known as Peter's Pence – would cease if Henry did not get his way. Then, in an astonishing outburst, he declared Henry would rather risk losing his kingdom than give up the right of investiture. To this the pope drily replied that he would rather risk losing his life than grant him any such right.

With his mission completed as fruitlessly as he had expected, Anselm set out again for England and was joined on the road by William. By the time they reached Lyons it was approaching Christmas and Anselm proposed staying there for the feast. William, however, was travelling on at once, and in parting gave Anselm a message he said came from the king. If Anselm in returning was prepared to concede to Henry all the rights his father had enjoyed, he would be welcomed. If not ...

Anselm was well able to read between the lines, so he settled down again to exile in Lyons, and Henry, confirming his meaning, took for himself the revenues of Canterbury. Even then, the relationship did not completely break down. Though bishops sent letters to Anselm suggesting he had run away from his duty and painting appalling pictures of the breakdown in Christianity in England without him, Henry's oppression seems, in general, to have fallen short of his brother William's. Those appointed to deal with the revenues of Canterbury were some of Anselm's own men, deemed more likely to treat gently those who were dependant on the church. Similarly he found a novel way of dealing with married priests, continually fining them when it proved impossible to keep them from their wives, and thereby paying lip service to church reform while at the same time filling his own coffers.

Letters still passed back and forth between Pope Paschal and the various parties, until Paschal finally lost patience. In March 1105 he excommunicated not only the bishops who had received investiture from Henry, but also the king's chief adviser, Robert de Meulan, whom he probably felt was behind Henry's obstinacy. Robert de Meulan had previously advised William Rufus in his earlier dispute with a pope, so Paschal may not have been far wrong.

Henry himself was also threatened with excommunication, though, possibly due to Anselm's influence, the threat was not immediately carried out. This was no meaningless threat, however. At that time, the future Emperor Henry V was leading a rebellion against his father, having sought and obtained the pope's backing for this on the grounds that as Henry IV had been excommunicated, there was no reason for his subjects to obey him, and he had no right to rule over a Christian empire. An excommunication would also have been a severe embarrassment to the English king, as he was, at this time, seeking to establish himself as a defender of the church in Normandy.

In the end it was the king's sister who broke the deadlock. Adela, Henry's favourite sibling, had married Count Stephen of Blois at around fifteen years of age. Stephen was some twenty years older than his wife and he it was who had returned early from the First Crusade after the siege of Antioch, bearing cartloads of treasure. Some said he returned due to illness, most declared that he had run away from the fight. The following year, however, he returned to the East, some say at the insistence of Adela, and he was killed at the Battle of Ramla in 1102. During his absences, and after his death, Adela proved to be a very capable regent, even continuing as co-ruler when her son, Theobald, came of age.

She had been particularly supportive of Anselm during his exile, and when she apparently fell seriously ill in the spring of 1105, the archbishop visited her at Blois. Adela made a full recovery, but was horrified to discover that her brother was about to be excommunicated. Through her intervention, Henry and Anselm were brought together at L'Aigle in Normandy, a meeting that quickly re-established their earlier friendship. Eadmer records with approval that whenever there were matters to discuss, it was the king who went to Anselm rather than sending for Anselm to come to him. The revenues of Canterbury were also restored to the archbishop and, finally, a compromise was reached on the major issue that had divided them.

Whether this was suggested by Henry, Adela or Anselm, or arose from all their discussions, it was proposed that Henry would give up the right of investing with ring and crozier, provided the pope would permit homage to be done for the temporal lands that went with the office. In addition, though nominations of bishops and abbots would be made by the king, he would accept the advice of the church in making these appointments.

There followed a delay while the agreement of Pope Paschal was obtained, and this was notified to Anselm in a letter dated March 1106. Clearly it was intended to be a temporary concession, 'until by God's grace the heart of the king is softened by your preaching,' but it was enough to end the impasse. The excommunication of the bishops was lifted and, after a further delay due to illness, in March 1107 Anselm finally returned to England to be greeted with general rejoicing.

On 1 August 1107 Henry met with his bishops, abbots and nobles in London and, after due consideration, the Concordat of London was agreed upon, binding the State and the pope to the compromise which had been reached. Some have claimed this was a ground-breaking agreement, giving the pope unprecedented power in England, but in truth it seems the king gave up little but a formality. On each side, however, honour was satisfied. Soon after this Anselm invested and consecrated the bishops Henry had appointed and, in England at least, the Investiture Controversy was at an end.

6

The Conquest of Normandy (1102–1106)

During the years in which Henry courteously but doggedly continued his dispute with Anselm and the pope, there were, of course, other matters on his mind. Though he was never in the position of the Holy Roman Emperor, Henry IV, nevertheless the play of secular affairs had a lot to do with his willingness to come to a final agreement and avoid excommunication. Indeed, some people at the time suggested that it was this return to harmony with the Church that led to the ultimate fulfilment of his ambitions later in 1106.

Whether or not the Treaty of Alton was modelled on the Treaty of Rouen, it had as little chance of being honoured. The seemingly contradictory terms referring to amnesty for barons on each side, but punishment of 'wicked sowers of discord', provided ample opportunity for different interpretations, while Henry probably had as little intention of paying the annual pension as his brother William had before him. Possibly Henry's only clear action in pursuit of the treaty was the reinstatement of Ranulf Flambard as Bishop of Durham, with all his lands restored to him. This might seem surprising since he was the prime instigator of Robert's invasion, but there appears to have been a major shift of policy on the part of Flambard at some point in the enterprise. We hear of him urging on the preparations in Normandy, and bribing the English fleet to betray Henry's trust. After that there is a strange silence. Robert de Bellème and William of Mortain are named as the chief negotiators with Henry's representatives, when we might have expected to find Flambard in a prominent position and it has been suggested that rather than pressing for the duke's advantage, he might have been the one now urging settlement. The reason advanced for this is that after his departure from England, Anselm sent a letter to the pope listing the shortcomings of Flambard as Bishop of Durham, in particular accusing him of simony. The reply from Paschal seemed to leave the matter in Anselm's hands, including the decision of whether Flambard should be dismissed from his office and even unfrocked. Flambard's future prosperity, therefore, now lay in the hands of someone who appeared to be favoured by Henry and opposed to Curthose, and he may well have shaped his policy accordingly.

For a long time it was believed that Flambard returned to Normandy with Curthose and remained there for the next five years. Suggestions have even been made that he was then, or maybe always had been, an agent of Henry's. Circumstantial evidence produced in support of this included the easy terms of his imprisonment in the Tower, the escape that allowed him to take his treasure away with him to Normandy, the settlement at Alton and his later smooth return to Durham. There is firmer evidence, however, that he was publicly present at Durham, preaching an interminable sermon, at the translation of the relics of St Cuthbert to the new cathedral in 1104, well before the time stated. Nor does the writer continuing the Chronicle of Symeon of Durham suggest any such prolonged absence. In fact, the only statement made there is that though Flambard continually tried to recover Henry's favour by generous gifts, he never succeeded in doing so.

More typical of Henry's reaction to the settlement of 1101 is the report of Vitalis that he 'began gradually to wreak his vengeance on the traitors who had infamously deserted him in his time of need.' It is either a measure of his cunning, or his respect for the principle of justice, that he did this strictly according to the law. Some lesser offenders got away with a fine. Others, such as Ivo de Grandmesnil, played into his hands by waging a Norman-style private war on their neighbours. Ivo wriggled out of his punishment by pledging his lands to Robert de Meulan and departing on crusade.

William of Mortain escaped, entirely until he 'voluntarily' left the kingdom in 1104 – but William of Warenne, who seems to have sided with Curthose even though his movements in 1101 are unclear, was one of the first to suffer. He lost his lands in England in the autumn of 1101, officially, at least, because of violently seizing the lands of the Bishop of Thetford. It has been suggested, however, that these actions were not so much the king's vengeance as a determined attempt to remove trouble-makers from the kingdom. This interpretation seems to be borne out by the major target of Henry's wrath, the Montgomery brothers.

Robert de Bellème and his brothers Arnulf and Roger were all major landowners in England. After the death of his brother Hugh, Robert had extensive lands in Shropshire and around Arundel in Sussex. Arnulf was Earl of Pembroke and also held Holderness. Roger, called the Poitevin since he had obtained that county through his wife, had lands throughout the Midland shires from Lancashire to Suffolk and Essex. Individually and jointly they had a record of backing the king's enemies, both in 1101 and earlier in 1088, their oaths of homage and loyalty having little meaning for them when better prospects came in view. Of the three, Robert was by far the most powerful. He and Henry had crossed paths a few times before, but now Henry was determined to deal with him once and for all, at least as far as his English kingdom was concerned.

According to Vitalis, Henry had him closely watched for almost a year by 'secret spies'. Presumably they followed him in Normandy as well as in England since the accusations eventually made against him covered both lands. Their findings were 'reduced to writing with great precision,' until the king had enough – more than enough – evidence to make specific charges against him, the tipping point apparently being the unauthorised building and occupation of Bridgnorth Castle.

At Easter 1102, Robert attended the king's court as usual, apparently all unsuspecting. What happened then was clearly not just a personal accusation but the full and correct process of law set in motion against him. Vitalis says he was 'summoned ... to plead in (Henry's) court to an indictment containing forty-five counts of offences,' and he was 'required to make a distinct answer to each charge.' At that time, the king's court was still effectively a court of law for serious matters affecting his vassals and this was clearly one of those occasions. What it meant, though, was that Henry was not just the accuser but judge and jury besides, with all the weight of the law behind him.

Unsurprisingly Robert asked for an adjournment while he considered how to answer these charges. Equally unsurprisingly, when that was granted he decided he had no answer and instead slipped out of the building, took to his horse and galloped away. The statement of Vitalis that Henry was 'vexed' at being thus duped, is probably underselling his reaction.

Still strictly according to law, the king summoned Robert again to answer the charges, and when he received a flat refusal was able to proclaim that Robert de Bellême was a traitor and an outlaw. Sending to his brother in Normandy, he informed Curthose that the charges made and the reaction to them required that the Bellême lands in the duchy should also be forfeited, in accordance with the Treaty of Alton. Poor Curthose did his best. He sent an army to put the Bellême castle at Vignats under siege, but then, as usual, did not pursue any further action. The castle garrison, apparently, were willing to surrender, but could not do so honourably unless they were attacked and made some sort of resistance first. The attack never came, and eventually one of Curthose's men, Robert de Montfort, lost patience with his duke's 'sloth and indolence' and defected, setting fire to the besiegers' tents and causing such chaos that Curthose had to withdraw, with the jeers of the garrison ringing in his ears.

Meanwhile in England, Robert de Bellême was clearly preparing for a long haul, calling up his supporters and strengthening his defences. Arnulf, who some accounts say was also charged before the court, quickly rallied to him, with a number of Welsh Princes. Arnulf had married the daughter of the Irish King of Leinster, but there is no mention of Irish support for the brothers. Clearly, however, that land could offer a refuge and a source of supplies if needed. In the meantime, William of Malmesbury tells of Robert and Arnulf gathering corn from all around, and others mention plundering raids into Staffordshire. Castles were mended, walls built, defensive trenches dug. The Montgomerys were preparing for sieges, and sieges were what they got.

Vitalis describes Henry calling up 'the whole military array of England'. By this he seems to suggest that not only the feudal levies were summoned but also the fyrd, the ancient Anglo-Saxon militia. This seems to be confirmed when later he talks of 3,000 'provincial troops'. The fyrd could, in fact, provide many thousands of men but by tradition only a part would be called up at a time, usually those closest to the area in dispute.

Although the general outline of the campaign is agreed – the castles besieged and the outcome – different accounts give the events in a different order. Vitalis gives the fullest picture, and it is possible he may have had inside information.

Arundel Castle was Henry's first target, possibly in the belief that Bellème was there. He had, in fact, already moved to his new and illicit castle at Bridgnorth in Shropshire, and was busily fortifying this stronghold, perched on its steep hill above the River Severn. Arundel was nevertheless put under siege and, after a time, the garrison asked permission to send messengers to Bellème, as custom allowed, to see if any relief was likely, or if they might be permitted to surrender to the king. The terse answer was that they might expect no relief, and the castle was duly surrendered.

Another Bellème stronghold at Tickhill in Yorkshire was also besieged and taken, either by Bishop Robert Bloet of Lincoln or with the later assistance of King Henry. Then, according to Vitalis alone, Henry 'allowed his people to enjoy a short interval of repose'. By this is understood that he stood down the army for a period at midsummer before resuming his campaign in the autumn. Although this might sound unlikely to modern ears, allowing Bellème extra time to improve his defences, it must be remembered that England in the early 12th century was wholly reliant on its own agriculture to feed the population. Midsummer was harvest time, and every hand was needed to get in the harvest or there would be famine in the winter. It is unlikely that Henry's army enjoyed much 'repose' in their break from soldiering. After an interval of probably no more than a few weeks, the army was summoned again with Bridgnorth as the next target. Again Bellème had moved on before they got there. He left behind a castle well-fortified and provisioned, with eighty mercenary men at arms as well as its usual garrison, but around this time Henry found a new and useful ally. William Pantulf, 'a brave and experienced knight', had been a vassal of Robert de Bellême until he was 'rejected with disdain', as Vitalis puts it, whereupon he offered his services to Henry. He proved his worth as a mediator, not only with Bellême's men but also with his Welsh supporters.

The Welsh were bought off with promises of land in Powys, Ceredigion and Dyfed, but the approach made to those holding Bridgnorth Castle was rather different. True, there was an offer of a gift of land, but with that was the threat that if they did not surrender in three days, Henry would hang all those he captured. The garrison decided to accept the king's generous offer and surrender, though the eighty mercenaries had to be locked up while Henry's men took over the castle. After that, though, because they had honourably tried to fulfil their commitment, they were allowed to march out with their horses and arms.

While all this was taking place, Robert de Bellême was sitting securely in Shrewsbury Castle, some 20 miles away. His security would not last much longer, however. The road from Bridgnorth to Shrewsbury was narrow, rough and stony, in parts passing through a dense forest offering many opportunities for ambush. It may have been as much for psychological impact as for safety that Henry now set men to improve this road, hacking down the forest on each side to made a broad, open highway for his troops. As a statement of commitment, it was clear – and Bellême took the hint.

There had been some division of opinion in the army as to how he should be dealt with. The Norman lords were for leniency, fearing if such a mighty lord was to be disinherited the king, 'will trample us all under foot like feeble women.' On the other hand, the 'provincial troops' urged Henry to 'make no peace till you take him, alive or dead.' Bellême himself, however, realised further resistance would be futile. In the account of Vitalis, he went out to meet the king as he approached Shrewsbury, confessed to his treasonable offences and personally laid the keys to the castle at Henry's feet. Another account declares that it was the Abbot of

Sées who negotiated the surrender and handed over the keys. This is entirely plausible since the newly founded Shrewsbury Abbey had been colonised with monks from Sées in Normandy and the abbot may well have been visiting on abbey business.

Whichever version is true, it marked the end of the Montgomery brothers in England. Robert and Arnulf forfeited their lands and titles and were banished. Roger the Poitevin was given the choice of either to go with his brothers or to remain and become the king's man. He, too, decided to leave.

It also marked the end of campaigning in England. Not only does Vitalis say that 'England was in a tumult of joy' at the banishment of the Montgomery brothers, but he further notes that throughout the remainder of Henry's reign, 'no-one afterwards dared to revolt in England, nor held any fortress against him.'

The removal of such mighty magnates, and with so little violence, brought Henry enormous prestige. More than that, it also brought him enormous wealth from the forfeited estates and, of course, those estates, or at least parts of them, could be distributed as rewards to his faithful followers. Vitalis speaks of the king finding humble but capable men and promoting them as courtiers, 'taking them, so to speak, from the dust, surrounding them with wealth and exalting them above earls.'

Pre-eminent among the nobles and advisors of the time was Robert de Meulan, now with the great estates of Ivo de Grandmesnil in England to add to his own Beaumont lands in Normandy. He would become 1st Earl of Leicester, though he rarely used the title. Eustace of Boulogne had also returned, recovering his English lands under the Treaty of Alton, and he was secured as a royal supporter by marriage to Mary of Scotland, the younger sister of Queen Matilda. Other staunch supporters included Henry Beaumont, Earl of Warwick; Robert Bloet, former chancellor and now Bishop of Lincoln; Robert Fitzhamon, Henry's long-time friend; and, of course, Richard, Earl of Chester, the eight-year-old son of Hugh d'Avranches, whose estates Henry was administering.

Almost the only rotten apple left in the barrel was William of Mortain, Earl of Cornwall. Henry had tried to enlist him as a supporter by offering him the hand of Mary of Scotland, but William had spurned the offer, partly because although she was of the ancient royal line, she had no property as a dowry. In 1104 William found himself facing a law suit alleging he had wrongfully occupied lands adjacent to his earldom. Taking the hint, he immediately decamped to Normandy where, in due course, he threw his support behind Curthose and Robert de Bellème. Henry, meanwhile, took away both the earldom and the lands he had held in England, not only Cornwall but also including important parts of Sussex.

If Henry was getting stronger in England, the opposite was happening to Robert Curthose in Normandy. Robert de Montfort had already deserted his cause when, in January 1103 another staunch supporter was lost. William de Breteuil, son of the Conqueror's great friend William FitzOsbern, had inherited his father's estate in southern Normandy in 1071. He had stood up for the rights of Curthose on that fateful day when William Rufus had died, and he had supported him solidly ever since. Now his death without a legitimate heir led to a violent struggle among rival claimants. It seems clear that if Curthose had acted decisively to back one party, he might have secured his allegiance for the future. Instead, typically, he let events run their course without intervention.

William's illegitimate son Eustace took immediate possession of the estates and castles, but was at once challenged by William's nephews, William de Gael of Brittany and Reginald de Grancey, a Burgundian. Vitalis declares that the local people supported Eustace, 'preferring a countryman of their own to a Burgundian or Breton', even if Eustace was illegitimate. The death of de Gael narrowed the field, but Reginald was prepared to wage war to achieve his ends and enlisted the support of a number of important neighbouring lords including William, Count of Evreux; Ralph de Tosny, and Ascelin Goel, Lord of Ivry. With no help from Curthose, Eustace appealed for support to Henry, who indicated his favour by marrying him to his own illegitimate daughter, Juliana. More than this, military aid was promised and Robert de Meulan, whose nearby Beaumont estates were also threatened by the turmoil, travelled to Normandy and managed to broker a peace deal that recognised Eustace as rightful lord of Breteuil. Further marriages followed. Ralph de Tosny was given his father's lands in England and married a daughter and heiress of Earl Waltheof, the last Saxon Earl of Northumbria. Also at this time Rotrou, Count of Perche, an area to the south-west of Breteuil, married another of Henry's illegitimate daughters, Matilda, so that by the end of this matrimonial flurry, the King of England had secured for himself a solid area of southern Normandy whose rulers were attached to him, rather than to their own duke.

Some have suggested that Robert Curthose failed to intervene at this time because he was distracted by events closer to home. In October 1102 his son was born and baptised William. He would be known as 'Clito', the Norman equivalent of 'Atheling', or 'throne-worthy'. This clearly put Robert ahead in the inheritance stakes since Henry's first legitimate child, born in the February of that year, had been a daughter, Matilda, also known as Maud. It would be the middle of 1103 before Queen Matilda finally produced the necessary son and heir for Henry, who would also be called William.

However, William Clito was to be Robert's only legitimate child. In March 1103 his wife, Sibylla, died. According to William of Malmesbury, she died 'by disease' as a result of following the advice of a midwife, 'who had ordered her breasts, when in childbed, to be bound with tight bandages on account of the copious flow of her milk.' It was not usual for high-born ladies to breastfeed their own babies and it seems probable the midwife was trying to deal with this. If however Sibylla indeed had a 'copious flow,' it is more than likely that this treatment led to a build-up of milk in the breast, causing the painful inflammation known as mastitis. This is particularly common in the first months after childbirth. The breast hardens and, if untreated, can become infected, leading to flu-like symptoms, pain and fever and, if severe, even death. Modern advice is to avoid tight clothing and, if necessary, to take a course of antibiotics. Such remedies were not available to Sibylla and one wonders how many other mothers the midwife killed with her mistaken advice.

Orderic Vitalis, however, has a different and more sinister version of the cause of Sibylla's death. According to him, Agnes, widow of Walter Giffard, 'formed an affection for Duke Robert and entangled him in an illicit connection by the blandishments of love.' In addition to love, she promised material help from her own extensive resources and the support of her powerful relations, both of which might have been even more attractive to the beleaguered duke at the time. Again according to Vitalis, 'she induced the silly duke to engage that on the death of his present wife he would not only marry her, but entrust to her the government of the whole of Normandy.' This sounds a little reckless, even for Robert Curthose. Nevertheless Vitalis declares that, 'not long afterwards the duchess Sibylla took to her bed, infected by poison, and died.' Against this account it can only be pointed out that unexpected deaths at the time were often attributed to poison, and Curthose certainly did not marry Agnes or anyone else. Furthermore, far from handing over the government of Normandy to a strong and capable woman, it remained in his own hands, rapidly going from bad to worse.

The arrival of the Montgomery brothers, expelled from England at the end of 1102, did nothing to improve the peace of a duchy already riven by deadly feuds. William of Malmesbury says, 'The torch of war now lighted up in Normandy, receiving fresh fuel by the arrival of the traitors, blazed forth and seized everything within its reach.' Robert de Bellème, taking all their father's lands for his own, soon fell out with his brothers. Roger the Poitevin retired to his wife's lands to carry on a lifelong feud with a neighbour, but Arnulf fought back. Instead of ravaging the land with his brother, he now did the same on behalf of the duke, briefly obtaining for him the useful castle at Almenêches, between Sées and Argentan. It didn't matter to Robert de Bellème who was against him. 'Almost all Normandy rose in arms,' says Vitalis, 'And there was a general league to resist his tyranny,' but all to no avail. His resources were immense. He had thirty-four strong castles of his own, and no doubt his reputation for barbarity went before him, causing opponents to quail before the fighting even started. Vitalis, however, puts the lack of success squarely on the lack of strong leadership from Robert Curthose.

In June 1103 the duke began to gather an army at Almenêches, but a lightning strike by Bellème caused them to withdraw, leaving prisoners to be tormented and imprisoned by the tyrant. A further attempt was made. Again Curthose gathered his forces and prepared to challenge the power of Bellème in a decisive battle. Once again he was forestalled. As Curthose and his men approached, Bellème already had his forces in battle order, and one mighty charge swept the duke and his army clean away. Among the noble prisoners taken was the duke's own brother-in-law, William of Conversano. Never again would Curthose face up to Bellème, who now continued to ravage the lands of Normandy as he pleased.

With the full weight of barbarous violence descending on the area, and with no help from their duke, both the bishop and abbot of Sées fled for safety to England. They were soon followed by Curthose himself. What he hoped to obtain from this visit is not clear – a respite from his troubles at home, maybe, or help to subdue his tumultuous subjects in accordance with the Alton treaty. Perhaps, in accordance with that treaty, he might also have been looking for the promised pension, which he desperately needed and which, in all likelihood, he had not received. A commonly accepted reason, however, was that he came to do a favour for one of his supporters.

Vitalis tells us that at some point in 1103, William of Warenne presented himself to the duke in great distress, pointing out the huge loss he had sustained when deprived of the earldom of Surrey through supporting the duke's abortive invasion of England. Presumably he believed that Robert was now on friendly terms with his brother, and he begged him to go to England and plead for the return of his lands. Possibly Robert also believed he was on friendly terms with Henry, because he immediately agreed to do this.

He very soon learned of his mistake. Travelling with just a small escort of knights and squires, he was soon met by a group of the king's men, sent by Henry and, according to some accounts, led by Robert de Meulan. Why, they demanded, had Duke Robert entered the country without the king's permission? And furthermore, Henry wanted to know why he was in breach of their treaty in failing to deal with the king's enemies, now running riot in Normandy? Without spelling it out in so many words, Robert was then clearly given to understand that he had put himself firmly in Henry's power, and if he wanted to see his own lands again, he had better find ways to placate the king's wrath.

After this softening-up process, he was then conducted to Henry's court, where appearances were preserved in his treatment as an honoured guest. Robert 'concealed his alarm under an assumed gaiety,' while Henry 'presented a smiling countenance,' or so Vitalis says. He also tells us that 'their deep counsels were kept private,' so we don't really know by what process Robert was induced to confess his failures under the treaty and to promise to do better in future. Both Vitalis and Malmesbury agree, however, that it was at a suggestion from the queen that he agreed to give up his promised pension. Robert, says Malmesbury, 'As if contending with fortune whether she should give or he squander most, discovering the mere wish of the queen silently entreating it, kindly forgave the payment of this immense sum for ever.'

The only person who came out of this ill-advised visit well was William of Warenne who got his lands and his earldom back, and if Robert had thought that this would secure him as a much-needed supporter, he was wrong about that as well. William had, by this time, realised on which side his bread was likely to be buttered, and changed his allegiance accordingly. It is Vitalis this time who tell us, 'The earl, having thus recovered his father's inheritance ... learned wisdom from his misfortunes, and afterwards adhered faithfully to the king during the thirty-three years they lived together.' So in the space of one short visit Robert lost his money, his prestige and a very valuable supporter. He was soon to gain two others, although their value might be very questionable.

By the spring of 1104, the anarchy in Normandy was such that Curthose gave up trying to oppose Robert de Bellême and instead formed an alliance with him. They were joined by Bellême's nephew (and the duke's cousin) William of Mortain when Henry finally succeeded in dislodging him from England. Thereafter, this unholy trio set about attacking lands and castles in Normandy that favoured Henry, either out of sheer devilment, or possibly to provoke a reaction that could be turned in their favour. Henry, though, planned a provocation of his own.

First he accused Curthose of breaking their treaty by making alliance with his enemies, then he sent some of his own men to Normandy, presumably to strengthen those castles that supported him in that land. Finally, in August 1104, he set off himself to visit his castle at Domfront. Had Curthose had any power at all, he might have reacted with fury to this unapproved visit, as Henry had done to his visit the year before. Clearly that was beyond him. Despite the fact that in order to reach Domfront, Henry's cavalcade had to pass a ring of castles at Mortain, Ger and Tinchebrai, all held by William of Mortain, he seems to have travelled unchallenged. The fact that he was supported by leading magnates from both sides of the Channel may have had something to do with this. Vitalis lists Robert de Meulan, Richard of Chester (then about ten years old), Stephen of Aumale, Robert Fitzhamon, Robert de Montfort, Henry of Eu, Ralph de Tosny and Eustace of Boulogne as being among those who welcomed him, while other sources add the royal sons-in-law, Eustace of Breteuil and Rotrou of Perche.

As if this was not provocation enough, the king then summoned his brother to meet with him, and when Robert arrived, surrounded by what Vitalis calls his 'parasites', he set about him as if he were being accused in a court of law. Not only had Robert broken their treaty by making peace with traitors, but he was also charged with neglect and incompetence in abandoning the people of Normandy to bullies, thieves and robbers, 'like sheep in the jaws of wolves.' Again thrown on the defensive, Robert had no answer to make and, apparently fearful that he was in imminent danger of being deposed, sought to appease his brother. He offered to transfer to him the homage of William, Count of Evreux, handing him over, as Vitalis puts it, 'like a horse or an ox,' to the service of a new master. The count, who had served the Conqueror at the Battle of Hastings, was no doubt taken aback at this easy way with his fealty, but, again according to Vitalis, made a dignified acceptance of the situation. 'I love both the king and the duke,' he is said to have declared, 'Both are the sons of the king, my lord, and I wish to respect both; but I will only do homage to one of them, and him

I will loyally serve as my lord.' Then Robert placed the count's hand in Henry's and the deed was done – yet another example of the duke throwing away the loyalty of a badly needed supporter. Apparently, though, he had averted the anticipated disaster for after this Henry returned peacefully to England.

There was a storm coming, however, that no appeasement could divert. If Henry's trip had been a testing of the waters, he had found them very much to his satisfaction. Back in England matters were already in hand to prepare for a full scale invasion of Normandy and, in particular, to raise the money needed for such an invasion. It is at this time that Henry threw discretion to the wind, and his money-raising activities were very similar to those used earlier by his brother William. He did things he had vowed never to do, taking money from revenues of vacant churches and abbeys, fining the clergy and in general imposing increasingly heavy taxes. The Anglo-Saxon Chronicle, sounding far less sympathetic than might be expected, declares, 'It is not easy to describe the misery of this land which it suffered at this time through the various and manifold oppressions and taxes that never ceased or slackened.' Of course the Chronicle was written by monks, on whom the king's hand fell particularly heavily at this time. It was now, too, that the groans of the English churches were brought to the ears of Anselm. The result was the excommunication of Robert de Meulan in the spring of 1105, such an action against a chief advisor usually being seen as a warning shot to the ruler that he will be next.

Had Henry in fact been excommunicated in the spring of 1105, it might have completely undermined his plans to invade Normandy, and would certainly have deprived him of his main excuse, the oppression of the Norman Church. His eagerness to meet with Anselm and to compromise on the investiture issue had probably a great deal more to do with his political position, therefore, than with any real change of heart, and it may well be that his sister Adela's illness was also politically convenient. Nor were Anselm and Pope Paschal the only ones being courted at this time by Henry's diplomacy. As well as renewing his treaty with Eustace of Boulogne, the king also gained the support of the rulers of Maine, Anjou and Brittany, while messages exchanged with the French king Philip, and his more active son Louis, ensured they would not intervene on Robert's behalf.

The situation in Normandy was, in reality, becoming desperate. Robert de Bellême and his adherents had reacted with fury to Henry's visit the year before, and vented that fury on any part of the land deemed sympathetic to the king. 'They presently stained the whole province with murder and robbery,' says Vitalis, who, living there, should have known. 'The country people with their wives and children fled into France ... their own gardens, left deserted, were overrun with thistles and nettles ... for want of cultivation. ... Amidst these calamities the holy church was grievously persecuted.' As a result, he says, 'Cries of distress from suffering Normandy were wafted across the channel ... addressed to the king of England.'

It is highly likely that Henry had intended to invade anyway but it was good to have a ready excuse and, of course, Vitalis, always sympathetic to the English view, may have exaggerated the suffering. In any case, the immediate trigger for the invasion is said to have been the capture of Henry's great friend Robert Fitzhamon early in 1105.

Fitzhamon was apparently reducing to submission the area between Bayeux and Caen on Henry's behalf when he was ambushed by, among others, William of Warenne's brother Reginald. According to Wace, writing some time after the event, he tried to take shelter in a church tower at Secqueville, which was burnt down around him, forcing his surrender. At the time, or possibly later (the sources are unclear) he received a severe blow to the head causing brain damage, so that for the next two years until his death in 1107, he was rendered incapable.

Whether in immediate response to this or otherwise, Henry and his invasion force landed at Barfleur in the week before Easter 1105, and took up their quarters at Carentan. There on Easter Sunday, the Bishop of Sées, who must have either preceded or accompanied Henry, preached a sermon inciting the king to seize the duchy from his brother and restore it to good government. The church was apparently filled with chests, furniture and other goods, put there by the villagers in an attempt to preserve them from those at present ravaging the land. The bishop drew attention to these and to the reasons for their presence and, as usual, Vitalis does not hold back from putting a noble speech in the man's mouth. 'The church of God which was once called the house of prayer, is now, as you see, indecently filled with this vile lumber ... The church is thus made the people's stronghold, but even there perfect security is not found,' and he recited the burning down of a church in his diocese to illustrate his point. Why was this happening? Because of the sloth of Duke Robert and his subservience to his evil counsellors. It is difficult to believe the picture he paints of Robert's state – lying in bed half the day, and unable to go out because the 'buffoons and harlots by whom he is constantly surrounded, carry off his clothes during the night while he is drunk and snoring.' If he was exaggerating, he was speaking to an audience very willing to believe him. 'Rouse yourself to action in the name of the Lord,' he told Henry, 'And with the sword of justice make yourself master of your father's inheritance.' Furthermore, he declared, it would be no sin to seize the land in order to defend it from harm. To this Henry is stated to have replied, 'In God's name, I will not shrink from toiling earnestly for the restoration of peace, and ... to give tranquillity to the church.'

This was all very noble and a perfect excuse for action, but the bishop had not finished yet. He abruptly launched into a diatribe against the prevailing court fashion of long hair, beards and long, pointed shoes. Long hair was for women, he declared, and beards made them like goats, both in appearance and in satyr-like behaviour. Men let their beards grow, 'for fear that if they shaved, the short bristles might prick the faces of their mistresses when they were kissing them.' Their shoes were 'things like scorpion's tails at the extremities of their feet.' None of these things, he claimed, were suitably manly or appropriate for a king and his courtiers, and he finished by beseeching Henry to 'set your subjects a laudable example, that they might see in your person, above all others, how they ought to adjust their own.' Whereupon he whipped out a pair of scissors that he just happened to have with him, and there and then gave the king and several of his nobles a severe haircut.

The whole event has a strong flavour of stage-management. While it is possible the bishop simply had an aversion to long hair and beards (similar rules had been laid down in Anselm's Council of London in 1102) it is impossible to resist the symbolism involved. He had exhorted Henry to go to war, and now he had shorn him of the trappings of soft court life and prepared him for battle. No doubt the message was not lost on those who witnessed the occasion.

The first blow was struck at Bayeux where Fitzhamon was being held prisoner. Henry's army must have been impressive as it approached, composed as it was not only of Normans and Englishmen but also men from Maine, Anjou and Brittany. Those holding Bayeux for Duke Robert might have been intimidated into handing over the king's friend, but they did not surrender the town. Bayeux was duly stormed and taken, though in the process the cathedral and much else was burnt down and the men from Maine allowed to loot the place – perhaps not the best advertisement for Henry's claim that he was coming to bring order and peace.

Fighting continued, with Caen, where Duke Robert was, as the next target. Vitalis simply states that the citizens of Caen were terrified by what had happened at Bayeux and managed to negotiate with Henry to hand over the city to him. Wace, however, gives a far more complicated tale, backed up by all manner of circumstantial detail. According to him, a group of Caen's finest citizens were travelling from Argentan to Caen when they were captured by Robert of Saint-Remy. Perhaps realising the value of what he had, he then sold them to one of King Henry's men, whom he identifies as Robert Fitzhamon. The king was informed, and by sundry bribes, including the rents from a village in England thereafter known as the traitor's village, he persuaded them to betray their fellow citizens by handing over Caen to him. Again according to Wace, an elaborate pretence was set up that the men were set free on their oaths to raise large ransoms to pay for this freedom and, in exchange, hostages were sent to the king. Then they plotted together in a garden next to the town wall of Caen to open the gates and let in Henry's men. Wace adds the detail that the garden never afterwards bore any fruit. Finally,

Robert, getting wind of this plot, was advised to leave Caen, and retreated so rapidly and in such poor order that his baggage train was looted by the gatekeeper and others as it passed out through the Porte Milet.

How much of this is believable is not clear. Wace could certainly play free with the facts when it suited him. For example, he declares that Henry and the duke were of equal strength in the war and that it lasted six years, both of which 'facts' are clearly untrue. However, it does go a long way to explain why, according to Vitalis, four principal townsmen of Caen were rewarded by Henry with a village known as the traitor's village. Whichever version is truer, the fact remains that Caen was surrendered without bloodshed, and Henry marched on, this time to Falaise.

Falaise, however, was a step too far. The fortress there was not the mighty stone stronghold seen today, but there was a stone keep strong enough to resist Henry's assault. Here, too, he met his first real setback; in mid-May Helias, Count of Maine, abruptly withdrew his men from Henry's army. It is possible that others, too, fell away from Henry at this time, and though we have no specific reason given for this, a plausible suggestion is that it was to do with the threat of excommunication hanging over the king's head.

This had been a fairly vague threat when the expedition began in early April, but now it was known that Anselm had left his refuge at Lyons and was on his way north. He had told Adela his specific reason for moving was to go to excommunicate Henry, and no doubt word of this was flying along the roads of France and Normandy ahead of him. Helias was known to be a man of great piety and a correspondent of Anselm's, and would probably not want to continue a campaign supposedly in support of the Norman Church, with a man who had been clearly condemned by that Church.

Without these forces Henry was unable to continue his siege of Falaise, a siege which had already cost the life of at least one of his noble followers. Roger of Gloucester had been killed by an arrow fired from the keep, and some suggest that it was here that Robert Fitzhamon suffered his disabling head injury, which might match with Wace's description of his earlier activities.

A meeting with Duke Robert was arranged at the end of May but no kind of agreement was reached, and instead Henry turned his attention to clearing the threat of excommunication that seemed to be blighting his efforts at the time. By the end of July, he had met with Anselm at L'Aigle and agreed the compromise that would end the dispute. Then in August he returned to England, ready to begin planning the next step of his campaign.

How much of his setback at Falaise was known in England is not clear. Neither the Anglo-Saxon Chronicle nor John of Worcester mention it. The latter, in fact, simply states that Henry returned to England, 'finding it was not in his power at that time to make himself master of the whole of Normandy, and intending to return the ensuing year.'

Henry's earlier successes, however, may have caused a falling out among the duke's allies in Normandy. William of Mortain is recorded as continuing his attacks on Henry's lands in revenge for losing his estates in England, but before Christmas Robert de Bellême suddenly appeared at the English court. He left in the middle of the Christmas festivities having apparently failed to achieve what he came for, but what that was we don't know. He may have been trying to act as an intermediary between Duke Robert and his brother, though it seems hard to believe the duke could not have found someone more acceptable to Henry for such a task. On the other hand, there is just a possibility he had hope to defect to the English king, perhaps in exchange for recovering his earldom and lands in England. Either way, he was disappointed.

He would barely have been back in Normandy before Curthose, too, turned up in England, meeting his brother at Northampton. The Chronicle says he came because Henry would not hand back what he had seized from him in Normandy, though surely he was deluding himself if he had ever thought he would. An earlier message suggesting Henry should be content with England (having no right to that land either) and leave Normandy to Robert had been rebuffed, and this personal visit fared no better. Considering his reception on his previous visit, it must be counted as brave of him to make the attempt.

Sometime after Easter 1106 the pope's response to the agreement with Anselm was received, and with the cloud lifted from him, Henry prepared again to campaign in Normandy. The Anglo-Saxon Chronicle for 1106 is full of strange stars and double moons, but whether or not these were to be seen as omens, the king seemed to take no notice. Sometime between Pentecost (May 13) and August, he returned to Normandy, and the Chronicle says that almost everyone in that land submitted to him. Given the quantity of money, land and even bastard daughters he was prepared to give away, this hardly seems surprising.

Robert still had his adherents, however. Robert de Bellême and William of Mortain were still solidly behind him, or at least solidly against Henry. The English king might have taken Caen, but Rouen and Falaise still held out against him, and there were still people who were prepared to betray him to his enemies. Vitalis tells of the Abbot of Saint-Pierre-sur-Dives plotting with Robert to trap Henry and hand him over. This abbot was very much a product of his times. He had bought his office from the duke, and had built himself a castle alongside the abbey. Now he suggested that he would offer this castle to Henry, and tell him to come quietly with few men to take possession of it without arousing the countryside to oppose him. Within the castle the duke's men, Reginald of Warenne and Robert d'Estouteville, would be positioned with a force of men to seize him as soon as he entered. The trap was duly set but Henry did not fall into it, perhaps knowing the background of this unlikely cleric and suspecting his motives. He took with him some 700 men at arms, and arrived at the castle unexpectedly, just at daybreak. Finding things exactly as he had suspected, he attacked the castle and burned it down, taking the duke's men prisoner and sending the reinforcements the duke had dispatched, scuttling back to Falaise.

It is likely Henry had hoped to make a public reconciliation with Anselm, and to have the archbishop beside him before launching his decisive assault on Curthose and his forces. In the event, although he met with Anselm in mid-August and was fully reconciled to him, the archbishop then suffered a serious bout of illness, and when he recovered travelled straight to England.

In the meantime the king changed his tactics. Instead of attacking the major fortresses of Falaise and Rouen as he had tried the previous year, he now took his forces south to besiege one of William of Mortain's castles at Tinchebrai. By now it was autumn and, according to the Chronicle, the weather was bad. The campaigning season was nearly at an end, and perhaps Henry felt it would be better to make some gains against softer targets.

At first the siege went badly. Although siege castles were built, William of Mortain was able to bring in men and supplies, and no real attempt was made to take the castle or starve out its occupants. Soon, however, Henry stepped up operations, bringing his whole army, now once again reinforced with men from Maine and Anjou, to isolate the castle and put it under a full siege. William of Mortain appealed to his duke for help, and with by now typical recklessness, Robert brought his own army down to challenge that of his brother.

He demanded that Henry either raise the siege or face him in open battle, a rare occurrence at the time. No doubt he thought that his experience of battles in the Holy Land would give him an advantage over an opponent who had never been in such a situation before. Henry responded with an offer of his own. He had not come, he said, out of greed or ambition, but to protect the Church and the poor people of Normandy from the 'cruel sons of iniquity' who oppressed them. Therefore he proposed that Robert should hand over to him the administration of the duchy, with all its fortresses, while remaining simply as a figurehead. Robert should have half of all the revenues of the duchy and Henry the other half, while the king would make up the loss to Robert out of his own English treasury. Thereafter, he said, he would have all the work of maintaining peace and order in the duchy, while Robert could simply enjoy himself.

Whether or not this was intended to be a deliberate insult that was certainly how it was received, at least by Robert de Bellême and William of Mortain. Vitalis implies that Curthose was actually prepared to consider it until deterred 'by their violent language'. The offer was rejected and both sides prepared for battle.

It was 28 September 1106, forty years to the day from when William the Conqueror first set foot in England. Vitalis gives a long list of all the nobles present in Henry's army, including Helias of Maine, William of Evreux, Robert de Meulan, William of Warenne, Ranulf of Bayeux and Robert de Montfort. On the other side, he says, Curthose had only Robert de Bellême, William of Mortain and a few of lesser standing. Henry, he says, had more knights, but Robert more infantry, and on the field of battle, 'brothers and kinsmen were arrayed on different sides ... ready to exchange blows with each other.'

Henry drew up his men in three divisions, all unmounted so as to form a solid defensive line. Ranulf of Bayeux, a long-time friend of the king, commanded the first, composed of men from Bayeux, Countances and Avranches, Henry's most solid area of support. Henry himself with his English and Norman troops, formed the second division, with the experienced Robert de Meulan (then in his sixties) in command. The third division was led by William of Warenne, proving that what Vitalis said was true since his brother, newly released, was fighting for the duke. In addition, Henry had a reserve led by Helias of Maine, with 1,000 mounted knights from Maine and Brittany, held at some distance from the field of battle.

Against this Duke Robert drew up his men in only two divisions, the first led by William of Mortain and the second by Robert de Bellême. Although Henry of Huntingdon declares that these, too, were all dismounted, some at least must have been mounted since other sources suggest that the first attack was a mounted charge, and Huntingdon implies that the duke was in it.

At 9 o'clock in the morning the battle commenced. 'The duke, with his few followers,' says Huntingdon, 'Boldly charged the king's numerous troops, and, well trained in the wars of Jerusalem, his terrible onset repulsed the royal army.' Despite being pushed back by the impact of the mounted charge, however, Henry's front line held, and when the two main forces clashed, they were soon so closely locked together that fighting was almost impossible. Wace declares that hardly any were killed, and Vitalis says 'it was out of their power to injure each other.'

The decisive blow, however, was struck by Helias of Maine and his mounted knights. Crashing into the flank of the duke's forces, it was claimed more than 200 men fell at the first charge, and more in the chaos that followed. Then, even more decisively, Robert de Bellème, instead of reinforcing the duke's struggling army, turned tail and fled, taking his men with him.

The battle was over in less than an hour, Henry victorious and Robert Curthose not only defeated but captured. Henry was now master of Normandy, and his English troops especially rejoiced. Forty years on, they had revenge for Hastings. There Normandy had conquered England. Now England had conquered Normandy.

7

Lion of Justice
(1106–1111)

In a letter to Anselm soon after his victory at Tinchebrai, Henry boasted that he had captured 400 knights and 10,000 foot soldiers in the battle, while those killed by the sword were without number. The actual figures were probably a great deal lower, but it was his first battle and he had defeated the veteran of the crusades, and no doubt he can be forgiven a measure of exaggeration. Among the captives, though, were some of the first importance.

Robert Curthose had suffered the indignity of being captured by Waldric, one of the king's chaplains. William of Mortain was also a prisoner, captured by the Bretons who were initially reluctant to hand him over to Henry. The most surprising figure, however, to have fallen into the hands of the king was his wife's uncle, Edgar Atheling, who had fought for the duke and who, not for the first time in his life, now found himself allied to a losing cause.

Robert, though, seemed perfectly happy to accept defeat, behaving more like an Edwardian gentleman than a Norman lord. If it had been 800 years later one could almost see him shaking Henry by the hand and exclaiming, 'Well played, old man.' As it was, he pointed out to him that with Robert de Bellême still on the loose, it would be a good idea if he acted swiftly to secure the castle at Falaise. It shows the level of trust he had in his allies that he had instructed the castellan to surrender it to no-one but Robert himself or to his loyal vassal William de Ferrers. William de Ferrers having also been taken prisoner, he was now duly dispatched to ride ahead and, on the orders of the duke, to secure the castle for Henry. Further orders followed for the surrender of Rouen and then to all those who still held castles for Robert to surrender them to Henry's men. Not only was the battle lost, but as far as Curthose was concerned, the entire war and the duchy with it.

At Falaise Henry met, probably for the first time, his nephew William Clito, then approaching his fourth birthday. It was here that Henry made a mistake which would have serious consequences. In general he was quite astute in dealing with his great haul of prisoners. Most, Edgar Atheling among them, were rapidly released, presumably after offering homage to their new ruler. Robert, of course, was far too important to be treated in this way and, with the father securely in his hands, it might have been expected that Henry would also hold onto the son. Keeping William Clito close, bringing him up in the English court, would not only have removed any focal point for rebellion in Normandy, but would also have given Henry an extra hold over Robert. It was possible, too, that this might have allowed Henry to influence the boy's attitude, turning him from a potential enemy into a friend. Instead, young William was handed over to Helias of Saint-Saens, the man who had married Robert's illegitimate daughter and who was, therefore, the boy's brother-in-law. Whether this was a kindly act on Henry's part, letting the young child go to his familiar relations, whether it was his own idea or suggested by someone else, we don't know. Some accounts suggest that Henry was worried he would be blamed if anything happened to the child while in his care, though who would blame him or what consequences he might fear are not obvious. For whatever reason, the deed was done and Robert's only son and heir was taken away from Henry's court to be brought up in Normandy by a man fiercely loyal to his father-in-law's cause.

No mistake was made with his other important prisoners. William of Mortain was stripped of his lands and title and sent over to England where he was held securely in the Tower of London. Though Henry of Huntingdon declares the prisoner was thrown into a dungeon, the accounts of his daily allowance for food and drink suggest something a little less harsh. The same author is the only one to say that William was also blinded, at the time a common way of neutralising a dangerous opponent. However, there is a later brief mention in a London record that after Henry's death, William became a Cluniac monk in the Abbey of Bermondsey, and this says nothing about blindness. In any case, William would have been approaching sixty at the time, having spent over thirty years in prison. At that age failing eyesight would not be unexpected, and that may have given rise to the allegation.

Robert Curthose would also spend the rest of his life as a prisoner, albeit one not denied any of life's comforts or even luxuries. First held at Wareham, he was later moved to Roger of Salisbury's newly rebuilt Devizes Castle, then later to Bristol Castle, and finally to Cardiff Castle. There he spent his later days learning Welsh and, if one account is to be believed, writing poetry in that language. It is claimed that one example of his poems survives, a lament containing the lines, 'Woe to a man when there are those who hate him', 'Woe to him that is in the power of his enemies,' and, 'Woe to him that is not old enough to die.' Whether written by Robert or not, these lines might be seen as an accurate depiction of his situation. On the other hand, if half the things that were written about his indolence and love of an easy life are true, life-long imprisonment in luxurious circumstances with no cares or responsibilities might have suited him down to the ground.

Although Anselm, in response to Henry's letter, addressed him as 'Duke of Normandy', there is no evidence that Robert was formally deposed. Instead Henry carried out more or less the scheme he had proposed before the battle, although without the substantial payments to Robert he had suggested. There was no doubt, however, about who was now the effective ruler of Normandy.

In October 1106 he called a council at Lisieux. There, before all the Norman barons, he issued by 'royal authority' a declaration establishing his peace over all Normandy. Robbery and violence were to cease, and for all else the clock was to be turned back to 1087 and the death of William the Conqueror. The Church was to recover all the lands it had held at that time, and all other grants made by Robert Curthose were to be cancelled. In rather the same way as the Conqueror had treated Harold Godwinson forty years before, Curthose's reign was to be airbrushed from history.

This council, too, gave an opportunity for any baron who had not yet done so to submit and pay homage to Henry. One of these, either then or very soon after, was Robert de Bellème. He had tried to persuade Helias of Maine to break his alliance and join him in attacking the English king. Instead Helias acted as a mediator to bring them to at least a show of agreement. Robert duly submitted and was allowed to keep his father's lands and to remain as vicomte (the Norman equivalent of the English sheriff) for the Falaise area. Everything else, however, had to be handed back, including the strategic castle at Argentan and more than thirty other castles he had taken and fortified during his reign of terror. Though apparently now tamed, perhaps the words Vitalis puts in Bellème's mouth during his discussions with Helias most closely reflect his true feelings at the time. 'Never,' he is deemed to have said, 'while my life is spared, will I permit the man to govern Normandy in tranquillity who holds in chains the prince who is my liege lord.' For a time, though, with the tide flowing strong against him and in favour of Henry, the great Robert de Bellème had to live his life in enforced peace.

Further councils held at Falaise in January 1107 and again at Lisieux in March of that year, reinforced the message. All unauthorised castles were to be destroyed, and the ducal courts, so long ineffective, were to be revived. Within a short time they were being used to reclaim lost lands, and increased confidence in their justice, as well as harsh punishments for violence, led to a sharp reduction in the private wars for which Normandy had long been famous. As Vitalis put it, 'All who set the law at defiance ... were filled with sorrow and dismay, knowing well that a yoke they could not shake off was now imposed ... on their stubborn necks.'

At some point before Easter 1107 (13 April) Henry returned to England. The final settlement of the investiture issue, confirmed at the Council of London in August of that year, meant that a priority was the consecration of a number of bishops he had appointed in earlier years. Among these were William Giffard of Winchester, who had been waiting since the day of William Rufus's death for his consecration, and Roger of Salisbury, appointed some five years previously. New bishops appointed at this time included Warelwast, who became Bishop of Exeter, and Reinhelm, formerly chancellor to Queen Matilda, who became Bishop of Hereford. All these appointments were approved and invested by Anselm and, in theory at least, represented the new reformed, independent Church. All of them, however, had long been in the service of the king or queen. In addition, Roger of Salisbury was possibly married, or at least had a long-term mistress and children, as was Richard of Beaumais who became Bishop of London the following year.

At about the same time, a new Bishop of Lisieux, appointed by Henry, was being consecrated in Normandy by William, Archbishop of Rouen. When Bishop Serlo of Sées had fled to England to escape the ravages of Robert de Bellème, with him was a young archdeacon called John. Vitalis says John was already known to Henry, presumably from his time as lord of Domfront, and he soon became a chaplain to the king. Already renowned for his 'singular judgement and eloquence', he was soon a sought-after adviser, even attending the king's councils.

From the time of his exile from England in 1101 Ranulf Flambard had been lord of Lisieux. He had used his influence to impose a number of unworthy bishops on that diocese for his own benefit, first his brother, Fulcher, described as almost illiterate, then his son, Thomas, who was still a child, and finally, when the scandal involved in this forced a change, one of his clerks who paid a large sum of money for the office. In September 1106, after this period when Lisieux had been 'more in the power of wolves than pastors,' Flambard sought to curry favour with Henry by handing over the city and see to him, and Henry, having already recognised the intrinsic worth of Archdeacon John, then appointed him Bishop of Lisieux. The appointment was made before Henry returned to England, but since the new bishop was not yet even a priest, he had first to be ordained by Bishop Serlo, before, in September 1107, being consecrated as bishop by the Archbishop of Rouen.

Over a period of more than a quarter of a century, John of Lisieux more than repaid Henry's faith in him, both as a bishop and as an administrator. Vitalis says, 'God's mercy sent John to be ... bishop for the consolation of the faithful,' but he was much more than that, becoming the king's right-hand man in the duchy. Accompanying the king when he was in Normandy, and representing him with virtually viceregal powers when he was not, John was the chief instrument by which peace and good government was imposed on that formerly troubled land.

And peace and good government was Henry's main policy, not only in Normandy but in England as well. He began as he meant to go on, starting with reforming his own court. The vast retinue of the king – household officers, clerks, knights and all their support staff, not to mention the magnates and their retinues that followed him about – had caused major problems in the past. William Rufus had allowed his followers to plunder wherever they went, spoiling, wasting and even burning what they did not consume. In the early days Henry's men had done much the same, causing sufficient outcry for complaints to be recorded in the Anglo-Saxon Chronicle. After 1104, however, he seems to have brought them under control as no further complaints are recorded. The year 1108 marks a major change. In that year detailed regulations were laid down by the king for his household. Precise allowances were made for food, drink and even candles for everyone from the highest to the lowest. Even magnates visiting the court had their own set allowances, and furthermore the provisions were to be bought, not requisitioned, with fixed prices laid down for the produce needed, and severe punishments for those breaking the rules.

We have no exact knowledge of the size of Henry's court at the time, and indeed the numbers would ebb and flow depending on where he was and what business or leisure activity he was engaged in. We do know that courts had been growing and their members becoming more specialised from the time of the Conqueror onwards.

The court fulfilled a great number of roles. It was a meeting place and a place where ideas could be exchanged. It was an administrative centre and a place where justice was dispensed. It displayed the wealth and power of the king. It was a ladder to higher things for those of good family, or even no family, who could catch the king's eye and impress him with their usefulness. It

Holy Trinity Abbey, Caen
This 'Abbaye aux Dames' was founded by the Conqueror's wife, Queen Matilda, as penance for marrying William when forbidden to do so by the pope.

St Stephen's Abbey, Caen
The 'Abbaye aux Hommes' was founded by William as his part of the penance. The extremely plain façade is believed to have been designed by Lanfranc.

Selby Abbey, Yorkshire
This was a joint foundation by William and Matilda, probably to commemorate the birth of their son Henry, in Selby, in 1068.

The tomb of Queen Matilda
Situated before the altar in Holy Trinity Abbey.

Memorial to William the Conqueror
William was originally buried beneath the lantern tower in his still unfinished abbey of St Stephen. In 1562 rioters destroyed his tomb and threw around the bones it contained. All that is left is one thigh bone, buried beneath this memorial slab before the altar in St Stephen's Abbey.

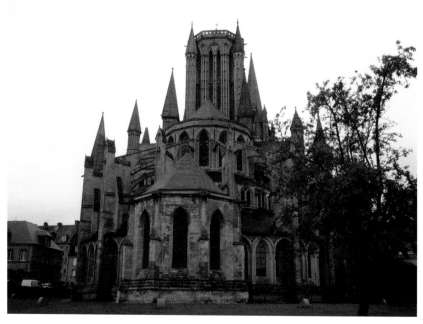

Coutances Cathedral, Normandy
This was the seat of Bishop Geoffrey of Coutances, who was not happy when Coutances formed part of the lands sold to Henry by Robert Curthose in 1088.

Avranches, Normandy
This was also part of Henry's lands at the time and a major centre of power in the area. Hugh d'Avranches, its lord, was also 1st Earl of Chester and became a friend and supporter of Henry.

Pevensey Castle
In 1088 Robert of Mortain and Odo of Bayeux were besieged here by King William Rufus after they launched a rebellion on behalf of Robert Curthose. They were starved into surrender.

Rochester Castle

After the surrender of Pevensey, Odo was to order Rochester Castle to submit; instead he joined the rebels inside, including Robert de Bellême and Eustace of Boulogne sent over by Robert Curthose. Robert himself never arrived nor sent any adequate relieving force. Eventually heat, thirst and a plague of flies forced the surrender of the castle, ending the rebellion.

Mont-St-Michel

Henry was besieged here in 1091 when his brothers decided to use force to recover the lands Robert had sold him. The lack of adequate drinking water forced him to surrender.

Domfront Castle
This belonged to Robert de Bellème until its castellan decided to hand it over to Henry in 1092. Henry promised the people of Domfront he would be their lord. He built the mighty keep at the centre of the castle and held it for forty-three years.

The Rufus Stone in the New Forest, Hants.
Left: This marks the spot where King William Rufus was killed while hunting in the forest, in August 1100.

Below left: The Rufus Stone tells the story of the death ...

Below right: ... and burial of King William Rufus.

HERE STOOD THE OAK TREE, ON WHICH AN ARROW SHOT BY SIR WALTER TYRRELL AT A STAG, GLANCED AND STRUCK KING WILLIAM THE SECOND, SURNAMED RUFUS, ON THE BREAST, OF WHICH HE INSTANTLY DIED, ON THE SECOND DAY OF AUGUST, ANNO 1100.

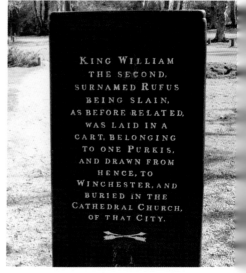

KING WILLIAM THE SECOND, SURNAMED RUFUS BEING SLAIN, AS BEFORE RELATED, WAS LAID IN A CART, BELONGING TO ONE PURKIS, AND DRAWN FROM HENCE, TO WINCHESTER, AND BURIED IN THE CATHEDRAL CHURCH, OF THAT CITY.

William Rufus was originally buried beneath the tower of Winchester Cathedral. Two years later, the tower collapsed. Some said this was because of the king's infamy, though others conceded it might have been bad workmanship. The tower was rebuilt and William's remains were later placed in a mortuary box.

Romsey Abbey
Henry's queen, Matilda, spent most of her childhood here, where her Aunt Christina was the abbess.

Westminster Abbey
Henry I was crowned here on 5 August 1100. Three months later he married Matilda here, and she was crowned as Queen of England.

ENTRY TO THE TRAITORS GATE

The Tower of London
Ranulf Flambard was responsible for building the first outer wall around the Conqueror's keep, the White Tower, and he was later the first prisoner ever held there – and the first to escape.

The church at Alton, Hants.
Near here, Henry met his brother Robert and negotiated the Treaty of Alton, which put an end to Robert's invasion and his challenge for the English crown.

Canterbury Cathedral, the seat of Archbishop Anselm
Anselm's long conflict with William and with Henry led to two periods of exile. The Investiture Controversy in England was ended by compromise in 1106.

Roger of Montgomery's tomb, Shrewsbury Abbey
Roger, prompted by the father of Orderic Vitalis, was the founder of Shrewbury
Abbey. Roger of Montgomery's was 1st Earl of Shrewsbury and the father of the
notorious Robert de Bellème.

Bridgnorth Castle
Building this castle without permission was one of the charges brought against
Robert de Bellème. Henry besieged the castle in 1102, but Robert had escaped to
Shrewsbury.

Shrewsbury Castle
Henry's show of force on the way to Shrewsbury persuaded Robert to surrender the castle without a siege. He was then exiled to Normandy.

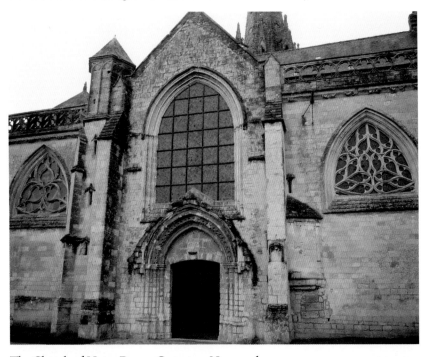

The Church of Notre Dame, Carentan, Normandy
When Henry invaded Normandy in 1105, he listened to a sermon here and had his hair cut by the bishop of Sées.

Bayeux Cathedral
Bishop Odo of Bayeux, who built the original cathedral here, was a trusted counsellor of Robert Curthose and an enemy of Henry. When Henry invaded Normandy in 1105, his men sacked the town of Bayeux.

Falaise Castle
Although Henry besieged this mighty keep in 1105, he was unable to force a surrender and withdrew to England.

Tinchebrai

This field below the town of Tinchebrai is a possible site for the battle fought in 1106, in which Henry defeated his brother Robert and won all Normandy.

Remains of Henry's castle at Caen

Left: Within the Conqueror's fortress at Caen, Henry constructed this mighty castle.

Pembroke Castle

Below: The castle was founded by Arnulf of Montgomery and later held for King Henry by Gerald FitzWalter of Windsor and his wife Princess Nest.

Carew Castle garderobe
When Prince Owain of Powys attacked Gerald's other castle at Carew, Gerald had to escape down the chute of this garderobe (toilet). Princess Nest and her children were kidnapped during this raid.

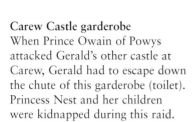

This plaque at Barfleur records that the mariner 'Stephen' commanded the ship that carried William the Conqueror to England in 1066. His son Thomas owned the Blanche Nef (White Ship), which would carry William Adelin and his companions to their deaths, shipwrecked on the rocks outside Barfleur.

The harbour entrance at Barfleur
This harbour was often used by Henry when travelling to and from Normandy. The treacherous rocks on either side meant careful seamanship was needed to enter and leave the harbour.

The tomb of Robert Curthose, Gloucester Cathedral
Robert spent twenty-eight years as a prisoner in England before his death in 1134.

The site of Woodstock Palace
This was one of Henry's favourite palaces. Ideally placed for hunting, in its grounds it also housed his collection of exotic animals. Today the site is within the park of Blenheim Palace.

Remains of Reading Abbey
Henry founded Reading Abbey for the salvation of the souls of his family, ancestors and successors. Of major importance later, it was still in its infancy when he died in 1135. He was buried before the high altar, but the destruction carried out at the time of the Reformation means the exact site is now lost.

was even a nursery and training ground for those who would play an important role in the next generation.

At the heart of this was the king's own support staff, his household, with its own hierarchy dedicated to providing for all his personal needs. It is traditional to divide this into four parts, the chamber, the hall, the yard and the chapel. Master of the chamber, and of the household as a whole, was the chamberlain. Not only did he serve the king in his private rooms, but he was also in charge of the money that would be needed daily for expenses. In the hall, the steward or dapifer was responsible for providing food for all, and the butler was responsible for the wine and ale. The outside servants of the yard and stables were the responsibility of the marshal, while royal escorts, bodyguards and security in general, that of the constable. Below these were all manner of cooks, ushers, cup-bearers, doorkeepers, clerks, masters of horse, grooms, huntsmen, armourers and so on, probably numbering in the hundreds. A separate group was made up of the king's personal retinue of knights, some serving for advantage and some for pay.

The chapel was not only the domain of chaplains providing the various services of worship engaged in by all members of the household, but it also housed a writing office, becoming increasingly important during Henry's reign. This was led by the chancellor, who at this time as well as being the king's chaplain was also his secretary, and in later years would become an ever greater figure. Even now the post of chancellor could be a major stepping stone for one rising from clerk level to be an important advisor and administrator for the king. We can see this from the list of those who held this office.

Robert Bloet was chancellor to William Rufus before becoming Bishop of Lincoln in 1093, but he was still close to King Henry as a trusted advisor at his death in 1123. In fact it is recorded that he was riding with the king and another advisor when he had what was described as a fit, but may well have been a stroke and, by one account, died in the king's arms. He was followed as chancellor by William Giffard, who Henry inherited when he took the throne. William, too, was rewarded for his support by becoming Bishop of Winchester, managing through the Investiture Controversy to remain on good terms with both Anselm and the king.

William' successor as chancellor was Roger le Poer, a companion of Henry's from his time of wandering in France. Roger's major talent was for administration and, though he held the post of chancellor for little over a year before becoming Bishop of Salisbury in 1102, still he remained in all but name Henry's 'justiciar' or chief minister for the rest of his reign. By then his family, including his son and nephews, had become one of the most powerful in the land. That the power had left the post of chancellor when Roger of Salisbury moved on is shown by the inferior quality of the next holder of the office. Waldric, too, had been a royal chaplain but he was described as a greedy and violent man. In the fashion of priests and bishops of old, he took part in the Battle of Tinchebrai, his chief claim to fame being the capture of Robert Curthose. Thereafter he persuaded Henry to appoint him Bishop of Laon in southern Normandy, where he so displeased the population that he was murdered in the crypt of the cathedral by the citizens during a riot at Easter in 1112.

Possibly one reason for Waldric's appointment was to tie Laon closer to England. The cathedral there was famous for its school, where Anselm of Laon taught a most practical course for aspiring clergy, combining a strong moral and pastoral side with sound administration. Many young clerks found their way from Laon to Henry's court, or to the household of an English bishop, and from thence became bishops themselves. Others came from schools at Liège and later at Salisbury or Lincoln, or rose from Henry's own household or those of other magnates. All were moulded under the hand of Roger of Salisbury to become a most efficient administrative machine to carry out the king's commands.

As well as those directly serving the king, at any one time Henry's court might also contain foreign visitors with their entourages, magnates from England and Normandy and their retinues, bishops and abbots, those seeking favours and those seeking justice. His own children, both legitimate and illegitimate, made up another group, along with others privileged to receive at least part of their upbringing at the royal court. Notable among the latter are Stephen of Blois, a younger son of his favourite sister, Adela, and Brian FitzCount, illegitimate son of Alan of Brittany.

At this time, of course, the court did not remain long in one place but moved around both in England, particularly southern England, and in Normandy. The royal and the ducal estates scattered throughout these lands were originally intended for the support of the ruler and his court, so that as he moved around produce would be brought to supply their needs. Staying too long in one place would, however, quickly exhaust the resources, and arriving unexpectedly caused an equal problem.

Increasingly through the reign, dues would be paid in cash rather than in kind, so that the court could buy what it needed from anyone in an area. Furthermore, for the most part Henry would plan his travels, letting it be known in advance where he would be staying. The writers of the time generally set this down as a sign of the king's good organisation and consideration for his people. It meant that markets could spring up in advance of the king's arrival, with people knowing that their goods would be bought. Instead of fleeing to the woods and hiding from the ravages of the court, as had happened in earlier times, people now saw a royal visit as a happy and profitable event.

The advantage of payment in money rather than in kind meant that the king could be more flexible in the way he acquired the goods and services he needed. Increasingly, for example, mercenary soldiers were paid for, rather than demanding the nominal knight service from his vassals, and men from Flanders and Brittany served in the king's army with Normans and Englishmen.

To pay for the needs of a substantial court, however, and for all the other demands on the king, a great deal of money would be needed. It has been noted as a major achievement of the administration that throughout his reign, whether in peace or in war, Henry remained solvent. Much credit for this must go to the efficiency of the methods developed by Roger of Salisbury to ensure that all the money due to the Crown was properly paid.

When the Normans conquered England in 1066, they took over not only the land but also a long-standing and sophisticated system of raising finance for the monarch's use. The geld – originally

Danegeld – was a form of tax based on landholding, collected on behalf of the king by his sheriffs. In the time of Athelred and even earlier, vast amounts of money had been raised in this way in order to buy off Viking raiders, and although the tax was abolished by Edward the Confessor, it seems to have been quietly reinstated before the end of his reign. Land was assessed in terms of 'hides', a measurement of area that varied in different regions according to the quality of the land. A usual level of tax was 2 shillings per hide of land held, and this may have been an annual demand, but the level was set by the king and higher rates could be levied in time of need. William Rufus called for 4 shillings per hide when raising the money for Robert's loan in 1095, for example. Not only was geld a useful source of finance for the king, but it also provided a way of rewarding faithful service, since exemptions from geld could be given either for a period of years or sometimes for life.

This money, increasingly payable in coin, was not the king's only source of finance. Royal estates, by and large, were let out 'at farm', meaning that those who occupied them and farmed the land paid a fee for doing so. The payment received for this, again increasingly in coin, produced something like half the total revenue in a normal year. Similarly, the majority of towns and cities also belonged to the king and rents and tolls could be demanded, along with extra payments for special privileges. London, for example, paid for the right to choose its own sheriff. If something extra was needed for the king's use, 'aids' could also be demanded from towns.

Royal justice produced regular funds in the form of fees and fines, as did feudal dues such as payments made in lieu of military service or when an heir inherited his lands. People paid for offices in the royal household, and sometimes again to give up an office, and revenues from forfeited land and vacant Church offices also came into the royal treasury.

English kings had long controlled the coinage and only licensed moneyers were allowed to issue coins. This, too, was a source of revenue since the moneyers had to pay for this privilege and also for the dies from which the coins were struck. Changing the coinage regularly provided a steady stream of money for the king, particularly since he took a share of the fees for re-minting existing coins, and only the new coins could be used for paying what was due to the Crown. Silver pennies were the main coins issued. Round halfpennies were first introduced by Henry. Prior to this they had been literally a silver penny cut in half.

There was a shortage of silver in Europe at the time and great problems were found later in the reign with debased coins and fraudulent moneyers. As payment in coin became more important to the king, harsh punishments were imposed for tampering with the coinage. A false moneyer could be castrated and lose his right hand if found guilty.

From time to time when the king wanted advice on matters of major importance he would summon all the great magnates and clerics to a *Magnum Concilium* or Grand Council. For the rest of the time all government was centred on his court, and in particular on his inner circle of advisers known as the *Curia Regis*, the king's council. From this would grow in time all the departments of government, the law courts and even Parliament itself, though that was a long way in the future. For the time being, this restless court travelled constantly on both sides of the Channel. The king's majesty must be seen and his presence felt wherever the affairs of state demanded it.

William the Conqueror, well knowing the power of ritual, had instigated regular 'crown-wearings', meetings of the court where the king would be seen crowned and dispensing justice and favour to those who requested it. These took place at the times of the major religious festivals, at Christmas, Easter and Pentecost, with a regular circuit of Gloucester, Winchester and Westminster. Henry's crown-wearings were just as important but gradually more flexibility crept in. Gloucester featured less often and other places such as Marlborough, Odiham and Windsor appeared. Still a festival without a crown-wearing was unusual enough to feature in the Anglo-Saxon Chronicle, and in 1111 it seemed almost front page news that the king did not wear his crown either at Christmas, Easter or Pentecost.

This mobile court, while good for some purposes, made others unnecessarily difficult. Twice a year the sheriff of every shire in England was required to account for all the revenues due from his shire to the royal treasury. This biennial audit took place at Easter (March/April) and Michaelmas (September), and had involved the sheriffs travelling to wherever the court might be so that the officials in charge of the treasury might check that all that was due had in fact been delivered.

Roger of Salisbury is credited with developing the system that grew up in the early years of Henry's reign and revolutionised this accounting procedure. For the first time, a group of officials from the *Curia* would go to Winchester, where the main royal treasury had been kept since Anglo-Saxon times, and there, under the supervision of Roger of Salisbury, the sheriffs would present their accounts to what became known as the Exchequer.

The name derives from the large table, 10 feet by 5 feet, spread with a checked cloth rather like a chess board, on which the money was counted. The cloth acted like an abacus, a fairly new introduction to Western Europe, which enabled complicated sums to be done before the adoption of Arabic numerals and zeroes. The money would often be assayed as well as counted to be sure of the silver content, and while some officials were involved with the counting, others noted down the sums and the sources from which they came on long parchment sheets. These, when rolled up for storage, resembled long pipes and therefore became known as Pipe Rolls. The earliest that we have dates from 1130, but clearly they had been in use long before this.

A similar process was carried out at Caen in Normandy under the supervision of John of Lisieux, indeed it may be that the chequered cloth was in use there before its adoption in England. There it was the vicomtes who had to account for the ducal revenue, which again came into a central treasury. Neither John of Lisieux nor Roger of Salisbury were officially given the title of treasurer, though this would come in later generations.

In England the main treasury was at Winchester, but a subsidiary began to be established at Westminster. Money needed for daily expenses was carried for the king by his chamberlain, both in England and in Normandy. When needed, money was also shipped from England to a treasury at Falaise via Southampton and Barfleur.

The checked cloth on the table gives us the word 'exchequer', which later came into general use for a department of government dealing with finance. In 1110 for the first time the officials dealing with this accounting process are referred to as 'Barons of the Exchequer'. This is not to suggest, however, that the exchequer was yet a separate department of government with a fixed membership. The biennial accounting was, though, the first occasion when 'government' business was carried out at a fixed place and time and in the absence of the king.

This detailed accounting system meant that a close watch could be kept on all the king's revenues. Debts unpaid in one period could be carried forward to the next, and long and short exemptions carefully noted. Inevitably this process threw up disputes and it is clear the officials had authority to deal with these. From this would grow, over many years, a judicial side to the exchequer, and eventually the Court of the Exchequer became a law court where pleas involving the king's rights would be decided. Later it extended its jurisdiction to other pleas as well, becoming the first of the great Common Law courts of England to come into existence.

The king's regard for the law may have come as a pleasant surprise to his subjects. He did at times, it is true, go back on many of the promises made in his coronation charter, but his justice was not arbitrary, as William Rufus's had been. Summoning Robert de Bellème to answer specific charges before his court may have been just as sure a way of getting rid of him as any other, but it did emphasise the importance of using a recognised legal process, rather than simple force. During Henry's reign the foundations were laid for almost the whole system of justice that exists in England today, and though most of the building was done by future generations, enough was done at the time to earn him the title 'Lion of Justice'.

In the main, the system of justice in England which Henry inherited was one stretching far back into the past. The main courts were the shire courts, presided over by the sheriff of that shire acting in his judicial capacity as the king's representative. He declared the 'judgement' of the court but did not decide it arbitrarily. Decisions were the job of the suitors, land-holders from the shire who were summoned to the court to contribute to local justice in this way.

The customary business of the court was deciding on compensation for injury, recovering debts due, and settling land disputes, such as the establishment of correct boundaries.

Within each shire were subdivisions known as Hundreds, some of which are still to be found on maps today. These, too, had their courts and their suitors, presided over by the Hundred Reeve, who would be the sheriff's deputy for that area. Smaller scale local disputes were dealt with, and in particular breaches of the peace, for which a fine was payable.

Overlaying this system from the time of the Conquest onwards, came two other sets of courts. The first of these, the ecclesiastical courts, not only dealt with matters of Church law and the discipline of the clergy, but also ruled on the validity of a marriage and the legitimacy of children. In addition, as they developed, any clerk in any form of holy orders (and there were many at the time) could claim 'benefit of clergy', and have any accusation against them transferred from a lay court to the ecclesiastical court, thereby escaping the most severe forms of punishment.

More importantly, it was the right of any lord to hold a court for his tenants. This might be the Manor Court of a smaller land-holder, or the Honour Court of a magnate holding a number of manors as an 'Honour' or 'Barony'. Such courts were like smaller versions of the king's own court, primarily concerned with the management of the holding, but also having jurisdiction to discipline tenants, enforce duties owed, and decide disputes between them.

Throughout the reign of Henry I the trend was to centralise justice in the king's hands. There was a wide overlap in the jurisdictions of the Manor and Honour Courts with that of the Sheriff's court, and not only was justice profitable, but also any strengthening of the magnates' powers would lead to a corresponding weakening of those of the sheriff. The sheriff was the king's representative. Indeed, he became a more important figure after the Conquest than he had been before, and increasingly was appointed from among the king's officials, instead of from among the barony.

It is probably for this reason that, when Henry was turning his mind to the re-ordering of the country in 1108, he issued a writ saying the Shire and Hundred Courts must in future be held at the times and places where they had been held at the time of the Conqueror. Not only did this put an end to any back-sliding that had occurred under William Rufus and in the earlier, more troubled days of Henry's reign, but it also signalled his firm intention to support the Shire Courts as dispensers of the king's justice.

Ruling by writ was another inheritance from earlier times. A writ was a command of the king, with strong sanctions including imprisonment and loss of lands for failure to obey. Increasingly writs were issued to sheriffs directing them to deal with matters outside their usual jurisdiction. By this means people became accustomed to the king's justice being dispensed by the king's representative on the issue of a royal writ. The king also sent his own officials to deal with matters in the Shire Courts. Their commissions from the king specified the kinds of cases they were empowered to deal with, and these included offences against the king's peace as well as other disputes and purely administrative matters. They were not yet called Justices nor organised on any regular basis. Still this was the seed that would grow into the system of justice still practised in England today, whereby itinerant judges still enforce the law of the land in local courts.

In general the king did not *make* law, in the way that Parliament today makes laws, though, if some problem was found on a regular basis, he might, after consultation with his advisors, lay down a new rule. Rather, when a writ commanded some dispute to be dealt with, it acted as a summons to appear before a court where the decision would be based on long-standing customs rather than newly minted laws. So the manuscript we have, entitled *Leges Henrici Primi* – The Laws of Henry I – is not a list of laws made by Henry himself. Instead it is an attempt to collect together laws that existed at the time. Probably written by a clerk of the curia sometime between 1115 and 1118, it is the first-known attempt to compile a treatise on the law, pre-dating the better-known treatise of Glanvil by around half a century.

It began, naturally enough, with a statement of Henry's Coronation Charter, but since that declared an intention to return to the laws of Edward the Confessor, many of the laws subsequently described derive from a much earlier time. Indeed, Edward himself had adopted the code of law laid down by Cnut, the Viking king who had been a predecessor on the English throne, and Cnut in turn claimed to be ruling according to the laws of King Edgar, who had died in 975 AD. It is unsurprising, then, that the majority of the laws described are Anglo-Saxon, though with an overlay of Norman adaptations.

Much of the *Leges* is taken up with procedural matters, suggesting it was probably written for the benefit of the king's justices carrying out their commissions around the country. It lays down, for example, the formal procedure for summoning a person to court, and that used in murder cases. Levels of judicial fines are also covered, along with rules about the administration of the forest laws, and about roads and highways.

Most importantly, however, from the point of view of the centralisation of justice, it lays down a list of 'Pleas of the Crown', matters that could only be tried by the king himself or by one of his officials. These included treason, murder, rape, robbery, some kinds of theft and arson. Of course any acts of violence against the king, his household or his servants would also be dealt with in this way, as well as actions against counterfeiters, while the concept of the 'King's Peace', confirmed in both the Coronation Charter and the *Leges*, would enable the king to draw all criminal matters into his jurisdiction.

As feudal overlord, Henry's court would also deal with all issues relating to his tenants-in-chief. This might involve punishment of offences, enforcement of dues and settling disputes over land. Increasingly, too, disputes about revenues owed to the Crown were being decided by the Exchequer, while, after 1111, it was decreed that any dispute between freemen who were tenants of different lords must be decided in the Shire Court, rather than a Manor or Honour Court. Little by little the king was extending his reach into all areas of law.

There was, of course, no police force at the time, to catch wrong-doers and bring them before the court. By and large it would be a complaint from the victim or his family that would begin an action. Then it was part of the sheriff's job to see that offenders were produced to answer for their crimes. They were helped in this by what was known as the frankpledge system. Under this system, every man over the age of 15 belonged to a group called a 'tithing', and regular reviews were held to make sure these tithings were properly constituted. If a crime was committed by one of their number, it was the duty of the tithing to produce him before the court. Failure to do this would mean that they themselves would be fined. Particularly onerous would be the 'murder fine', stated in the *Leges* as forty-six silver marks. Originally this was payable for the death of a Norman, but later it was extended to cover all murders.

Methods of proving a case were also developing at this time. Before this there was a strong reliance on the judgement of God as to which side might be telling the truth. This might sound primitive to us, but in a strongly religious society with no forensics and few other methods of collecting evidence, it was logical enough. The Anglo-Saxons had had two basic methods, trial by ordeal and compurgation. The ordeal, under supervision of the clergy, might be to carry a red hot metal bar for a certain distance. The injured hand would then be bound up, and a few days later inspected by the supervising clergy. If the burns had healed sufficiently it would be deemed that God was witnessing that the accused had spoken the truth.

Compurgation or oath-swearing, whereby a specified number of people would swear to the truth on a Bible, might sound to us an easier option. It must be remembered, however, that, at the time, lying on oath was seen as a major sin, condemning a person to eternal damnation in hell, a very real prospect to the people of the twelfth century. It would not be something done lightly, and a person may well fall short of the number required to prove his innocence. Interestingly, when Earl Godwin was accused of treason by Edward the Confessor, he cleared his name by compurgation – though he did also have an army at his back.

The Norman equivalent was Trial by Battle. Individuals or their champions would fight to the death or until one yielded, with God giving the victory to the one telling the truth. William of Eu, accused of treason against William Rufus in 1095, underwent a trial by battle at Salisbury. He was defeated by Geoffrey Baynard, nominated to fight for the king, and being, therefore, declared to be guilty, he was duly blinded and mutilated. At first only Normans could claim trial by battle, but later this right was extended to the English as well, and in fact it was only abolished in 1819, after an enterprising claimant in court wanted to use it to prove his case.

By the time of Henry I, however, there was already a move towards requiring what we would regard as evidence. In particular, charters and other documents would be produced in court to establish claims to land and other rights and exemptions. This was especially true in the Exchequer and in other places where the king's officials were dealing with a matter. Now, too, more use began to be made of 'jurors'. These were not independent lay people deciding truth on the basis of evidence laid before them, as we have today. Instead they were local people with a knowledge of the facts, who would give sworn evidence as to those facts to enable the king's justices to come to a decision. We would call them witnesses rather than jurors, and their precursors were probably those who gave evidence to the commissioners sent by the Conqueror for the compilation of the Domesday Book.

These superior methods used in the king's courts by his proto-justices made them a popular place in which to have disputes decided, despite the fees that had to be paid. Equally, quite apart from enhancing the king's authority, the additional cases and the increased fees involved made royal justice highly profitable. The *Leges* recognised that anyone unhappy with the quality of justice achieved elsewhere could appeal to the king, and this developed into a new procedure under what came to be called the Writ of Right. Here anyone could apply to the king on the basis that his lord was refusing or unreasonably delaying to give judgement in a case, and thereby denying him his rights. The king would then issue a writ requiring the lord 'to do right' or the king would see that right was done. No doubt dealing with genuine complaints at first, over time this simply became a way of removing a case from the Manorial Court into the hands of the king's justices. Once again the Manorial Courts would be weakened and the king's courts strengthened by this device as not only criminal matters, but more and more disputes of every kind were brought within the scope of the king's centralising justice.

The years from 1106 to 1111 were the most peaceful of Henry's reign. After that time, although peace reigned in England, for the majority of the king's life troubles elsewhere took him out of the country for long periods. Nevertheless, the reforms set in motion during the years of peace gave rise to systems of finance, government and law that were strong enough to survive, and even to keep developing under the guiding hand of Roger of Salisbury, during the times when the king was away. There may have been complaints about the taxes needed to fund wars and other enterprises but there were no rebellions, and increased confidence in the justice dispensed by the king's courts meant that private wars and violent struggles became, for a time at least, a thing of the past.

8

Prestige and Problems
(1111–1120)

Victory at Tinchebrai and the rapid capitulation of Normandy brought Henry, perhaps in equal measure, increased prestige and increasing problems. In the tranquillity of the early years, however, the problems seemed far away and the prestige a more immediate and satisfying reality. Henry, the landless younger son, was now not only king of one of the wealthiest countries in Europe, but also clearly master of Normandy, whether or not he chose to use the title of Duke. Other rulers, including Philip of France, were quick to recognise the fait accompli, and some were almost equally quick to pay court to the new and rising power, and to seek a connection to Henry's royal line.

As early as 1108, the King of the Germans began negotiating for the hand of Henry's daughter, Matilda. At the time he was in his early twenties and Matilda was six. Typical of its time, this was not a love match but a business arrangement, with advantages sought and promised on both sides. Unusually, however, at least some of the bargaining seems to have been carried out through the intervention of Matilda's mother, Queen Matilda. We know this from a letter which thanks her for her good offices in helping him achieve his bride.

Henry V, King of the Germans, had received that title as long ago as 1099. At that time his father, Henry IV, had had him crowned as such, to cut off and spite his elder brother Conrad who had led a revolt against him in Italy. The title was bestowed after a sworn undertaking that the young Henry would not meddle in his father's affairs of state during his father's lifetime. That promise, however, came to nothing when, in 1104, the youth was persuaded to take part in a revolt of his own. Claiming horror at his father's excommunication, he obtained the backing of Pope Paschal, who hoped by this means to end the Investiture Dispute and depose the rival antipope set up by Henry IV. By 1105 it was clear the son had the upper hand in the struggle and Henry IV was forced to abdicate, being briefly imprisoned before his death in August 1106. The new king, Henry V, had by then also acquired the title King of the Romans, or King of Italy, on the death of his brother, but the title he really wanted was Holy Roman Emperor, which, by tradition, could only be bestowed by the pope. It soon appeared, however, that he was no more willing than his father had been to give up the right of investing bishops. Attempts to persuade Paschal to compromise failed, and it was clear that some show of force would be needed if he was to achieve the coronation he required. An expedition to Italy was planned but military expeditions were expensive and, in looking round for a source of money, Henry was, of course, attracted to the wealthiest nation, England.

An English connection had other advantages. It would form an alliance against France where changes were afoot that could have unpredictable results. It might also persuade the pope to compromise, as he had done so recently in negotiations with Henry and Anselm. Nor was the least attraction that the English princess was young enough to be trained up in ways fitting her to be a German Empress.

For the English Henry, too, there were advantages, the greatest of which was probably the prestige involved in the close connection with the Holy Roman Empire. That Henry V was at loggerheads with the pope and not yet crowned as emperor, probably mattered little to Henry with his own compromise safely achieved. He was, no doubt, confident that the problem would be smoothed over, sooner or later, and his daughter would then be an empress. In any case, an ally against France was always worth having.

The details were hammered out, and when Henry returned from Normandy to England before Pentecost 1109, German envoys arrived at his court to agree the marriage contract.

These ambassadors, says Henry of Huntingdon, were 'remarkable for their great stature and splendid attire', as well they might have been. The king was offering a dowry of 10,000 silver marks with his daughter, a staggering sum at the time, and splendour on all sides was necessary to underline the importance of the match. 'Oaths were sworn,' says the Anglo-Saxon Chronicle, and 'stipulations ratified', but the entry for the following year, 'a year of much distress from the taxes which the king raised for his daughter's dowry', gives an idea of the practicalities involved.

Perhaps in line with her new status, the seven-year-old Matilda appeared with her parents at a royal council held in October 1109. Then, early in the New Year, having just passed her eighth birthday, the royal bride set out in company with a distinguished party of Normans and Germans to Utrecht, where, on 10 April 1110, she was officially betrothed to Henry, King of the Germans. They would not be married for another four years, and in the meantime the little princess would be crowned Queen of the Germans and handed over to the care of Bruno, Archbishop of Trier, who would have responsibility for her upbringing.

That both the English and the German rulers were seeking an ally against France was the result of a major change in that country. The death of Philip in July 1108 had brought to the throne his more vigorous son, Louis VI, and Louis was already showing he was not prepared to rule in as relaxed a manner as his father had recently done. Indeed, Suger declares that in his later years Philip had shown no interest at all in State affairs, being wholly besotted by his second wife, Bertrada de Montfort. They had married in 1092 but the marriage was bigamous on both sides, and although Philip's wife died the following year, Bertrada's husband, Fulk IV of Anjou, lived until 1109.

Fulk, nick-named 'the ill-tempered', had married and repudiated at least three, probably four, wives before Bertrada, and her departure with Philip of France has been referred to variously as an abduction and a rescue. On a number of occasions Philip was excommunicated for this bigamous marriage, and returned to the Church only by promising to give up Bertrada. On each occasion, however, he returned to her after a very short time. Suger's opinion can be gleaned from his statement that Bertrada was particularly skilled in the strange female arts by which women could trample their husbands under their feet, even after tormenting them with many injustices. As an example, he recounts that Fulk apparently became totally reconciled with the situation, and would sit on a stool at her feet and obey her every wish, as if under the power of a sorcerer. No doubt as a monk Suger fundamentally disapproved of the whole situation. Vitalis, too, declares that, as a result of his bigamy, Philip was struck with toothache and scurvy, and on his deathbed declared himself to be too great a sinner to be buried with his ancestors in St Denis. He too mentions powers of sorcery, though in a more serious context, accusing Bertrada of trying to kill Prince Louis by such means, in order to put her own son, Philip, on the throne. In spite of this, Louis seems to have had little difficulty in succeeding to the throne, and in putting his stepmother and her children firmly in their place. Bertrada entered a convent and lived on until 1117.

The particular problem presented to Henry by the change of monarch in France was the issue of homage. As effective Duke of Normandy, it was his duty to do homage to his overlord the King of the Franks, and formally to receive the duchy from his hand. As a king himself, though, Henry was extremely reluctant to do this. His father, as Duke of Normandy, had done homage to Philip's father, but when William the Conqueror became king of England he had avoided doing homage to Philip, presenting his son Robert to do so in his place. Possibly Henry was hoping to do something similar. There was a procedure known as *homage en marche*, whereby one king could acknowledge the overlordship of another at the boundary of their lands, without any loss of prestige. This had occurred when Malcolm of Scotland had acknowledged William at the time of the Treaty of Abernethy and it was Malcolm's refusal to offer anything more that led to his angry departure from the court of William Rufus shortly before his death.

Henry, though, seemed reluctant even to offer this much. Henry of Huntingdon refers to his refusal to pay 'an enormous contribution' to Louis, and this may well have been a 'relief' or payment demanded by an overlord in exchange for confirming a new vassal in his fief. Philip had been happy enough for Henry to bring peace to Normandy, but Louis was determined to exact all his dues from those holding lands from him, however high and powerful they might be.

As well as Henry's delaying tactics in the matter of homage, a specific point of conflict between him and Louis concerned certain castles of the Vexin. Suger refers to an earlier agreement between them that does not seem to have survived in any other record. By this agreement, if the castles at Gisors or at Bray-et-lu fell into the hands of either of them, they should be destroyed within forty days. After Tinchebrai, however, Henry had taken possession of the mighty castle at Gisors, garrisoning it with his own men, and he showed no sign of destroying it. According to Suger, this brought about a sudden hatred between the two men, who had previously been on good terms.

As a preliminary to talks between them, Louis gathered his men and attacked the lands of Henry's friend and advisor Robert de Meulan, thereby 'paving the way favourably' for a meeting of the kings. They met at Planche-de-Neaufles near Gisors in March 1109, Henry on one side of the River Epte, Louis on the other, and each backed by an army. Suger comments, with what sounds very much like sarcasm, that the place chosen for the meeting was one where, by tradition, talks were hardly ever successful, and from the detail he gives us, he must have been present.

There was, apparently, a very rickety bridge across the Epte, likely to tip into the river anyone crossing without appropriate care. Across this came a noble French delegation to present their case to Henry. The English king, they said, owed his position in Normandy solely to the goodwill of Louis, and furthermore he was in breach of the agreement concerning Gisors Castle. They demanded that the matter should be settled in the traditional way through trial by combat.

Having said this they withdrew across the bridge, closely followed by a delegation from Normandy carrying Henry's response. He refused trial by combat, but was prepared to submit the matter to trial by law. Suger believed this was simply a further delaying tactic.

Louis then nominated his ally, Robert, Count of Flanders as his champion in a trial by combat, and when this was turned down, apparently offered to fight Henry himself, if the armies would withdraw and they could find a suitable place for such an encounter. After this, things seemed to become more confused, with various people shouting suggestions as to where they could fight, including on the rickety bridge over the river. At one point both armies 'rushed to arm themselves', and according to Suger, only the impossibility of crossing the river prevented a massacre taking place. The arguments continued into the night. Next morning, however, the French made an early attack across the river, pushing their opponents back to Gisors Castle. The situation ended in a stalemate as both kings withdrew, but from then on a rather on/off state of war existed between them, as each strove to damage the other wherever and whenever any opportunity arose.

For much of the rest of 1109 Henry seems to have been taken up with arrangements for his daughter's betrothal, but early the following year events in Normandy claimed his attention again. At Easter, there appears to have been an attempt to renew the long-standing treaty with Robert of Flanders, but that may not have been completely successful. William of Malmesbury says that having considered the matter, Henry decided that 'the kings of England were not accustomed to pay tribute to the Flemings', and refused to keep up the annual payments that had previously been made, thereby causing a rift between the two countries. A more serious matter, though, was the death of Helias of Maine early in July of 1110. Helias had been a firm supporter of Henry, but his only child and heiress, Ermengarde, was married to Fulk V of Anjou, who had recently succeeded his father as the count. Fulk now claimed the county of Maine as his wife's inheritance, and from being a friendly state, Maine now became a source of trouble and a potential threat to the southern borders of Normandy.

With potential enemies stacking up against him, Henry seems belatedly to have realised what a trump card he had left lying around in Normandy. The son of Robert Curthose, William Clito, had all this time been growing up in peace, in the care of his brother-in-law, Helias of Saint-Saens. He had a perfectly valid claim to the duchy, and with Henry failing to do the required homage, it would be quite possible for the boy to be presented to Louis, perform the necessary ritual, and be granted the duchy from the hand of its overlord. Furthermore, it was abundantly clear to Henry that, if that were to happen, there would be many in Normandy who would back the son of Curthose, and he would have a major struggle on his hands to retain the duchy. It was certainly high time the boy was brought under the control of the English king.

In August 1110 he sent Robert de Beauchamp to arrest him. According to Vitalis Robert arrived unexpectedly on a Sunday morning when Helias was away from home. Instead of handing over the boy, however, the household roused the nine-year-old from his bed and hid him away. They then smuggled him out to Helias, who fled with him and began to appeal to anyone he could think of who might be powerful enough to support the boy's claims to the duchy.

Robert de Bellème was the first to champion him. A staunch friend of Robert Curthose and ever ready to take up arms against Henry, some accounts suggest he took in William Clito and his protector and gave them a home. Vitalis, though, seems to describe a more distant relationship, saying that 'Helias carried the boy with him in all his wanderings', and that the connection with Bellème involved a 'frequent interchange between them of hasty messengers.' Nonetheless, Bellème seems to have been active in urging the French king to support the boy, and added one more to the alliance that had formed against Henry. With Robert of Flanders to the east, Louis to the south, and Fulk of Anjou stirring trouble in the south-west, the English king must have felt himself ringed around with enemies.

About this time Henry took action against a number of his own nobles, exiling them and seizing their lands both in England and in Normandy. Very little explanation has been recorded for these moves, and they are generally credited to Henry's excellent network of spies giving early warning of possible plots against him.

Even the elderly Count of Evreux, who had fought for Henry at Tinchebrai, was banished from his lands in Normandy. His fault, if any, was probably his close connection to the de Montfort family, who were his nephews and nieces. One niece, Bertrada, was the widow of the French king but also the mother of Fulk of Anjou, while a nephew and heir-apparent was Amaury de Montfort, an enthusiastic supporter of Louis and opponent of Henry.

By the summer of 1111 matters in Normandy were serious enough to draw the English king back across the Channel. According to Henry of Huntingdon, the aggression of Fulk of Anjou in Maine was a major cause, and Henry 'wasted his territory with fire and sword according to the laws of war'. Meanwhile, as Louis was continuing his attacks on the lands of Robert de Meulan, that count retaliated by invading French lands and attacking and plundering Paris itself.

There were other ways of waging war, however, and diplomacy (along with bribes of various kinds) played a large part in Henry's strategy. In 1111, Count Theobald of Blois, possibly on the advice of his mother Adela, left the alliance with his overlord Louis to instead support his uncle, Henry of England. A disagreement about the building of a castle is given as the reason for his defection, but it marked a turning point in the hostilities. Theobald incited a large number of French barons to rebel against Louis, and the French king found himself facing a major insurgency within his own territory of the Ile de France.

It was in the course of this that Louis lost another ally. In October 1111 Robert of Flanders was killed while fighting with the French king near Meaux, to the east of Paris. Accounts differ as to how he met his death. In one he was on a bridge that collapsed and he was drowned. Another version persuasively describes how he fell from his horse while riding fast through a narrow way, and was trampled under the horses that were following him. Either way, it was the end of the hero of the First Crusade, and the men of Flanders withdrew to regroup around their new count, Robert's son, the eighteen-year-old Baldwin.

Hostilities continued through 1112, but now the tide seemed to be flowing more strongly for Henry. In the autumn of that year he seized the opportunity to remove another opponent from the game. At the beginning of November Robert de Bellême arrived at Henry's court at Bonneville-sur-Touques, near the Norman coast. He was apparently there on behalf of King Louis, possibly to try to negotiate a truce between them, and possibly to request that Henry release his brother, Robert. He certainly believed he was under a safe-conduct from Louis or he would never have approached Henry in this way. His belief, however, was not shared by Henry, who was playing to an altogether different set of rules.

Twice before he had had this man in his power, and let him go, and on each occasion, despite oaths of fealty, Bellème had again taken arms against him. Henry would not make the same mistake again. No doubt to his complete astonishment, Bellème found himself arraigned before Henry's court on charges that sound relatively trivial – not attending the court when summoned, failing to account for some revenue and acting against his lord's interests. Unsurprisingly he was found guilty on all counts, and the sentence of the court was life imprisonment. The notorious Robert de Bellème was taken away, first to Cherbourg, then the following year to Wareham, and drops out of the records entirely. The latest reference to him comes in 1130 when he was still clearly alive after eighteen years imprisonment, but the date and place of his death is unknown.

Robert's eighteen-year-old son, William Talvas, succeeded him, and called on his Mortain relations to join him in attacking Henry but to little avail. A major stronghold of theirs at Alençon was besieged and taken in a very short time, but already the English king had his mind on other plans. With two important allies lost to him, and rebels of his own to deal with, Louis was already weakened, but Henry intended to cut away his other main supporter if he possibly could.

Around the turn of the year he began negotiating with Fulk of Anjou to end the hostilities between them, and by late February 1113 the deal was done. Henry and Fulk met near Alençon, where Fulk was confirmed as Count of Maine, recognising Henry as his overlord for that county. The basis and seal for this agreement was the betrothal of Henry's son, William Adelin, to Fulk's younger daughter, Matilda. Again this was a purely political arrangement designed to secure an important friendship and destroy the French alliance, while, on his side, Fulk could look forward to a grandson becoming King of England. The two principals involved, William and Matilda, were respectively nine and two years old.

This was the final straw for Louis. Within a month he had met with Henry near Gisors, where all the trouble had started, and negotiated a peace treaty, which on the face of it appeared to give Henry all and more than he had wanted. He kept Gisors and was recognised by Louis, not only as overlord of Maine but of Brittany too. In return there seems to have been an unwritten understanding that homage would be paid to Louis for all of these, either by Henry or, more likely, by his son at some point in the future. Nothing, however, took place at the time.

As Henry had already pardoned William of Evreux and members of the de Montfort family for earlier actions against him, peace seemed to be breaking out all round. The only one excluded was William Talvas, who lost all his father's lands in Normandy (though some luck and an underhand trick was needed to wrest Bellême Castle from its garrison), and had to fall back on the title of Count of Ponthieu, which was his mother's inheritance.

In the summer of 1113, then, Henry was able to return triumphant to England and turn his mind to some matters that needed his attention in that part of his domain. In Scotland his brother-in-law Edgar had died in 1107, and the Scottish throne had passed to Edgar's brother, Alexander, who soon after had married Henry's illegitimate daughter Sibylla. It was claimed that there had been an agreement that Alexander would share Scotland with his younger brother David, giving him control of lands on the borders with England. So far, however, he had not done so. Both boys had spent time at the English court in their youth and, according to Vitalis, David had remained there. In the words of William of Malmesbury, he had, 'rubbed off the rust of Scottish barbarism' in England, and may possibly have been fighting with the king in Normandy. It may have been Queen Matilda who proposed a rich marriage for her brother but Henry certainly approved. In 1113, therefore, David married Maud of Senlis, widow of Simon of Senlis, and daughter of the ill-fated Waltheof. David was in his late twenties and she around forty, with three children already from her earlier marriage. Until these children grew up, however, she brought with her to the marriage the Honour of Huntingdon, with rich estates in Northamptonshire, Huntingdonshire and Bedfordshire. With this boost to his prosperity, and with Henry's support, David was soon established in the borderlands of Scotland.

It is clear that no rift with Alexander resulted from this. He had always acknowledged Henry as overlord and behaved as a loyal vassal throughout. Indeed, the following year he was to be found helping the English king impose his authority in Wales.

There, too, there were matters that needed attention. In the north, Gruffydd ap Cynan was taking advantage of the youth of Richard of Chester to raid into lands that had once been part of his kingdom of Gwynedd. In mid-Wales, the kingdom of Powys had been entrusted to Cadwgan ap Bleddyn, but he proved quite incapable of controlling the murderous feuds between his brothers, sons and nephews. His son, Owain, had a particularly wayward youth. As well as carrying on dynastic feuding, he extended his violent activities into the south-western kingdom of Dyfed, which had long been under the control of the Normans. Arnulf of Montgomery had been the first to establish a castle at Pembroke, and when in 1102 he fell from grace, one of his men, Gerald FitzWalter, had gradually worked his way into Henry's favour and been sent back to hold the area for the king. As well as this, Henry had settled a large contingent of Flemings in the area. Veterans of his mercenary armies, their presence also helped to keep the peace.

In spite of this, however, Owain's raids became an increasing nuisance. He murdered a leading Flemish citizen, abducted the wife of Gerald FitzWalter, carried on a no doubt lucrative trade in captured slaves for Ireland, and raided the lands of another Norman, Gilbert FitzRichard, in Ceredigion. Surprisingly, when his father was murdered by his cousin, Madog, in 1111, Owain was allowed to succeed as king, but the capture, blinding and imprisonment of Madog in 1113 was probably the last straw that persuaded Henry to take action.

In 1114 three armies were assembled to march into Wales. One in the north was led by Alexander of Scotland and the nineteen-year-old Richard of Chester. A second in the south was led by Gilbert FitzRichard, while Henry himself led a third into Merionethshire. We have few details of the numbers involved, but clearly there were enough to overawe the usually defiant Welsh. The aim was not slaughter but intimidation and it worked. Gruffydd ap Cynan submitted to Henry and was confirmed in his lands with Henry as overlord. Thereafter he caused no trouble but devoted himself to promoting the old Welsh culture of music and poetry, supporting the bardic traditions within his realm of Gwynedd.

Owain was taken prisoner and for a time travelled with the English court, perhaps to rub the Welsh 'rust' off. Certainly he was not treated as a dangerous enemy. He was knighted by Henry, and was with him in Normandy the following year before being allowed to return to Powys. There his uncle Maredudd had been acting as steward after submitting to Henry in 1114. Owain was not to have long as ruler, however. In 1116 he was ambushed and killed by Gerald FitzWalter and a group of Flemings, no doubt in revenge for his earlier wrongdoing.

Henry spent only about a year in England before returning to Normandy, but before he left there were vacancies to be filled and rewards to be distributed to those who had served him well, or who had gained his favour. Among the latter was Stephen of Blois, a younger brother of Count Theobald. Brought up initially by his formidable mother Adela, he had almost certainly been with his uncle Henry during his Norman campaigns of 1111 and 1112. He was knighted by Henry in 1112 when in his late teens, and accompanied him to England. There Henry bestowed on him the title (but not the lands) of Count of Mortain, together with the Honour of Eye and most of the lands that had been confiscated from Roger the Poitevin some years before.

Among the vacancies filled at this time were both English archbishoprics. Anselm had died in April 1109 but no successor had yet been appointed. To the end he had kept up an insistence that the Archbishop of York must profess obedience to the Archbishop of Canterbury, and when Archbishop Thomas of York died in 1114, Henry did his best to smooth over this dispute. On the advice of Robert Bloet and Roger of Salisbury, Ralph, Bishop of Rochester was nominated to the See of Canterbury. He was another who had fled from Sées earlier, with John of Lisieux. The nomination for Archbishop of York went to Thurstan who had been Henry's secretary, and whom the king felt would not cause any trouble. Unfortunately, when Thurstan arrived in York he was strongly advised that he must not profess obedience to Canterbury, and so he, too, refused to do so and the dispute rumbled on. Almost all the vacancies for bishops and abbots at this time were filled with Normans, especially Norman monks, and even Eadmer was driven to comment that the prospects of promotion for any English cleric were poor indeed.

Henry's return to Normandy in the autumn of 1114 seems to have been more precautionary than a response to a specific crisis. Following the fall of Robert de Bellême, the cause of William Clito had been taken up enthusiastically by the young Baldwin of Flanders, who was some ten years older. Baldwin had given the boy and his ever-faithful supporter Helias, a place at his court, and was pressuring Louis of France to recognise him as rightful heir to Normandy. Henry, quite rightly, had suspicions that, if that were to happen, he would not be able to rely on the loyalty of many of the great Norman lords. No doubt his famous network of spies was keeping him informed as to underground murmurings, and it seemed imperative that his own son should be formally acknowledged as heir, both by the Normans and, if possible, by the French king himself.

It was a Norman tradition that the heir should be formally invested and paid homage within the lifetime of the reigning duke. This had happened with William the Conqueror and with his son Robert. Early in 1115, then, the great lords of Normandy were assembled and formally paid homage to William Adelin, aged eleven, as rightful heir to Normandy. At the same time Henry offered Louis the homage of his son, together with a large sum of money, if he too would acknowledge him as rightful heir. Initially it looked as though Louis would agree. He took the money, and then, on reflection, refused the homage.

By one account it was the Count of Nevers who dissuaded the king, pointing out that he had already committed himself to the cause of William Clito. In retaliation, Theobald of Blois had the count imprisoned, and in turn found himself and his followers excommunicated by the papal legate, Cuno, as a result of pressure from Louis. The 'cold war' was about to get hot again.

Henry had returned to England where, in March 1116, a similar ceremony took place at Salisbury to that which had been held the year before in Normandy. Now it was the turn of the English magnates to take an oath of fealty to William Adelin, and swear faithfully to transfer the crown to him on his father's death. Soon after this Henry gathered his forces and left once more for Normandy. It would be more than four years before he set foot in England again.

For the next two years, details are hard to come by. Vitalis records a 'serious misunderstanding' between Henry and Louis, as Louis gave help to William Clito for the recovery of his inheritance. He also declares 'a great number of the Normans espoused his cause with all their might.' For Suger it was mutual malice that revived the earlier civil wars, while the Anglo-Saxon Chronicle has it that Henry went to the aid of his nephew, Theobald, who was being attacked by Louis. For the Chronicle, the major concern was the exaction of oppressive taxes to pay for all this, both in England and in Normandy.

What is clear is that again France, Flanders and Anjou were lined up against the forces of England, Normandy and their allies of Blois and Brittany, and that 'there was much plundering and taking of castles between France and Normandy.' In 1117 Baldwin of Flanders invaded north-eastern Normandy, meeting up with French forces near Mortemer. In the same year Louis attacked lands belonging to Blois in Brie and around Chartres, while the Vexin again saw a great deal of indeterminate bloodshed. It was 1118, however, that became Henry's *annus horribilis*.

As usual Vitalis is full of strange omens and portents. In one particularly bizarre tale, a pregnant cow was found to be carrying, not a calf, but three little piglets. This was deemed to foretell (goodness knows how) that there would soon be three deaths that would be important to England. Sure enough, three deaths are then recorded.

The first, on 18 April, was that of William, Count of Evreux. The significance of this was that his nominated heir, Amaury de Montfort, was the last person Henry would want in control of Evreux in the heart of Normandy. Denied succession, Vitalis says, Amaury 'flew to arms with all his force,' and 'nearly the whole of France espoused his cause.'

The second death, on 1 May, was that of Queen Matilda. Though they had recently spent more time apart than together, her contribution to Henry and to England, both as regent and as a major influence on culture and smooth administration should not be under-estimated. Her passing gets only a short mention in the Chronicle, but Henry of Huntingdon devotes a touching poem to the occasion, ending, 'At the earliest dawn of May / Ent'ring on an endless day / Thou wert wrapt in clouds of light, / We were left in Darkest night.' Circumstances in Normandy kept Henry from her funeral, but on his orders it was a magnificent affair in Westminster Abbey, and thereafter he paid for a candle to be kept constantly burning before her tomb.

On 5 June, the third death was that of Robert de Meulan. This great warrior was at least in his late sixties, if not his seventies, but his heirs were twin boys of fourteen years. The succession was clear, though. One boy, Waleran, was to have his father's Norman estates, and the other, Robert, those lands in England, while Henry was to be guardian for both. It was, however, the worst possible time for him to lose his most experienced and trusted adviser.

More and more Norman magnates were turning against Henry. Some were firmly in support of William Clito, while others simply had a grudge against the English king, often relating to some issue of succession to lands. Vitalis records that 'treason chilled and numbed the hearts of eighteen of the noble castellans of Normandy.'

Among them were Henry of Eu and Stephen of Aumale, both in the north-east of the duchy.

The English king held the castle at Eu, and Baldwin of Flanders joined with Henry of Eu and Stephen in trying to wrest control of the area from him. In an action near Arques, however, Baldwin received what Suger describes as a light blow in the face from a lance. Retreating to Aumale, he is said to have 'scorned to look after so small a wound'. Furthermore, according to Vitalis, he 'supped on meat which was too young, drank mulled wine and slept with a woman', as a result of which his wound developed into a mortal disease. William of Malmesbury repeats this tale, though for him it was 'garlic with goose' rather than over-young meat. Either way it is hard to see how it could have triggered a mortal disease, even when the facial wound was added, let alone one which caused him to languish in great pain for some ten months. It was September 1118 when he was wounded and withdrew with his men to Flanders, but he did not die until the following June. Nevertheless, the withdrawal and death of a Count of Flanders weakened the alliance against Henry at a time when he most needed it to be weakened.

Suger says Henry was attacked on all sides, not only by 'foreigners' but by his own men, while Vitalis records that he so doubted the loyalty of the Normans that his army largely consisted of English and Breton troops. 'Even those who ate at his table,' he says, 'favoured his nephew and other enemies, and by betraying his secrets rendered them essential service.' Both Suger and William of Malmesbury report a plot within his own household to kill the king. The plot was discovered and the 'assassin', named only as a chamberlain whose name began with H, was blinded and mutilated, but for some time Henry wore his sword at all times, even within his own house.

Possibly in an attempt to divide up the area that needed defending, in the autumn of 1118 Henry handed over Sées, Alençon and all the former Bellême lands to Theobald of Blois, who, with the king's permission, passed them on to his brother Stephen. This proved to be a big mistake. As noted by Vitalis, Stephen was 'a very young man', probably in his mid-twenties, and this was likely to have been his first major responsibility. He did not handle it well. Failing to treat the citizens with respect, 'by his outrages and exaction, and changing the customary payments and services (he) made himself odious and the vassals disloyal.' Within a very short time his mismanagement would lead to a serious setback for the king.

In the meantime Henry was rushing hither and thither, trying to stamp out the fires of rebellion wherever they flared. An example of the confusion occurring at this time is the situation at L'Aigle. Richer, Lord of L'Aigle, had inherited his Norman lands and castle from his father Gilbert, who had been a faithful vassal of Henry. However, Gilbert had also had lands in England, and when Richer tried to claim these, Henry refused, saying his brothers had a better claim. In a fit of pique, Richer went off to Louis of France and told him he would hand over the castle at L'Aigle on the southern borders of Normandy unless Henry gave in to his demands. In the meantime, on the advice of Rotrou of Perche, Henry's son-in-law and Richer's uncle, Henry had changed his mind and granted the request. Richer then tried to call off the deal with Louis, but Louis and his forces were already on their way to L'Aigle. Finding unexpected resistance, they burnt the place down and took possession of the citadel. Henry immediately set out to re-take it but before he could do so, received apparently reliable information that Rouen, his capital, was in immediate danger, and about-turned to defend that instead. When he arrived at Rouen, however, he found the danger to have been greatly exaggerated.

In October 1118 Henry suffered another severe blow. After successfully keeping Amaury de Montfort out of the castle at Evreux for almost six months, his castellan there decided that Amaury did, after all, have right on his side, and simply handed the castle over to him. Amaury took possession immediately, filling the castle and countryside with his men, and causing the Bishop of Evreux to flee for safety to Henry's court.

Worse was to follow. Henry now set out to besiege L'Aigle but found the French garrison there more than ready to fight him. In one encounter Theobald of Blois was unhorsed and taken prisoner, and it took a spirited action on the part of Henry and Stephen of

Blois to rescue him. Soon afterwards Stephen's heavy-handedness with the citizens of Alençon caused his uncle another loss.

According to Vitalis, Stephen, young and unsure of himself, became convinced that all the citizens of Alençon were potential traitors. As a result, he demanded hostages for good conduct to be delivered to the castle, and in one particular case the respectable wife of a prominent citizen found herself being held by 'depraved men'. At the time it is likely that Stephen was not present at Alençon, but he, of course, got the blame for this incident. Nor was it reported to Henry who, it was felt, would take the side of his nephew. Instead the outraged husband and others like him sent to Fulk of Anjou, inviting him to come to their aid. Come he did, with knights, archers and foot soldiers, to take possession of all but the citadel at Alençon. This was late in December 1118 and Henry immediately brought an army (Vitalis specifies English, Norman and mercenaries) to retake the place. Fulk, however, was equally ready to defend his position, marching out in battle array to meet the English king.

In some accounts Stephen of Blois and his brother Theobald were in the first division of Henry's army. In others they were riding ahead to try to get provisions to the garrison in the citadel. Either way, they met with Fulk's forces and suffered heavy losses. The bulk of the armies then came together in fierce fighting, and again the heavy losses were on Henry's side. Finally, with a combination of cavalry and archers, Fulk forced Henry to withdraw and, the relieving action having failed, the garrison inside the citadel had no choice but to surrender.

It was the first and only time in Henry's career that he was defeated in battle and, of course, gave great encouragement to all those who had turned against him. Vitalis records that Normandy was 'polluted in every direction by blood, robbery and fire', while the Anglo-Saxon Chronicle summary for the year, putting it rather mildly, states that Henry was 'most harassed by his own men who continually revolted and betrayed him and went over to the enemy.'

The year 1119 began equally badly. Henry tried to negotiate a peace with Amaury de Montfort, offering to confirm him as Count of Evreux if he would hand over the castle at Alençon. The offer was scornfully refused. Amaury had already had his countship confirmed by the overlord of both, Louis of France, and he now proceeded to further undermine Henry by causing trouble in the area of Breteuil.

Eustace of Breteuil was Henry's own son-in-law, married to his illegitimate daughter Juliana. He owed his position as lord of Breteuil to Henry, and it was a wealthy and strategically important honour, again on the southern borders of Normandy. Eustace, though, had a rather vague claim on the castle at Ivry, even more importantly placed right on the border with France, and close to the French lands of Amaury de Montfort. According to Vitalis it was Amaury who now incited Eustace to demand this castle as the price for his continued loyalty. Possibly not entirely believing the threat, Henry prevaricated, suggesting that he could have the castle at some future time, no doubt when the present troubles had been resolved. As a sign of his commitment, a hostage exchange was arranged, as was common in such situations. Eustace would have the son of the castellan at Ivry as hostage, and would in return hand over to Henry his two daughters, Henry's own grandchildren.

What happened next is again put down by Vitalis to the interference of Amaury, 'who used every artifice that malice could suggest to renew the quarrel.' Somehow he persuaded Eustace to put out the eyes of the boy he held as hostage, and then send him back to his father. Outraged, the father appealed to Henry who was apparently horrified at what Eustace had done. With what regret we don't know, but entirely in accordance with the laws and customs of the times, he then handed over his own grandchildren to the boy's father, who 'savagely tore out their eyes and cut off the tips of their noses, in retaliation for the cruelty shown to his son.' If Amaury had intended to cause a rift between Henry and Eustace, he had certainly achieved his aim. The pain and suffering caused to 'innocent childhood' seemed lamented by no-one but Vitalis.

Immediately Eustace put his castles on a war footing, and he dispatched Juliana to Breteuil to do the same there and hold the castle against Henry. The citizens of Breteuil, however, sent for the king and opened their gates to him, leaving Juliana besieged in the citadel. She invited her father to come and see her to negotiate face to face. When he did, though, all unsuspecting, he found her holding a drawn crossbow, and as soon as he appeared she shot at him. She may have been a very poor shot, or perhaps at the last minute found she could not kill her own father. Vitalis declares it was God who protected him. Whatever the cause, the bolt missed and Henry immediately ordered his men to destroy the castle drawbridge. Juliana, recognising that she was now helpless in the hands of her foes, did the only thing she could to obtain leniency and surrendered the castle.

Again it is Vitalis who records Henry's revenge on his daughter for the shock of her attack. Apparently set free to go and rejoin her husband, she was not allowed to leave through the door or across the destroyed drawbridge. Instead she was 'compelled to let herself down from the summit of the walls without support, and as there was no bridge she descended into the foss indecently with naked legs.' All the while, no doubt, being watched by hundreds of jeering soldiers and townspeople. Furthermore, he adds that this took place in the third week of February when 'the castle ditch was full of snow-water which, being half-frozen, her tender limbs of course suffered.' Perhaps the burning humiliation of the situation kept her warm.

While all this was going on, Louis of France was busy elsewhere, openly championing William Clito and launching attacks on Normandy. By a trick, he obtained entry to the castle at Andely, which had been held by Richard, Henry's illegitimate son. Richard was allowed to leave freely, but Louis was then able to use the castle as a base for raiding all over the Vexin and up the River Seine as far as Pont-St-Pierre, barely half a dozen miles from Rouen itself.

Not all Norman magnates deserted Henry. Perhaps to make a point, Vitalis gives a list of those who remained loyal, including William of Warenne, Ralph de Tosny, Walter Giffard and Richard of Chester, now in his mid-twenties. He also singles out for special mention Ralph the Red, lord of Pont-Echanfray, giving sterling service against his fellow Normans. Among the fortresses still rock solid for the English king he lists not only those one might expect in traditionally loyal territory, such as Bayeux, Avranches and Falaise, but places such as Argentan, Arques, Vernon and Nonancourt, which were far more exposed to attack and betrayal. Nevertheless, early in 1119, it seemed to be time for Henry to engage in some serious diplomacy.

His overtures to Amaury de Montfort had been rejected, but he found more fertile ground with Fulk of Anjou. Possibly his spies had informed him that Fulk was thinking of a trip to Jerusalem. There was, of course, the existing betrothal between their children, and no doubt Henry reminded him of the benefits he had expected to receive through that alliance. A considerable amount of money also changed hands – Suger declares that Fulk put greed before loyalty – and, much to the fury of the French, a deal was done. In May 1119 the fifteen-year-old William Adelin crossed over to Normandy and was duly married at Lisieux to the eight-year-old Matilda. The County of Maine was her dowry as Fulk again recognised Henry's overlordship and immediately transferred to him control of a number of castles, including Alençon. He also seems to have mediated a number of reconciliations between Henry and rebellious magnates. Certainly he was involved in the pardoning of William Talvas who now had the Bellême lands returned to him, though Henry continued to garrison the castles with his own men. Immediately after this Fulk left for the Holy Land.

Henry announced the marriage at a council in Lisieux in June, and at the same time the death of Baldwin of Flanders was revealed. Baldwin had died on 17 June having named as his successor his cousin Charles, son of Canute of Denmark, who had grown up at the Flanders court. At once Charles let it be known that he was not interested in continuing the contest with Henry. He had enough to deal with at home without pursuing foreign adventures so, within a month, Louis of France had lost both his major supporters.

Clearly the wind was again blowing in Henry's favour, and he lost no time in taking advantage of it. With renewed vigour he set about punishing those who had betrayed him, making a 'terrible expedition through Normandy.' First he sacked and burnt the

Castle of Pont-St-Pierre belonging to Eustace of Breteuil, then, setting down before Evreux, he put that city under siege. With him, as well as his usual followers, was the Bishop of Evreux who had fled the year before. Henry now called the bishop and put a proposition to him. Evreux was strongly defended and he believed the only way to take the citadel was by fire, but if he set fire to the city, many houses and churches would be destroyed. Would the bishop sanction this on the clear understanding that when Henry was victorious, he would rebuild the churches better than before, with his own money? The bishop agreed, the fire was set, and the city was burned to the ground – but the citadel still held out against them.

Amaury, who was not there at the time, now appealed to Louis for help, and Louis, who had been besieging one of Henry's castles on the frontier, gathered his forces and returned to Andely. By now Henry himself was at Rouen and appeared to be preparing to move south into the Vexin where Louis had been ravaging the land for some time. Some have suggested that Henry did not want to face Louis directly and stayed in Rouen until his spies told him Louis had moved away south to collect reinforcements. If so the spies must have failed to mention that Louis was on his way north again, aiming for one of Henry's castles on the River Andelle, which he believed would be handed over to him by traitors.

Henry, now moving south, was unaware of Louis moving north until scouts ahead of his army spotted the movement of French knights. Then, as Vitalis puts it, 'both kings were present at the head of their armies and, if they wished, battle might be joined.' Unusually, this time they did wish, and Henry took up a position on a level plain known as Brémule.

It is estimated that Henry was accompanied by some 500 knights, along with his illegitimate sons Robert and Richard, and a number of seasoned campaigners such as William of Warenne and Walter Giffard. It is also claimed that William Adelin was present, but how much he was involved in the fighting is not clear. Accounts vary as to the composition of either three of four lines of battle that were drawn up. It is likely that William of Warenne, Walter Giffard and other nobles made up the first line, with the king and his household knights in the second, while his sons and their followers stiffened the bulk of the infantry making up a third line.

The French appeared to be outnumbered as far as knights were concerned, and also to be less organised. Along with Louis was William Clito, who, according to Vitalis, 'armed himself for the liberation of his father from his long imprisonment and the recovery of the dominions of his ancestors.' No doubt he was hoping for a swift and decisive victory in his favour. There were among the French, too, some Norman nobles still at loggerheads with Henry, notably William Crispin who had already been pardoned twice for treachery.

Little is said about Louis's battle array, except that Henry of Huntingdon tells us he put William Clito in command of the first division. Possibly his inexperience as a commander explains why these men then rushed at the enemy with what Suger describes as much courage but little sense. Their furious pace was initially successful in shattering Henry's front line, but then coming up against the second line that fought with solid discipline, they were themselves thrown back. Then, says Henry of Huntingdon, 'the battle raged fiercely; the lances were shivered and they fought with swords.' The impetuous French were partly surrounded, and William Crispin made a bold attempt to kill the English king. He struck him twice on the head with his sword with such force that, although the helmet withstood the blows, it was forced into the king's forehead, 'so that blood gushed forth.' Henry of Huntingdon has it that Henry himself returned the blows, felling his opponent to the ground. Others, however, give that honour to Richard FitzRichard, one of the Clare family, who then had to throw himself on top of William Crispin to prevent him being cut to pieces by Henry's supporters. At this point Henry's third line, led by his sons, 'levelled their spears and charged the enemy', whereupon Louis retired as honourably as he could, as Suger puts it, or 'fled at a gallop', in the words of Vitalis.

It was not the end of the war but it was a decisive turning point. The French had suffered heavy losses, mainly in the form of prisoners rather than the slain, since, through love of God and the thought of rich ransoms, the knights had generally refrained from killing each other. Henry's own losses were slight and, of course, winning a battle was a sign of God's favour. As Huntingdon put it in one of his many celebratory verses, 'Conqu'ring Englands' mighty son the spoils and laurelled trophies won.'

Louis was apparently cut to the heart by the result of his own rashness. Amaury de Montfort was able to persuade him to return to the offensive, burning Ivry and attacking Breteuil and Chartres, but Breteuil was another humiliation. Ralph de Gael who had been given the castle by Henry, showed his scorn for the French army by deliberately leaving the gates of the fortress open while fighting off Louis's attack, and the attempted siege was quickly relieved by a force led by Henry, his son Richard and Ralph the Red. It was becoming clear that the end was in sight and the time for negotiating was rapidly approaching.

In October 1119 the pope arrived at Rheims, convening a great papal council attended by Church leaders from France, England, Normandy and elsewhere. This was not Paschal, who had died in January 1118, nor yet his successor Gelatius, who had lasted barely a year. The new pope, elected in February 1119 at Cluny by only nine cardinals, took the name Calixtus II. He was a French pope from the leading Burgundian family, and had been Archbishop of Vienne, a French diocese. Queen Adelaide of France, Louis's second wife, was his niece. Though his primary purpose in calling the council was to discuss the ongoing crisis with the Holy Roman Emperor over investitures, Louis could not let slip an opportunity to put his grievances against Henry before this higher authority, and no doubt hoped to obtain some declaration in his favour from one who must surely back the French cause.

At first it appeared he would get all he wanted. Even before the council began, the pope defied the English king by consecrating Thurstan as Archbishop of York. Though appointed some half dozen years before, Thurstan had never been consecrated because he had refused to profess obedience to the Archbishop of Canterbury, who had in turn refused to consecrate him. Thurstan had accompanied Henry to Normandy in 1116 asking to put the matter before the pope, but Henry had refused. Thereafter Thurstan had remained in Normandy, building a reputation for holiness, but also making useful friendships among the bishops and papal representatives. Having received his consecration, Henry refused him permission to return to England, so Thurstan remained for some time with the papal court, continuing to win friends and gain influence.

When the council opened on 18 October, Louis of France appeared to state his case against Henry, who had pointedly stayed away. The English king, he said, had violently invaded Normandy, which was part of Louis's realm; he had imprisoned his brother and disinherited his nephew; he had unlawfully imprisoned Robert de Bellème, the king's envoy; and had incited rebellion among his vassals, notably Count Theobald of Blois. At the end of all this the Archbishop of Rouen began to present a reply on behalf of Henry, but was unable to proceed because of the furious uproar that greeted his words. So far, so good for Louis. When a little later the Bishop of Evreux tried to condemn Amaury de Montfort, he too was shouted down, being told it was not Amaury but Henry who should be condemned for burning down all the churches in that city.

It looked as though Louis would get what he wanted but when the pope responded he spoke only of the need for peace and then called an adjournment. Now, however, Thurstan began to work on behalf of his king. He was so successful at this that some have suggested the whole dispute about his consecration had simply been a set-up to enable Thurstan to use his extensive powers of persuasion on the pope and his inner circle. He had been close to Henry when he was his secretary, and they had still apparently been on friendly terms in the course of the dispute. That had been going on far too long, however, to be simply a ruse to ingratiate Thurstan, though the suggestion is that it may have been exaggerated for the purpose. Be that as it may, he now began to impress on anyone who would listen how hard Henry was working to make peace with his former enemies, and how they were beginning to respond to his overtures.

This was no less than the truth. Amaury de Montfort had recently decided to accept the offer Henry had made him early in the year and ended the siege of Evreux. Richer de L'Aigle had, through the intervention of his uncle Rotrou of Perche, been reconciled with the king, and a number of other rebellious lords had also made their peace with him. Even Eustace and Juliana had appeared, barefoot and penitent, at Henry's camp and, through the mediation of his son Richard, Juliana's half-brother, had been forgiven and returned to favour, though not to the lands they had lost.

Stephen of Aumale was still resisting, however, and attempting to persuade Charles of Flanders to join him in continued defiance. In response Henry moved his army to Eu and began to build a siege castle, but then sent William of Warenne to negotiate. Here again peace would eventually be agreed without further violence.

It was while Henry was in the area of Aumale that he met with William Clito. The boy, now just seventeen-years-old, came to beg for his father's release. If Henry would set him free, Clito promised that the two of them would go away to Jerusalem where Robert had been a hero before, and would never bother Henry again. It must have seemed a possible solution, but with the events of the previous year in mind Henry was not prepared to take the risk of releasing his brother. Instead he offered Clito money and authority over three English counties. It is recorded that Clito departed weeping, with the ever-faithful Helias of Saint-Saens by his side.

By November 1119, Thurstan's persuasion had borne fruit. The pope agreed to meet Henry near Gisors to hear his side of the case. There, faced with the charges against him, Henry was eloquent in his defence. He had won Normandy according to tradition by right of battle. Neither Robert nor his other brother William Rufus could properly claim to have possessed Normandy since it had been in a constant turmoil of revolt and banditry. He had offered his help to Robert in order to protect the Church, but that offer had been refused. His actions afterwards had been solely aimed at restoring his father's laws to a lawless land. Finally, although Robert was indeed captive, it was a captivity more like the comfortable retirement of a worn-out pilgrim, and Robert's son had been committed to the care of a kinsman who had betrayed Henry's trust and stirred up discord on his behalf. Throughout, Henry emphasised that he had never had designs on the kingdom of France, that he wanted only peace with Louis and was prepared to perform whatever was due from the Duke of Normandy to the King of the Franks.

Calixtus was clearly impressed with Henry's response, but when they moved on to the issue of the English Church and the debate between Canterbury and York, this threatened to sink the fragile barque of a peace settlement. Again there may have been a certain amount of bluff on both sides. Calixtus, coming down firmly in favour of Thurstan, decreed that York need never profess obedience to Canterbury, and ordered Henry to allow Thurstan to return home as a consecrated archbishop. Henry prevaricated, was threatened with excommunication and, as before, his sister Adela was drawn into the delicate negotiations. It has been suggested that Thurstan saw the situation as a test of his merits, and that, if he could help along the peace negotiations now clearly underway between Henry and Louis, his own position would benefit. He certainly seems to have been engaged in some advanced shuttle diplomacy, moving between the papal court and that of Adela and Count Theobald of Blois. While not himself visiting Louis, he clearly called on his friendship with the papal legate, Cuno, who did, and the peace deal finally achieved between Henry and Louis in the spring of 1120 is generally attributed to the combined efforts of Thurstan, Adela, Theobald and the papal legate.

With an arrangement of this importance it might be thought that there would be a fanfare of trumpets and an elaborate ritual to seal the formalities. In fact we know neither the time nor the place where this was done. Possibly a certain coyness on the part of the French might be a reason for this, since the deal Louis was now accepting was substantially the same as Henry had offered years before. Louis would grant Normandy, not directly to Henry but to his son, William Adelin, who would do homage for it. Nor could the homage be paid directly to Louis, who had to overcome the difficulty that he had previously accepted homage for Normandy from William Clito. One account, which may well be accurate, declares that the solution to this was found by William Adelin swearing homage not to Louis, but to the king's infant son, Philip.

It had taken years of war and caused hardship and poverty on all sides, but by September 1120 Henry had achieved exactly what he wanted. Secure in his possession of Normandy, he was also at peace with Anjou, Flanders and all those rebellious nobles who had caused such trouble two years before. Not only was *he* secure, but the futures for both his legitimate children, William Adelin and Matilda, seemed thoroughly settled. What could possibly go wrong?

9

All the King's Children

In the midst of his extensive eulogy on the many qualities of Henry I, William of Malmesbury includes the firm declaration, 'He was free during his whole life from impure desires.' Given that Henry acknowledged and provided for at least twenty illegitimate children, this might make one wonder whether Malmesbury was blind, stupid or deliberately telling lies. Orderic Vitalis seems to come closer to the truth when he writes of the king that he was 'criminally addicted to one vice from the days of his youth until he was advanced in years, having several sons and daughters by concubines.' The only quibble there might be the use of the word 'several'.

Malmesbury, however, has his justification at hand. 'He was led,' he says, 'by female blandishments not for the gratification of incontinency, but for the sake of issue; nor condescended to casual intercourse, unless it might produce that effect; in this respect the master of his natural inclinations, not the passive slave of lust.' As excuses go, this certainly has the flavour of originality. Henry did not indulge his lust, but merely sought to provide sons and daughters for the good of his kingdom, while thoughtfully sparing his lawful wife this onerous task. If that is so, one can only presume he was blessed with an uncanny degree of foresight, since several of these numerous offspring were born before any opportunity arose for him to become king of England.

Of course Malmesbury had to be a little careful here since he was writing under the patronage of Robert of Gloucester, probably by far the most famous of Henry's illegitimate offspring. He was also, however, reflecting, as a monk should, the Church's traditional attitude to sex and marriage. It was St Paul who famously wrote that 'it is better to marry than burn', though in the context of the advice he was giving, 'burn' refers to burning with lust rather than burning in hell. Nevertheless, the Church's squeamishness on the subject meant that it had no clear role to play in marriage before about the mid-eleventh century. Marriage, according to St Paul, was an admission of failure to live the ideal celibate life, a second best in the holiness stakes, and therefore not something the Church was primarily concerned with. Only in the eleventh century, with the moral reformers of the Church getting into their stride, did the basic principles of marriage as we would recognise them begin to be laid down by the Church.

Before that time, marriage was seen as a private arrangement and, for the upper levels of society at least, a business deal. In Old English a 'wed' was a pledge or something deposited as security for the fulfilment of an obligation. Hence a wedding was an exchange of 'weds' or promises, made secure by the marriage of the man and woman concerned. Most commonly the promises involved an alliance of families or lands, or an exchange of property, and such deals were usually made by the fathers of the couple. They were far too important to be left to those actually getting married. Nor was their consent involved. In many, if not most cases, they were children at the time the deal was struck and had never even met each other.

The other aspect of marriage, of course, was the begetting of children. The Church regarded this as the only excuse for sex, even within a marriage. St Jerome wrote that 'excessive love' even for a man's own wife was disgraceful, and that nothing was worse than to love a wife like a mistress. Hence William of Malmesbury's emphasis on the outcome of Henry's activities.

In this aspect of marriage the upper levels of society were entirely in agreement with the Church. Quite apart from the political/

business side, the purpose of marriage was to secure the family line, to pass the genes, along with the property, safely down to the next generation. Any wife who failed to do this should be discarded, whether or not such failure was her fault, and a new one tried in her place.

It was onto this background of the traditional approach to marriage that, from the eleventh century onward, the Church struggled to graft some more moral, even religious, principles. First the marriage should become a public rather than a private act, a sacrament rather than a signing of contracts. No specific ceremony was laid down, however, and though publicity was desirable and rules for publishing banns date from 1200, it was not until 1563 that a priest was needed.

As a Christian sacrament, the idea of consent also became more important. This involved not only the consent of the parents or guardians, but also that of the man, and more importantly, the woman involved. It has been suggested that this had the effect of improving the status of women, and this may well be true at the lower levels of society, but the effect at the top was likely to be more limited. The children of kings, barons, knights and even more lowly landowners would have been raised from infanthood to know their duty. On a purely practical level, daughters were the property of their fathers until they were wed, and the only alternative to the marriage bed would have been the nunnery. No doubt there were some who chose this when a proposed marriage was not to their liking, but they were probably a small minority. For a son, too, his father would have held a secure grip on the purse-strings and there was always a risk of being disinherited. A landless son, without the support of his family, would probably have led a wandering life, as did Henry himself after his expulsion from Mont St Michel. A likely outcome would be joining some band of mercenary fighters, or trying his luck in the Holy Land or some other frontier territory.

The emphasis on consent, however, led to a different set of problems. With no required ceremony for marriage, the Church would have to recognise as valid any exchange of promises, even if this was done in secret. 'I here take thee as my husband/wife' would be good enough, especially if intercourse followed, and this could render a subsequent more formal marriage to another person null and void. There is at least one notable example of this in later history, when Joan, the so-called 'Fair Maid of Kent', revealed after several years of marriage to William de Montacute that she had earlier secretly married Thomas Holland. With the second marriage annulled, and after the death of Thomas Holland, she later went on to marry Edward, the Black Prince, and was the mother of Richard II.

The other major way for a marriage to be annulled was on grounds of consanguinity. At the time the prohibited degrees of relationship for marriage were far more extensive than at present. Even sixth cousins were, in theory at least, forbidden to marry, relationships that, in all likelihood, went well beyond the knowledge of the current generation, but which could be conveniently 'discovered', or more often invented, as a way of blocking a marriage or getting rid of a spouse who had proved barren or incompatible. Fulk IV of Anjou is believed to have disposed of four wives in this way, before he received his comeuppance when Bertrada left him for Philip of France.

With such a restrictive rule, and with families at the highest level seeking someone of equal status to marry, a degree of flexibility crept in. The pope could give a dispensation for a couple to marry within the prohibited degrees and, of course, this was more easily obtained by a family with influence (and money) who properly requested it. This happened retrospectively in the case of William the Conqueror whose marriage to Matilda of Flanders was finally sanctioned, at the cost of building 'his and hers' abbeys in Caen as a penance for jumping the gun.

With this rather fluid approach to marriage, it was sometimes difficult to decide whether any offspring were legitimate or illegitimate. A secret earlier marriage should, of course, render illegitimate any children of a later formal marriage. Similarly, if a marriage was annulled for reasons of consanguinity that should mean that the children of that marriage were also illegitimate, but no firm ruling seems to have been applied to this situation.

Henry I lived at a time when such issues were only just beginning to become important. The idea of primogeniture, the eldest son takes all, had some way to go before it became firmly established, and before this it was common, if not usual, for property to be shared between all the sons at least, if not between all the children. Thus, William the Conqueror had, albeit reluctantly, split his property between his three sons with no great controversy.

A little further back in time, no distinction was made between legitimate and illegitimate sons. It was their ability and usefulness that counted, rather than the status of their mothers, and any acknowledged son could expect some share in the 'family business'. This idea persisted in Wales long after it had been abandoned in England, and it is largely as a result of Church influence that it *was* abandoned in England. As the Church became more involved in promoting 'regular' marriage as a sacred undertaking, there was felt the need for some practical form of incentive to comply with its rules. Frowning on bastardy was one thing, but giving it practical consequences was another. The rule gradually became established that illegitimate children could not inherit as of right, even if acknowledged by their fathers. In order to pass property and titles to the next generation, as the rules hardened in this area, there had to be a proper marriage and legitimate offspring.

On the other hand, while the Church might disapprove (as Vitalis clearly did), society in general took a rather more benevolent view of people in Henry's situation. As a young prince he could not make a marriage agreement for himself but had to wait on the whim of his father for such a deal to be made. What more natural than that he should, in the meantime, seek 'comfort' elsewhere? Indeed, it is commented on as unusual that his brother William Rufus did not do the same. Even when a prince or lord was married, the chances were that he had had no say in choosing his wife, and as long as the requisite heirs were produced in wedlock, there was little discouragement from finding a more compatible mate (or mates) outside the marriage bed. Needless to say, this benevolence applied only to the male of the species. In order to ensure that no little cuckoos were being brought up within the family nest, the wife was, in general, required to be a virgin until marriage, and thereafter would be strictly punished by Church, family and society, for any adultery that might be discovered.

It is not at all strange, therefore, to find Henry I proving his fertility both before and after his marriage, though he does not have the excuse that the marriage was forced upon him. Indeed he did declare when he married Matilda in 1100 that he intended to give up his mistresses and settle down, which he did – for a while. Maybe Vitalis was right when he said Henry was 'addicted' to this one vice, or possibly it was the extensive time he spent away from his wife that brought about a return to former ways. Matilda, for her part, seems to have made no complaint and simply got on with running her household, sharing in the running of the country and being the patron of music, art and literature that she was.

What is perhaps strange is the number of offspring from these liaisons that Henry acknowledged, brought up and made use of, and also, in many cases, the status of the women who became his partners, some of them for long periods of time. We know the names of at least five of them, though there were doubtless many more, and though by and large they were not drawn from the highest level of society, neither were they nameless, friendless serfs.

We don't know, however, the mother of the son who is generally accepted as the eldest of his children. This was Robert, sometimes known as Robert of Caen and later Robert of Gloucester. He was almost certainly born around 1090, and despite efforts to tie him into the Gayt family of Oxfordshire, his mother is now usually referred to as a 'woman of Caen.' Considering Henry's activities at the time, this is likely to be correct, as indeed is his birthplace in the city of Caen. For at least part of 1087 Henry was in Caen, arranging his father's funeral. The following year he obtained his lands in Western Normandy from his brother Robert, and again is likely to have spent part of the time in Caen. Then, after a short trip to England from autumn 1088 to early summer 1089, he was imprisoned at Bayeux, following which he was again in the Cotentin area, with lands perhaps extending as far as Caen, before rescuing Robert from William Rufus in Rouen. If his son Robert was born any time within five years of 1086 the chances are that it was sometime around 1090 and in the Caen area.

We have no details of Robert's upbringing, but since Henry was about to enter his wandering phase, followed by his 'banditry' in the Domfront area, it is likely he spent his early years with his mother. It has been suggested he spent some time in the household of Robert Bloet, Bishop of Lincoln, but if so this was probably after Henry became king, when the boy would have been about ten years old. He certainly received a good education at some point in his childhood. Then, some ten years later, he surfaces again, fully grown and supporting his father in the French wars, and playing a decisive role in the Battle of Brémule.

In 1107 Robert married Mabel Fitzhamon, eldest daughter and heiress of Henry's long-time friend and supporter Robert Fitzhamon. The marriage may have been arranged long before, but it took place in the year her father died, at a time when Mabel would have entered the king's wardship. It also set the policy the king would follow with all his illegitimate sons, not setting them up in estates taken from the Crown lands, but marrying them into wealth and property. Mabel brought to her husband the extensive lands of Robert Fitzhamon comprising the Honour of Gloucester, with the lordship of Glamorgan stretching far into south Wales, as well as lands in Normandy around Bayeux.

Robert was to become one of the most able and trusted supporters of his father throughout his life, particularly when Henry's carefully laid plans for the future were abruptly thrown into disarray in 1120. The following year, or possibly in 1122 Robert became Earl of Gloucester, and at one point there was even talk that he might be offered the crown itself. That did not happen, and after his father's death he became the most important supporter of his half-sister Matilda in the anarchy that ensued.

Robert and Mabel had at least eight children together, one of whom became Bishop of Worcester, while an illegitimate son became Bishop of Bayeux. Robert's eldest son and heir, William, 2nd Earl of Gloucester, was the father of Isabel of Gloucester who married John 'Lackland', youngest son of Henry II. She never got to wear a crown, however, since the marriage was annulled on the grounds of consanguinity – they were second-cousins, both great-grandchildren of Henry I – before John came to the throne as King John. Robert himself died at Bristol Castle in 1147 and was buried in the nearby St James Priory, which he had founded.

With Robert in Normandy, and again prominent at the Battle of Brémule, was his half-brother Richard, known as Richard of Lincoln. He was the son of Ansfride who seems to have been a mistress of Henry's for a period of years in the early 1090s, and maybe even earlier. We know a little more about Ansfride than about most of the other mistresses. She was apparently born in Berkshire and married a man called Anskill, a tenant of Abingdon Abbey. The story is that she was widowed and approached Henry for help in relation to her situation with the abbey. The chances are that this was in 1088 during his stay in England, and given the likely birth dates of the children attributed to her as Henry's mistress, she may either have accompanied him or followed him back to Normandy.

The first child generally acknowledged as hers was Juliana, who must have been born around 1090 in order to be of marriageable age when she married Eustace of Pacy in 1103, when Henry helped him secure the Honour of Breteuil. We have already followed the ups and downs of Juliana's career until she and her husband were forgiven their rebellion in 1119. They never recovered the lands they had lost around Breteuil but still had Eustace's own lands at Pacy, and Henry is said to have granted them an annuity of 300 silver marks. As well as the two daughters caught up in the quarrels of their elders, they also had two sons, William and Roger. Either before or after the death of Eustace in 1136, Juliana became a nun at the abbey of Fontevrault.

A total of three of Henry's children are attributed to Ansfride. A son, Fulk, became a monk at Abingdon, bringing the story full circle. It is reasonable to suppose he might be the younger son, possibly born around 1094, since it is his brother Richard who gets all the notice, and who was clearly brought up to be a soldier rather than a cleric. Richard is likely to have been born around 1092 and is probably known as Richard of Lincoln through being brought up in the household of Robert Bloet, though it is just possible he was born in that city. Like his half-brother Robert, he figures prominently in Henry's French wars. He was clearly trusted to be in charge of Henry's castle at Anderly when it was taken by a trick by Louis in 1119, but no doubt felt he had got his revenge sharing the command of the infantry that forced Louis to flee at Brémule. It is clear that Henry loved both these boys very dearly and a bright future was in store for Richard. In 1120 he was betrothed to Amice, daughter of Ralph de Gael, and through her he would have received the Honour of Breteuil and secured the southern boundary of Normandy for his father. It was not to be. His sudden death that same year not only robbed Henry of a beloved son, but also meant another of his well-laid plans came to nothing.

We don't know what happened to Ansfride when Henry became king. Possibly she had already died, though one account says she lived until 1164, by which time she would have been approaching her nineties. For a period, though, she had clearly held the king's affections, though not exclusively. In the years before he became king, Henry had at least three more daughters and probably another son.

We can calculate the approximate birth dates of the daughters because we know of their marriages. In one case that is all we know. A daughter known as Matilda or Maud married Conan III, Duke of Brittany, some time before 1113. They had either two or three children, the confusion arising because, although a son called Hoel, born around 1116, was brought up as a child of the family, Conan later declared that the boy was not his and disinherited him. A daughter, Bertha, born around 1114 was then declared to be sole heiress. Her first marriage was to Alan the Black, who became Earl of Richmond, and the couple lived in England, producing a son, Conan, who would later become Duke of Brittany. When Bertha's father died in 1148, however, young Conan was only ten years old, so Bertha and her second husband, Odo, Viscount of Porhoet, ruled in his place. From this second marriage came a daughter, Alix, who became a mistress of Henry II of England.

Another Matilda or Maud, whose mother was called Edith, must also have been born around 1090 as she was married to Rotrou of Perche in 1103, once again securing for Henry an extremely useful ally on the southern borders on Normandy. She was his second wife, and he must have been at least ten years older since he had already taken part in the First Crusade. Serving under the command of Bohemond, he was reputed to have been one of the first over the walls at the end of the Siege of Antioch. He would fight again in Spain in the early years of his marriage, before becoming a solid supporter of his father-in-law in his French wars. After the death of his wife in 1120, he would fight again in Spain, but he was close enough to Henry to be present at his deathbed in 1135. Philipa, a daughter of Matilda and Rotrou, married Helias of Maine, a younger brother of Geoffrey Plantagenet. He tried to claim the County of Maine from his brother, but was unsuccessful and ended his days in 1151 as a prisoner at Tours.

The other daughter we know about from this period was the first fruits of a liaison that must have continued for a considerable time. Sybilla the was daughter of Sybil Corbet, who is believed to have had at least five of Henry's children. Sybil herself was the daughter of Robert Corbet, lord of Alcester, and how she came into Henry's orbit we don't know. She must have been with him in Normandy in the early days, however, for it is claimed that Sybilla was born at Domfront, probably around 1092. The other children attributed to Sybil are Rainald or Reginald, William, Rohese and Gundred, and the spread of their birth dates runs from 1092 to a probable 1114, with a gap in the middle. It is likely that Sybil was one of the mistresses Henry vowed to give up on his marriage to Matilda in 1100. Around 1114 Sybil herself was married to Herbert Fitzherbert, the oldest son and heir of Henry's chamberlain. This match was almost certainly arranged by Henry, as Herbert then became Lord of Blaen Llyfni near Abergavenny in the Welsh Marches.

We know a fair amount about three of Sybil's children, Sybilla, Rainald and William, but very little about the other two daughters, Rohese and Gundred. Sybilla married Alexander, King of Scotland, soon after he succeeded to the throne. This led to the rather bizarre situation that Henry, who was already Alexander's brother-in-law, now became his father-in-law as well. Nobody seems to have mentioned the perils of consanguinity or made any comment on her illegitimacy. In the event, the marriage proved childless. We don't know what part Sybilla played in the reforms Alexander carried out in Scotland but his court was described as splendid, and he is credited with bringing together the older, wilder Scotland of the Highlands and the more civilising Anglo-Norman influences. Despite some disparaging comments from William of Malmesbury, Alexander and Sybilla seem to have been happy together. When she died in 1122 it is claimed he planned to found an abbey in her memory, but his own death two years later meant the project was never realised. Sybilla is buried in Dunfermline Abbey.

Sybilla's brother William followed her to Scotland and seems to have had a position at the Scottish court. He is mentioned as the first Constable of Scotland. He may have been a dozen years her junior, and following her death returned to England where he married a woman known only as Alice. If Henry stuck to his policy Alice was likely to have been an heiress, and certainly William later appears as a substantial landowner in Devon and Cornwall. There is a possibility he may have lived until 1187, though the records tend to confuse him with other Williams active at that time.

Sybilla's other brother, Rainald or Reginald, was known as Rainald de Dunstanville, possibly indicating that he was born at Dunstanville in Normandy, a little way south of Dieppe. His birth date is usually given as around 1110, but, if Sybil was accompanying Henry, it may have been a year earlier or later, at which times the king is known to have been in Normandy. Little is heard of him in Henry's lifetime, but in the anarchy which followed the king's death, he came out as a strong supporter of his half-sister Matilda, and received from her the earldom of Cornwall in 1141. At about this time, too, he married Beatrice, heiress to William FitzRichard, and thus acquired extensive lands in Cornwall. The fortunes of war deprived him of these lands, but he recovered them from Henry II and in 1173 was named High Sheriff of Devon. Rainald and Beatrice had four daughters, one of whom, Maud, married Robert de Beaumont, eldest son and heir of Waleran de Beaumont, and grandson of Robert de Meulan.

Sybilla's sister Rohese, who may have been born as late as 1114, married Henry de la Pomeroy, who was serving as a captain in her father's household troops at the time. Promoted within the household, he later served and prospered under Henry II. He died in 1167 and Rohese survived for another decade or so as a widow. Of her sister Gundred we know nothing except that in 1130 she held land in Wiltshire, and we only know that because she is described as 'sister of Rainald de Dunstanville.'

Another son of Henry's born before he became king was Robert FitzEdith, also referred to as Robert the King's son. His date of birth has been given as 1093 and, as his name suggests, his mother was called Edith. In fact we know a great deal more about his mother than we do about Robert himself. She was a daughter of Forne Sigulfson, lord of Greystoke in Cumberland, and is sometimes known as Edith Forne or Edith of Greystoke. As well as Robert, she is said to have had a daughter by Henry, who was called Adeliza, although her date of birth is unknown. Her existence, in fact, is only deduced as she signed charters along with her brother Robert.

As with many of Henry's known mistresses, Edith later made a good marriage, though the form of words used to describe it has possibly sinister overtones. It was said that in 1120 Henry 'caused her to marry' Robert D'Oyly, though this may mean no more than that he arranged the marriage, and need not necessarily imply any reluctance on either side. Robert D'Oyly was Constable of Oxford Castle, and nephew of the Robert D'Oyly who had fortified Wallingford Castle for William the Conqueror. Edith and Robert had at least two sons, and Edith is credited with the idea of founding a priory at Osney, near Oxford Castle. The story goes that she had a dream of chattering magpies, which was interpreted as being the crying out of souls in purgatory who needed to be prayed for. She then persuaded her husband to found the priory of St Mary, which later became Osney Abbey. Edith herself was buried in the church there in the habit of a nun, with a similarly garbed effigy on her tomb and a picture of chattering magpies nearby.

Of Robert FitzEdith himself we know only that around 1142 he married an heiress, Matilda d'Avranches, a distant relative of the d'Avranches family who had provided the first two Earls of Chester. Through her he became Lord of Okehampton in Devon. He died in 1172.

Henry's vow to give up his mistresses when he got married may have lasted a matter of a few years, possibly until after the birth of his legitimate son William in 1103. He and Matilda seem to have had no more children, although one chronicler refers to another son, Richard, who survived only a short time. Possibly after that Matilda could have no more children.

Certainly he was soon tempted away and the temptress could well have been the famously beautiful Welsh Princess Nest. Nest was the daughter of the last king of Deheubarth, a kingdom in west Wales now largely covered by Pembrokeshire, Carmarthenshire and Ceredigion. Her father was killed in battle with the encroaching Normans in 1093 when Nest was about eight years old. Her younger brother Gruffydd escaped to Ireland, but Nest was captured by the Normans and was probably brought up in the household of Robert Fitzhamon and his wife Sybil de Montgomery at Cardiff.

At some point she came to the attention of King Henry, and probably around 1103, when she was seventeen or eighteen years old, became his mistress. Their son, known as Henry the King's Son, was born soon after, but the liaison was fairly brief as Nest was married off in 1105 to Gerald FitzWalter of Windsor.

This was the same Gerald who had been steward at Pembroke Castle under Arnulf of Montgomery, and having fallen from grace with Arnulf, he had now worked himself back into Henry's favour. Indeed, he seems to have been a resourceful fellow if the story told of his time under siege at Pembroke is anything to go by. Besieged by the Welsh, he had the last four pigs killed and roasted and thrown over the wall to the besiegers to persuade them that the castle had enough food to give away. Then he made sure they intercepted a letter he had written to say that no relief force was needed as they could easily hold out for at least four months with the resources they had. The demoralised Welsh then gave up and abandoned the siege. Of course the story may be untrue or exaggerated, but if not Gerald would appear to have been a man of 'infinite resource and sagacity'.

He was certainly, in Henry's eyes, the man to return to Pembroke to hold it on behalf of the English king, and it was felt his task would be easier if he was married to the last surviving princess of the royal line. That was not the end of Nest's adventures, however. Though their main fortress was at Pembroke, it is known the family favoured as a home a castle at Carew, a few miles away and easily accessible by water. They certainly built the first stone tower there, still standing and now forming part of the east range of buildings. It was almost certainly from there that Nest and her children were abducted by the scandalous Prince Owain in 1109.

It may be that he intended to attack Gerald, though another version declares he had heard of Nest's beauty and came deliberately to carry her away. In yet another version, Nest was more than willing to be abducted. We will never know. There seems to be general agreement however that while Owain fired the outer wooden buildings and battered his way in, Nest urged her husband to escape by the only route possible – down the chute of the 'garderobe' or toilet. At Carew this now emerges inside the inner gateway to the courtyard, but at the time it would have been outside the castle. Gerald made good his escape, and Nest and her children, including the king's son Henry, were carried away by Owain.

Again depending on which version of the story is told, she remained with him three, four, or even five years and had a number of children by him. More prosaically her release was probably negotiated two years later, possibly about the time Owain's father died and he was permitted to become King of Powys. No children are recorded, and her other children were released rather sooner than their mother.

Henry, who seems to be the only child of the king to bear his father's name, was given estates in the area of Narberth, and later fought in Anglesey at the time Henry II was attempting to regain control of the Welsh kingdoms. He was killed in battle in 1158. His son Meilyr joined the invasion of Ireland launched in 1169 and, with many of the descendants of Nest and Gerald, became a powerful Irish baron. He became Lord Chief Justice of Ireland and was the founder of Dublin Castle.

William de Tracy is another son of Henry I about whom we know very little. He died in 1136, but whether he was born before or after Henry's marriage is not certain. We know nothing at all about his mother. He married Gieva de Tracy, the daughter of the Lord of Barnstaple, and was given by his father the feudal barony of Bradninch in Devon. His daughter and sole heiress, Grace, was born about 1130 and married John of Sudeley. Their younger son was Sir William de Tracy, adopting his mother's name and inheriting Bradninch, and he was one of the four knights involved in assassinating Thomas Becket in Canterbury Cathedral in 1170. For this he and his fellows were excommunicated. They visited Rome and had an audience with the pope who then passed the sentence that to make up for their grievous sin, they must go and fight for Christendom in the Holy Land for fourteen years, and then remain there in religious retreat for the rest of their lives. One story says that Sir William died on the way to Jerusalem, but others say he fulfilled his sentence exactly, becoming a hermit near Jerusalem when he finished his military service. When he died he was either buried in Jerusalem before the door of the Temple, or another version says his body was brought home to England and buried on Brean Down in Somerset.

Of Henry's remaining son, we know almost nothing. He was known as Gilbert Fitzroy and his birth dates have been given as wide apart as 1114 and 1130. He was born at Westminster, and died there sometime after 1142, but exactly when that was and what he did in between is a complete blank.

The only other mistress whose name we know is probably the last one, and also one of the highest in rank. She was Isabel de Beaumont, daughter of Henry's closest adviser Robert de Meulan. At the earliest, she was born in 1105, and possibly as much as ten years later, and Henry would have been at least fifty before she became his mistress. Her daughter, also called Isabel, was born at some point in the 1120s. She is believed to have remained unmarried and lived with her mother for all or most of her life. Sometime before 1130 Isabel de Beaumont made an excellent marriage to Gilbert de Clare, known as Strongbow, who had extensive estates in Normandy and in South Wales, including Chepstow Castle. The marriage was almost certainly arranged by Henry, though whether to reward Gilbert or Isabel for services to the Crown is not clear.

There are three other daughters of whom we know something, though their mothers are not named. One was Maud, who became a nun and ultimately Abbess of Montivilliers in northern Normandy. Another, Constance, married Roscelin de Beaumont, hereditary vicomte of Maine. She may have been born around 1109 and married in the 1120s, and it was her granddaughter Ermengarde who, in 1186, married the Scottish king known as William the Lion. Their son, Constance's great-grandson, would become Alexander II of Scotland.

Finally, another daughter called Aline or Alice was also born around 1110, and in 1126 was married to Matthew of Montmorency in France. It has been suggested Henry arranged this marriage in the hope of wooing Matthew away from loyalty to the French throne. If this was his aim it was a failure since Matthew later became Constable of France, the highest officer of the Crown serving the French king.

Beyond these known and named children we have hints and rumours of several more. An unnamed 'wife of Fergus of Galloway' is likely to have been an illegitimate daughter, since her son, Uhtred, was referred to as a cousin of Henry II. Galloway would have been a useful ally for England at the time, giving security to the border areas in the north-west.

Then there is Sybil of Falaise who is referred to as Henry's niece. Some believe she too was an illegitimate daughter, since such children were commonly referred to as nephews and nieces. On the other hand, with so many children openly acknowledged as illegitimate offspring, it seems odd that she alone would be called a niece, and it is possible she was an illegitimate daughter of Robert Curthose. Sybil married Baldwin de Boullers and four children are named, though only a daughter called Matilda is definitely attributed to Sybil. Matilda in turn married Richard FitzUrse, and their son Reginald was another of the murderers of Thomas Becket.

Writing with hindsight William of Malmesbury could certainly claim that Henry effectively used his by-blows to achieve alliances for the benefit of his lands, though it is stretching credibility to believe that was in his mind at the time they were conceived. He did, however, by skilful diplomacy attain a network of relatives across Wales, Scotland, Brittany, Normandy, Maine, Blois and even part of France. Nor did his mistresses suffer from the connection. Those we know of seem to have married well and comfortably, and while no doubt there were others of lower birth whose names have not come down to us, there seems no reason to believe they would have been treated less generously by the king.

As for the children carrying this royal blood, they too seemed to suffer no taint. They married kings, dukes, counts and heiresses, and in their turn produced earls, monks, crusaders, a large part of the Anglo-Irish nobility, a Welsh chronicler, kings and at least one Constable of France.

With all this wealth of flesh and blood carrying forward his plans, by and large with a generous dose of love and loyalty, it seems ironic that the future security of Henry's kingdom and legacy should have hung on the slender thread of only one legitimate son. William of Malmesbury, writing of Queen Matilda, rather delicately states: 'Satisfied with a child of either sex, she ceased having issue.' This seems to imply that this was Matilda's choice. It could also be, however, that Henry, remembering his own family struggles, thought that one son with a clear line to the throne was enough. Possibly he felt he was giving the young William a definite advantage, particularly since there were two well-loved older half-brothers who would almost certainly offer their loyalty and service to the legitimate heir.

Life in those times was precarious, however, and maybe Henry should have foreseen how easily his precious thread could be snapped. Malmesbury declares that Henry had spent four years trying to achieve peace in Normandy and with the French king, finally attaining that with the agreement of 1120. 'Nevertheless the calm of this brilliant and carefully concerted peace, this anxious universal hope, was destroyed in an instant by the vicissitudes of human estate.' Tragedy was about to strike.

10

The White Ship and After (1120–1125)

By the autumn of 1120 William Adelin, the only legitimate son of Henry I of England, was a little over seventeen years of age. According to William of Malmesbury he had been 'educated and destined to the succession with the fondest hope and surpassing care.' Enjoying the full favour of his father, he had had all the freemen of England and Normandy submit themselves to him by homage and oath when he was only twelve, a ritual that had recently been repeated after Henry's triumph over his enemies in Normandy. For a time he had acted as regent in England after his mother's death, albeit with the guiding hand of Roger of Salisbury, before joining his father and half-brothers in Normandy in time for the Battle of Brémule. By his father's indulgence, says Malmesbury, he 'possessed everything but the name of king.' Added to this, he had a new wife, though she was 'scarcely marriageable' being only about nine years old. Nevertheless, through her he had the prospect of gaining the County of Maine if her father, Fulk of Anjou, failed to return from his trip to Jerusalem. With all that in his favour it would be a very level-headed seventeen-year-old who did not get a little above himself at times.

In fact Henry of Huntingdon records a sour note. 'But unpleasing thoughts suggested themselves to my mind,' he says, 'when I observed the excessive state with which he was surrounded and his own pride. I said to myself, "This prince, so pampered, is destined to be food for the fire!"' This was written a very long time later, however, and no doubt with a gloomy hindsight that saw the hand of God behind the events of a fateful November night, rather than the unthinking high spirits of youth.

It was certainly in a celebratory mood that Henry and his court came to the port of Barfleur in November 1120. 'King Henry,' says Vitalis, 'having now after great exertions put his affairs in Normandy into excellent order, resolved on re-crossing the sea and bestowing large rewards on his young esquires and most distinguished knights, some of whom he proposed to raise to high honours and ample wealth in England.' There must have been a great crowd of them for a fleet of ships was demanded and fitted out at the king's command.

Between them William of Malmesbury and Orderic Vitalis give us the fullest account of what happened then, complementing each other's stories and adding detail until we can almost see the events unfolding. It is Vitalis who tells us about a certain Thomas, son of Stephen, who came to Henry and offered to put his ship, the *Blanche-Nef*, or White Ship, at his disposal. His father, he said, had served William the Conqueror as a mariner all his life, commanding the very ship that had carried him across the Channel to invade England in 1066. Thomas wanted to serve Henry in the same way, 'having a vessel, called the *Blanche-Nef*, which is fitted out in the best manner, and perfectly adapted to receive a royal retinue.' His manner obviously impressed the king, but Henry replied that he had already selected a ship for himself and would not alter his plans now. However, he added, he was prepared to 'entrust to you my sons, William and Richard, whom I love as myself,' with others of his court who would travel with them.

It seems highly likely that the division between the ships reflected something of a generation gap. Henry was now well into middle age and his son seventeen. Already, Malmesbury tells us, almost all the young nobility were flocking round William, hoping to serve or amuse him and thereby gain reward or advancement. It is very easy to see a parallel situation in modern terms when young people throw a party and their parents go away for the night to avoid the row. For whatever reason, the older, more established members of Henry's court, such as Theobald of Blois and Rotrou of Perche, would travel with him in his ship, while the younger, wilder element would accompany his sons, 'by the king's command'.

The *Blanche-Nef* was, according to Malmesbury, 'of the best construction and recently fitted with new materials,' but it may well be that the prospect of, in effect, crossing the Channel with his own court, went to William's head a little. Certainly his actions over the hours prior to sailing on the evening of 25 November, smack of 'showing off'. It is Vitalis again who tells us that the crew of the White Ship were delighted to be favoured in this way by Henry, and that, 'greeting the king's son with fair words, they asked him to give them something to drink. The Prince,' says Vitalis, 'gave orders that they should have three muids.' A muid is an old French liquid measure. In modern wine-making terms, it is the equivalent of 159 gallons, though something like 60 gallons has been suggested for the medieval version. We are told elsewhere that there were casks of wine stowed on the ship, making the journey to England, and it is likely that three of these were then broached and shared out – close to 180 gallons of wine. A 'great drinking bout' ensued.

Whether any of this was witnessed by the king we don't know. Malmesbury simply tells us that 'the king set sail from Barfleur just before twilight ... and the breeze which filled his sails conducted him safely to his kingdom.' Since the White Ship was also carrying 'the king's treasure', it seems unlikely he would have entrusted either that or the life of his son to the hands of a crew of drunken sailors. We can only suppose that the party had not reached its riotous stage before he left. It certainly did soon after.

There were fifty experienced rowers on the White Ship along with an armed marine force, and it is probable that the great casks of wine were emptied not only by the crew but also by the passengers. It still appears, however, a very great quantity of wine to be consumed before taking a ship to sea and, since the wine was presumably destined for the king's court, we must assume it was good quality wine. Vitalis says the men at arms became very drunk and disorderly, taking possession of the rower's benches and driving away with contempt a number of priests who came to bless the ship with holy water for a safe voyage. Some of the more prudent passengers even disembarked because the ship 'was overcrowded with riotous and headstrong youths.' Among them was Stephen of Blois. We are not told whether or not he had indulged in the drinking, but Vitalis supplies the detail that he was suffering from diarrhoea so he was probably not really in the mood for a party.

It was by now, apparently, fully dark on a calm, cold night with only the sliver of a new moon. All of a sudden, as is the way with drunken parties, someone produced a brilliant idea. Henry, who had at least several hours start on them, must be overtaken. It was to be a race to England. Thomas, who had probably had as much wine as the rest, was confident that it could be done. He would 'soon leave behind him all the ships that had started before them.' Thus, as Malmesbury puts it, 'these imprudent youths, overwhelmed with liquor, launched the vessel from the shore.'

In many cases, on many shores, they may not have come to much harm, possibly going round in circles until they became exhausted. The entrance to Barfleur harbour, however, is treacherous in the extreme, with long arms of rock reaching out to sea on either side and more of the same along the coast to north and south. Even in daylight with a sober crew, care would be needed to get safely to sea. This particular crew took no care at all.

As Vitalis tells it, 'the sailors seized the oars' and 'joyously handled the ropes and sails and made the ship rush through the water at a great rate.' 'She flies swifter than the winged arrow,' adds Malmesbury. But not for long. Vitalis again: 'But as the drunken rowers exerted themselves to the utmost in pulling the oars, and the luckless pilot steered at random and got the ship out of its due course, the starboard bow of the *Blanche-Nef* struck violently a huge rock, which is left dry every day when the tide is out and covered by the waves at high water.'

No-one knows exactly which rock was struck, there are many to choose from on all sides. Malmesbury says it was not far from the shore, but it proved to be quite far enough. He describes how the mariners, probably rapidly sobering, spent a considerable time trying to free the ship, but it was inexorably stuck with two planks shattered. No doubt the more they tried to free it, the more water gushed in. 'Now, too,' he says, 'the water washed some of the crew overboard, and entering the chinks, drowned others.'

He describes how a decision was taken to save the life of the heir to the throne. A boat was launched and William 'might certainly have been saved by reaching the shore.' On board the stricken vessel, however, the Countess of Perche, William's half-sister, 'struggling with death ... implored her brother's assistance.' Touched by pity, William turned back and 'met his death by an excess of affection,' for as soon as the little boat came near, all those still alive on the White Ship tried to jump into it to save themselves. The boat, 'overcharged by the multitudes who leapt into her, sank and buried all indiscriminately in the deep.'

Vitalis estimates there were some 300 people on board the White Ship. Of all that mighty company now only two remained alive, clinging to the yard from which the sail had been set – and Thomas. Thomas, apparently, could swim, possibly the only one who could, or the only one sober enough to do so. After his first plunge into the sea, says Vitalis, he 'gained fresh energy and, recovering his senses, raised his head above the water.' Seeing the two clinging to the yard, he asked them what had happened to the king's son and was told, 'he and all who were with him had perished. "Then," said he, "it is misery for me to live any longer",' and he sank beneath the waves. Vitalis adds that he 'abandoned himself to his fate in utter despair, preferring to meet it at once, rather than face the rage of the king ... or drag out his existence and expiate his crime in a dungeon.'

Still through the dark, frosty night the two remaining survivors clung on, an ill-assorted pair. One was Geoffrey, son of Gilbert of L'Aigle, and the other a butcher from Rouen called Berold. For some time, we are told, they encouraged each other and called on God to save them. That they survived more than a few minutes in, or clinging above, a November sea is amazing, but finally the cold of the night and the icy waters took their toll. Geoffrey, 'after severe sufferings from the severity of the weather, lost his power of endurance and, commending his companion to God, fell into the sea and disappeared.'

The last survivor, Berold, was the poorest of the company, so Vitalis says, and that may well have saved him. While the lords and other had more fashionable clothes, Berold 'wore a sheepskin dress,' probably a rough cloak or tunic, the thickness of which likely kept him warm enough to survive the night. At dawn the next morning he was spotted and rescued by three fishermen, and so the tale of the disaster was told.

Those on shore had heard the cries and screams of the doomed company but, in the heavy darkness with no moonlight, had not been able to tell where they were or do anything to save them. It is also claimed that Henry and his companions on their way to England had heard the cries, though they could not have been very far out to sea if that is so. Again they had apparently wondered where they came from, but hadn't suspected the truth.

'No ship was ever productive of so much misery to England,' says Malmesbury, and looking at the list of those lost we can understand the sentiment. Henry lost not one but two sons, for Richard drowned alongside his half-brother. With them were Richard of Chester, 'distinguished for his bravery and kindness of heart,' with his wife, Matilda of Blois who was Henry's niece. The earl's older half-brother Othuer, who was tutor and governor to William Adelin, also drowned. Vitalis says that, as the little boat went down, he 'took ... the young prince in his arms, and sinking with him, they were never seen again.' Among the young nobility named as lost were Theodoric, a nephew of the Holy Roman Emperor; William of Rhuddlan, son of Robert, coming home to take possession of his inheritance in north Wales; two sons of Ivo de Grandmesnil, and William Bigod. Ralph the Red, hero of the recent wars and certain to be in line for high honours, was also among the dead, as was Geoffrey Riddel, one of Henry's travelling justices. He was married to the sister, or possibly half-sister, of Richard of Chester, so his widow, who was not on the ship, was left mourning three family members. Vitalis tells us that 'of those who perished ... there were no less than eighteen females who were either daughters, sisters, nieces or wives of kings or earls', one of whom was the Countess of Perche.

It was not only the nobility that suffered, however. The Anglo-Saxon Chronicle records that 'very many of the king's court, stewards and chamberlains and butlers and other men in office and an innumerable multitude of all ranks were lost,' while Malmesbury concludes his list of the dead with, 'almost every person of consequence about court, whether knight or chaplain or young nobleman training up to arms.' The county of Mortain in Normandy seems to have suffered particularly since, apart from Stephen and two men at arms who presumably got off the boat with him, 'almost all the lords and men of distinction in the county' were lost. Indeed, Vitalis seems to regard himself as unusually fortunate when he records, 'For myself, I have no-one to mourn, except from common feelings of pity, as no-one of my kindred was swallowed up in that horrible gulf.'

News of the shipwreck spread rapidly, in Normandy and presumably to England as well, since Theobald of Blois seems to have heard of it at some point on the following day. No-one, however, had the nerve to tell the king, though Vitalis says he was in a state of great anxiety and made many enquiries. Those who had lost relatives and friends seem to have mourned in private and kept their countenance before the king. Finally, the next day, Theobald devised a plan so that none of his fellows should be the one to break the news to Henry. A boy, blameless and unpunishable, was found to play a part. He 'threw himself at the king's feet weeping bitterly,' and when asked what was the matter, blurted out the news. Thus 'the king learnt from him the shipwreck of the *Blanche-Nef*,' says Vitalis, adding, 'So sudden was the shock and so severe his anguish that he fell instantly to the ground, but being raised up by his friends, he was conducted to his chamber and gave free course to the bitterness of his grief.'

It was a 'twofold grief', so the Chronicle tells us, 'first because they lost their lives so suddenly, and next that few of their bodies were ever found.' The wreck of the ship was secured and dragged to the shore and the king's treasure was recovered, 'and almost all that was in the vessel, the crew and passengers excepted.' Huge rewards were offered for any bodies that might be found and the shore on all sides was scoured for some time after. All they ever recovered, however, was the body of Richard of Chester, identified by his clothes, and a few others whose names were not important enough to record.

Henry's grief, bitter though it was at losing three of his children, was not only a personal matter, however. All that he had achieved, all his plans for the future had been bound up in William Adelin. The most pressing issue was that of the succession. Henry, now in secure possession of the kingdom of England and the Duchy of Normandy, had no wife and no legitimate offspring except his daughter Matilda, married to the Holy Roman Emperor. There is some evidence that he had already contemplated a remarriage of his own, the partner of his choice being Adeliza of Louvain, the so-called 'fair maid of Brabant'. She was the daughter of Geoffrey, Count of Louvain, Landgrave of Brabant and Duke of Lower Lotharingia. Since he owed these latter titles to the Holy Roman Emperor, it has been suggested that Matilda may have had a hand in arranging this match for her father. There were certainly advantages for both sides. Henry would get a young, beautiful wife who could boast descent from Charlemagne, while the emperor could cement the loyalty of Geoffrey, who before this time had shown a tendency to rebel. Whatever stage the negotiations had reached by November 1120, they were now rapidly accelerated and Henry and Adeliza were married at Windsor on 29 January 1121.

It is clear the new queen knew her duty. Though renowned as a patron of the arts, unlike her predecessor she did not set up her court in England but travelled extensively with her husband, the better to have a chance of producing the longed-for heir. She was about eighteen at the time of her marriage and would go on to produce seven children with a second husband. Henry, however, was now over fifty, and though he had regularly produced bastards until recent years, probably his last child was the illegitimate Isabel, born a few years earlier. Father of some two dozen children,

Henry was now unable to get the one needed for a quiet succession to a legitimate son.

If not a new heir, what then were his other options? Of his own children Robert was now the only one left of an age and ability to command respect. Intelligent, constantly supportive and proven in battle, he already had sons of his own to carry on the royal line. He had held the Honour of Gloucester for some considerable time, and now he became Earl of Gloucester, one of the few earldoms create during Henry's reign. Against him, however, was his illegitimacy, already less acceptable than it had been in previous times, and certain to cause conflict if favoured over any legitimate claimant.

Apart from his own children, Henry had his nephews, the sons of his sister Adela of Blois. The eldest of these, William, had already been put aside as mentally limited, and while Count Theobald had been a staunch friend and supporter of his uncle, there is no sign Henry thought of him as a possible successor to his throne. The third son, Stephen, Count of Mortain, had already been favoured with titles and lands, both in England and in Normandy, and some have seen his later marriage to Matilda of Boulogne as further evidence of Henry grooming the young man for higher things. Matilda was the daughter and sole heiress of Eustace III of Boulogne and his wife Mary, who was the sister of Henry's first wife, Matilda of Scotland. As such, she was Henry's niece and she also carried the old royal Anglo-Saxon bloodline, which might have made her an acceptable queen to the English. Possibly Stephen himself believed this marriage was intended to mark him out as an heir, though his failures in the past might indicate that Henry was simply setting him in a position appropriate to his abilities.

It may be that Henry gave some consideration to both Robert of Gloucester and Stephen as potential successors. It seems more likely, though, that their promotions early in the 1120s were intended to provide secure support for any new heir he might produce. He may have calculated that he would probably die before a new son could grow to manhood – though his brother Robert was entering his seventies, apparently hearty and strong – and an infant king would certainly be in need of powerful, established friends. If he was considering his daughter as heiress, the same point would be equally true, her husband the Holy Roman Emperor having more than enough to do with his own domains.

Of course the other nephew, and in some eyes the obvious person next in line to the throne, was William Clito, alive and well and living freely in France with the support of the French king. Henry, however, seems to have been absolutely determined that under no circumstances would Clito ever succeed to the throne of England.

Aside from the succession there were other immediate problems arising from the loss of the While Ship, as one by one Henry's carefully laid schemes began to unravel. The first area to be affected was Wales. Hearing of the death of Richard of Chester and his wife, Maredudd of Powys immediately began raiding across the border into Cheshire. In the summer of 1121 Henry assembled an army and marched into Powys via Shrewsbury. As before, the aim was to overawe rather than to seek battle. There were a few light skirmishes, in one of which Henry was targeted by Welsh archers and saved by his armour, but by and large the plan worked. Maredudd fled to Gruffydd ap Cynan in Gwynedd, but Gruffydd was not prepared to risk all he had achieved by submission to the English king, so Maredudd in turn was forced to submit. The enterprise cost Maredudd gifts and hostages and some 10,000 head of cattle by way of compensation for his behaviour.

To secure the area for the future, Henry gave the earldom of Chester to a long-time friend and supporter Ranulf le Meschin (Ranulf the Younger). Ranulf's father, also called Ranulf, had been the most powerful magnate in the Bessin area around Bayeux in Henry's younger days as Count of the Cotentin. Ranulf's mother was a sister of Hugh d'Avranches, making him a cousin of the last earl and a logical successor. In addition though, he was an experienced ruler of borderlands, having been lord of Carlisle for more than twenty years by right of his wife.

His move south left something of a gap in the north-west, as these lands were given up to the king in exchange for Chester.

The death of Henry's daughter, Queen Sybilla of Scotland, the following summer may have caused further anxiety about the relationship between the countries. Certainly Henry himself went north at the end of 1122, visiting Nottingham, York and Durham, as well as Carlisle where he ordered the castle to be strengthened. It might be that it was at this time that his illegitimate daughter was married to Fergus of Galloway, thus obtaining at least one ally in the region.

Things were beginning to unravel across the Channel, too. Late in 1121 Fulk of Anjou returned from his visit to Jerusalem. His daughter Matilda had not travelled on the White Ship with her husband, instead making the crossing in the more sober company of her father-in-law and his friends. Since then she had remained at Henry's court, where, according to Vitalis, he treated her 'with the greatest affection, and entertained her in England with the highest honours.' It is suggested that he had intended to marry her to someone of the highest rank in England, though no clue is given as to who that might be. Instead Fulk demanded that his daughter be returned, and not only his daughter but her dowry too. Henry was happy to return Matilda, who later became a nun at Fontrevault. The dowry was more troublesome consisting largely of a number of castles on the frontier between Maine and Normandy, which he was reluctant to give up.

His refusal to do so caused a rift between Fulk and Henry that Amaury de Montfort was quick to exploit. Amaury had his own quarrel with the English king. Though now clearly recognised as Count of Evreux, his castle there was still garrisoned with Henry's men, and his lands in Normandy were subject to the administrative regime set up by Henry and John of Lisieux. This was something that had not applied to his lands in France, and clearly the men carrying out the administration were not the most honest of officials. 'Corrupt officers are worse than thieves,' comments Vitalis, describing how, 'they exacted extraordinary imposts and perverted justice at their pleasure, laying heavy burdens on men both of high rank and low degree.' He claims, however, that Henry in England was unaware this was happening.

Vitalis credits Amaury with having taken up the cause of William Clito and persuading Fulk to marry his daughter Sybilla to the young man. Fulk agreed, William moved himself to Anjou and was duly married, receiving Maine as Sybilla's dowry, 'until he should recover his hereditary dominions.' There is some evidence that Clito then began attacks on the castles in dispute on the border, but Amaury was not content to let matters rest there. Instead he began inciting rebellion among mostly young Norman lords who also had some complaint against Henry.

Chief among these was Waleran de Meulan, the elder of the twin sons of Henry's friend and adviser Robert. Waleran had inherited the Beaumont lands along the Risle valley in Normandy, including the castles of Beaumont, Brionne and Pont-Audemer, with another castle north of the Seine at Vatteville.

His younger twin, Roger, had inherited the English lands, with the title Earl of Leicester. As Henry had had the care of these boys since their father's death and had endeavoured to treat them scrupulously fairly, he must have been surprised at this betrayal of trust, and a number of suggestions have been made as to why Waleran should turn against him.

Possibly Waleran was angry that his sister became Henry's mistress, though there is no record of this. More plausibly he may have felt slighted when his brother was married to the daughter of Ralph de Gael, with the Breteuil inheritance as her dowry. She was to have married Richard, the king's son who drowned in the White Ship, and Waleran may have felt he should have been considered as a husband rather than his brother. It is likely, however, that Henry didn't want such a large area of Normandy in the hands of one very young lord. Possibly Waleran had already shown signs of being unreliable.

For whatever reason, he intended his rebellion to be effective, and to that end consolidated alliances with three other lords by giving them his three sisters in marriage. Adeline married Hugh de Montfort. Aubree married Hugh of Chateauneuf-Thimerais, and Maud married William Louvel. Thus, says Vitalis, he 'gave them in marriage to three lords of castles, whose vassals, wealth and strong places made them very powerful.'

Also in the league of rebels were Baudri de Brai and Paganus of Gisors, whose castle in the Vexin was still held for Henry by his own men. William of Roumare was another with a grudge. He felt he should have had the lands in England that Ranulf of Chester had given up for his earldom, since these had come to Ranulf through his wife, Lucy, who was William's mother. Rather than join with the concerted action of the others, however, he seems to have carried on a lone nuisance campaign of burning and plundering until Henry gave him a large part of what he wanted.

The conspirators almost certainly believed they were acting secretly in building up to their rebellion, but it seems likely Henry's spy network had picked up that something was in the wind as early as April 1123. That was when Robert of Gloucester and Ranulf of Chester crossed the Channel to take up positions, one in the Cotentin and the other in the citadel at Evreux. Soon afterwards Henry himself travelled to Normandy, and about this time began a major programme of strengthening key fortresses at Rouen, Caen, Domfront, Falaise, Argentan and Gisors, among others.

In September 1123 the league of rebels met at a newly built castle thrown up by Waleran, near Evreux. Here they began to plan their war on Henry, still believing their secret was intact. Henry, however, had assembled an army at Rouen and planned to take them by surprise. He did this, as Vitalis explains, by 'marching out of this city on a Sunday, after dinner, without telling anyone where he was going or what he intended to do.' In fact he summoned Hugh de Montfort to meet him and, when he arrived, demanded he hand over to the king his castle at Montfort-sur-Risle.

Hugh, completely taken aback at this, was 'thrown into a state of great anxiety,' and fearing he would be 'immediately loaded with fetters,' agreed to the demand. He was then sent, accompanied by some of the king's men, to fetch the keys of the castle but, as soon as he was away from the king's presence, he apparently recovered his courage. He 'put spurs to his fleet charger and gave his companions the slip at the entrance of the forest.' Then galloping on to the castle, he warned his wife and his brother, who was also there, that the king was coming with an army and they must defend the place, before continuing on to Brionne to tell Waleran of Henry's approach.

Finding he had been tricked, the king marched quickly to Montfort-sur-Risle and put the castle under siege before the inhabitants had time to fully prepare for this. The town around it was burnt, and reinforcements arrived for Henry in the form of Nigel d'Aubigny and Robert of Gloucester, bringing with them men from the Cotentin and from Brittany. Repeated assaults wore down resistance and though the defenders held out for a month, hoping their fellow rebels would relieve them, at last the castle was surrendered. Vitalis reports that Henry was prepared to pardon Hugh and allow him to retain part of his lands, all except the castle and the forest, because his wife was the daughter of his old friend and had a baby son. Hugh, however, refused, preferring to remain with his co-conspirators.

The castle at Pont-Audemer was the next target, and far from being depressed at yet another rebellion, Vitalis makes it sound as though Henry was enjoying himself. 'He himself carefully looked to everything, running about like a young soldier. He taught the carpenters how to construct a berfrey (siege tower), jocularly chid the workmen who made mistakes and encouraged by his praise those who did well to greater exertions.' Again the town was burnt and all the land around it to isolate the defenders from any possible resources, and constant attacks were made, resulting in serious losses on their part. The castle held out for something like seven weeks, from October to December, but the end result was another surrender. Coming to terms, the defenders were allowed to march out with their gear and depart to Waleran at Beaumont.

On the same day Pont-Audemer fell, however, Henry came close to losing his stronghold at Gisors. Paganus of Gisors had made a plan to assassinate Robert de Chandos, who was holding the castle for Henry. It was a Monday and market day, and Robert had been invited to meet Paganus at his house in the town. As the people from the surrounding countryside came in for the market, however, with them came a strong force of soldiers, dressed as peasants and mingling with them. When the appointed time came when Robert should have been with Paganus, in fact he was delayed – Vitalis says delayed by his wife to discuss some household matter. Not knowing this Baudri de Brai sprang the trap, uncovering his armour and calling for the soldiers to attack. Robert, who had just left the castle, heard the noise and hurriedly turned back. Amaury and his forces were nearby and joined the attack and knowing he had not enough men to repel them, Robert fired the houses nearest the castle, whereupon the wind fanned the flames, spreading the fire through the town and forcing the attackers to withdraw. Soon afterwards Henry's army arrived on the scene and the rebels fled.

Henry now expropriated the lands of the traitors, taking back the county of Evreux and giving Gisors to the second son of Paganus who was serving under Stephen of Mortain. 'Thus,' says Vitalis. 'The treaty of peace which the pope had lately concluded between the kings was broken, and fresh hostilities of the fiercest character commenced on both sides.' It was by this time, however, mid-winter, and there would be no more fighting until the spring as Henry, out of consideration for the toils and suffering of the people, called a temporary halt.

Through an unusually wet winter, Henry instructed those holding his castles, particularly those recently taken in the Risle valley, to protect the local people. This protection was certainly needed as raiding and plundering continued on the part of the rebels, who had been joined by some two hundred French knights. With Louis still supporting William Clito, it might be wondered why he had not so far taken a greater hand in the uprising. The answer lay with Henry's son-in-law the Holy Roman Emperor. Having finally settled his differences with the pope and with his own nobles, he was able to oblige his father-in-law by distracting the attention of the French king. All through the early part of 1124 and probably even earlier, rumours grew in France that the emperor was planning an invasion. While Louis could spare a few knights to support action against Henry in Normandy, his main focus was on strengthening his own defences and preparing to hold off the might of the German Emperor.

Serious action in Normandy began again at the end of March 1124. A garrison of Henry's men had been gradually exerting control over Waleran's castle at Vatteville from a siege castle nearby. Over the night of 24/25 March Waleran set out to give some relief to those defending his castle. It seems to have been a stealth expedition, moving quietly through the surrounding forest of Brotonne to take supplies to the castle and then attack the siege tower. For some reason all the rebel commanders were there, Waleran himself and his three brothers-in-law, together with Amaury de Montfort.

The raid itself seems to have gone off perfectly. The castle was re-provisioned and the siege tower taken, its commander, Walter of Valiquerville, being plucked from the rampart, or, as Vitalis puts it, 'ingeniously caught by someone with an iron hook.' In the morning the relieving force took the opportunity to plunder the surrounding area for more supplies for the castle, and a particularly savage and seemingly unnecessary incident is recorded, where Waleran, coming upon some peasants gathering wood, savagely cut off their feet. This might have been an act of pure frustration since, if he was plundering peasants for supplies of food at the end of March, he was not likely to have found much.

It was when Waleran's force set out to return to Beaumont that things began to go wrong. Their secret expedition had been discovered and reported to Ranulf of Chester at Evreux, and he had immediately called up three of Henry's commanders in the area, Henry de la Pomeroy, Odo Borleng and William Harcourt, to take their men and ambush the raiders on their way home. They set out their forces, some three hundred men, on an open plain where the road from Vatteville to Beaumont emerges from the forest of Brotonne. Though the subsequent action is usually referred to as the Battle of Bourgthéroulde, a town some 8 miles away, Vitalis places it more precisely just outside the village of Rougemontier.

When the raiders emerged from the forest, at first it seemed there would be no action since Henry's men were far outnumbered by their opponents. Some were in favour of a quick retreat, but Vitalis credits Odo Borleng with rallying them to fight. Giving him a fairly typical Vitalis speech, he has him declare that if they deploy their forces correctly – some mounted, some dismounted, and with archers in the front line to bring down the unarmoured horses of the opposition – they should have a fine victory. Furthermore, they must not abandon Henry's commander, Walter, who had been taken prisoner. If they fail to fight, he finishes, 'We shall justly forfeit both pay and honour, and in my opinion ought no longer to eat the king's bread.'

On the other side, too, there were misgivings. Though Waleran 'exulted with boyish delight' at the thought of action (he was about twenty at the time), and was 'eager to win the honour of knighthood,' the more experienced Amaury urged caution. Seeing Odo's deployment of men, including himself, on foot, he pointed out that that meant they had no thought of retreat but would fight to the last, they 'must either conquer or die.' He was overruled. Waleran had no fear of 'peasants and common soldiers,' when he had 'the flower of chivalry of France and Normandy' on his side.

To prove his point he set out on a reckless charge with some forty men-at-arms and promptly had his horse shot from under him. The same fate befell his forty companions, and the whole party was surrounded and made captive within minutes. Altogether from the brief engagement there were some eighty prisoners, including Waleran and the two Hughs who were his brothers-in-law, while Vitalis tells a delightful story about the third brother-in-law, William Louvel. Somewhere in the confusion of battle, or more likely in fleeing from the scene, he was taken prisoner by a peasant. He then bargained to give up his armour in exchange for his freedom, cut off his long hair so he would not be recognised as a knight, and set out to walk home to Bréval. When he came to the Seine he gave his boots to the ferryman to take him across, and so eventually arrived home safe and well but barefoot.

Another with a lucky escape was Amaury de Montfort. He was taken prisoner by one of Henry's knights, William de Grandcourt, who seems to have had a very advanced idea of chivalry for the time. Knowing that, if he was delivered to the king, Amaury would be lucky ever to walk free again, he decided to set him free, and accompanied him to France where he remained an exile.

Other captives did not get off so lightly. Three are specifically mentioned as being condemned by Henry to being blinded. Two of them captured in the battle had taken arms against him after swearing fealty and therefore, under the rules of the time, their lives were forfeit. Blinding was seen as being more merciful. The third, Luc de la Barre, had been one of those who surrendered and was allowed to go free when Pont-Audemer fell to the king. Again the rules of war said he should not rejoin the fight, but he, too, had been taken prisoner at Rougemontier. Vitalis places Charles, Count of Flanders, at Henry's court at this time and says he protested at the punishments. Henry thereupon explained fully why the punishments were due, and in fact rather on the lenient side, adding that Luc's was additionally deserved because he 'made scurrilous sonnets on me and sang them aloud to bring me into contempt.'

To modern ears that seems like a poor excuse for blinding a man, but we need to look no further back than Henry's father to find harsher punishments for ridicule. When those holding the fortress of Alençon mocked him for being the bastard of a tanner's daughter, he had thirty-two citizens paraded before them and cut off their hands and feet. Even in the 15th century, Henry V hanged a trumpeter who had dared to ridicule him from the walls of the besieged town of Meaux. In fact the sentence of blinding was never carried out on Luc de la Barre. Resisting his gaolers at every step as they struggled to take him for his punishment, he escaped their grasp long enough to smash his skull against the stone wall of the cell until he fell dead.

The complete and unexpected victory at Rougemontier caused a number of lords in other parts of Normandy who had sympathised with the rebels, to change their minds and fade out of the conspiracy. Not all were yet ready to surrender, however, and Henry turned his attention to mopping up the last of the resistance. Vatteville was quickly taken and, on the king's orders, razed to the ground. Brionne was then besieged about the end of April and surrendered peacefully, leaving only Beaumont holding out under Waleran's steward, Morin de Pin. There might have been a more prolonged siege there but for Henry's change of tactics. With Waleran securely captive, he put it to him that all else was lost and that he might as well tell Morin to hand over Beaumont as well. Waleran, reflecting that he had 'deservedly fallen from his high estate,' and 'fearing also to expose himself to still greater peril,' agreed. The castle was handed over and Morin was sent into exile. He had earlier been Waleran's tutor, and Vitalis declares that Henry blamed him for leading the young man astray with his 'pernicious counsels'. Waleran himself, with his brothers-in-law, would later be moved to England, and he and Hugh of Chateauneuf-Thimerais would be held for the next five years. Hugh de Montfort, however, who had spurned Henry's offer of a pardon, would still be a prisoner at the time of the king's death.

By the time the army of the Holy Roman Emperor began to move towards Rheims in the summer of 1124, it had already achieved its purpose as far as Henry was concerned. Far from aiding the rebels who had fled across the border to France, Louis had been busy calling up support from all over his land. From every province men responded, perhaps inspired by his invocation of St Denis, the protector of France, and his carrying before him the great standard, the oriflamme, taken from the altar of the abbey church of St Denis. There were, we are told, men from Aquitaine and Brittany, from Flanders, from Blois and Burgundy, from Poitou and Anjou – everywhere, in fact, except from Normandy.

In the end there was no attack. It has been speculated that the Germans were overawed at the size of the French army, or perhaps it was an eclipse of the sun occurring at the time that put them off. It is possible that by then Emperor Henry V was already suffering from the illness that was to end his life. For whatever reason, the army moved away again – a failure for the empire, but a most decided success for Henry of England.

With Louis neutralised and the rebels defeated, Henry had had a very good year. There was only one other thing needed, the breakup of the alliance between William Clito and Fulk of Anjou, and this was a problem that Henry fought not with soldiers, but with diplomacy.

At the latest sometime in early 1124, he submitted to the pope that the marriage between Clito and Fulk's daughter Sybilla should be annulled because the couple were within the prohibited degrees of kinship. This was true, but the relationship was exactly the same as that between Henry's son and Fulk's other daughter, which no-one had mentioned at the time. As we have seen, the prohibited degrees were extensive, stretching to sixth cousins, and despite a recent pronouncement that such marriages were 'abominable', the Church usually turned a blind eye unless someone objected. Henry did object to this one, loudly, with detailed arguments and, more importantly, very large sums of money to help focus the pope's mind.

Pope Calixtus adopted delaying tactics, sending a succession of papal legates to look into the matter. The last of these, John of Crema, pronounced definitively that the marriage was void on the grounds of consanguinity, and the pope officially annulled it in August 1124. Fulk of Anjou was furious. He locked up the papal envoys who brought the news and burnt the letters declaring the nullity but, in the end, under sentence of excommunication, he was forced to accept the verdict.

Yet again William Clito was homeless, and virtually friendless as well, after Amaury de Montfort and William Louvel abandoned his cause and grovelled for a pardon from Henry. Vitalis gives a rather touching picture of the young man again setting off on his travels, accompanied as always by the faithful Helias of Saint-Saens. 'He became a wanderer from cottage to cottage in foreign lands ... in great fear and want,' he says, adding, 'he had to dread the grasp of his uncle's long and powerful arms, whose might and wealth, or the fame of them, were spread everywhere from the west to the east.'

Vitalis seems to have had a rather ambivalent attitude towards William Clito. At one point he speaks of him sympathetically, saying, 'This young prince was born to misfortune,' and calling him, 'brave, handsome and high-spirited.' Then, in the same sentence, declares that he 'recommended himself more to the various nations who supported his pretensions, by hopes which were illusory than by his merit.' It is possible Vitalis had some personal dealings with him or knew fellow monks who had, since he says the young wanderer was accustomed to seek hospitality among monks and canons, presumably in the guest halls of various monasteries. There, he says, 'he was so sumptuous in his way of living, though an exile, that his visits brought more charge than honour on his hosts.' Clearly William Clito was an expensive guest. Furthermore, in a more general summary, Vitalis declares, 'he was the cause of more misery than profit to the multitude who adhered to him,' and 'a great number of persons were mistaken in him.' It seems that, overall, Vitalis was not a big fan of the son of Robert Curthose.

As usual, war in Normandy, even on this limited scale, was felt in England in the form of heavy taxes, which felt heavier still in a year of bad weather and poor harvests. The Anglo-Saxon Chronicle bemoans that anyone with any property had it taken from him in taxes, while anyone with no property simply starved. The situation was made worse by the activities of the men operating the mints to produce the silver pennies that were the currency of the time. They had, in fact, so debased the coinage that the Chronicle again declares that a man with a pound at market could only obtain a shilling's worth of goods, that is to say, one twentieth of its nominal value.

The coin shipped overseas to pay Henry's army was equally debased, causing the king to take severe action. He issued instructions that all the moneyers operating the mints be rounded up and mutilated, and this was carried out under the supervision of Roger of Salisbury at Winchester, each of them losing his right hand. Some accounts say they were also castrated. Rather than causing outrage, the Chronicle presumably reflecting the opinion of the time, says this was done 'with much justice, because they had ruined this land with the great quantity of bad metal,' their silver pennies being found to be largely tin. After this, the number of mints was severely reduced and the coinage produced more closely supervised.

By the end of 1124, then, the cards had once more fallen in Henrys favour. The rebels were defeated and there was peace in England and in Normandy. William Clito, the joker in the pack, was still at liberty in France, however, and well able to cause more trouble in the future.

More importantly, in Henry's mind at least, he still had no son and heir with whom to trump Clito's potential challenge and secure the future of Henry's hard-won lands.

11

A Surfeit of Lampreys
(1125–1135)

It is possible Henry hoped his problems might be solved by the birth of a grandson. Even though there would likely be a long period of regency, no doubt he felt he could count on his son Robert of Gloucester to watch over the child's interests, and a boy in direct descent from himself, even if through the female line, would have a greater claim to English loyalty than any nephew. His daughter Matilda had been married for more than ten years, however, and so far no surviving grandchild had been produced, though one source claims there was a child who died soon after birth.

The situation might owe something to the unrest within the Holy Roman Empire throughout this period, as the emperor's ongoing dispute with the pope over investitures undermined his support at home. Even during the period before the actual marriage of Matilda and Emperor Henry V, the money she had brought as a dowry was being put to use to further that dispute. Almost immediately after their formal betrothal, Henry had gathered an army and marched into Italy. His dispute with the pope was already four years old and perhaps he thought he would have an advantage in further negotiations with control of Lombardy and an army at his back. He might have been right. Negotiations duly took place and, surprisingly, in February 1111 resulted in an agreement between emperor and pope made at Sutri: Henry would give up the right to invest bishops and archbishops with their symbols of office, the ring and crozier, In exchange, Pope Paschal would direct the German churches to return to the empire all lands and properties that had been granted to them from the time of Charlemagne onwards.

On the face of it, it seems an unusual agreement and one unlikely to succeed. Nonetheless, preparations were quickly made in Rome for Henry's coronation as Holy Roman Emperor. When the day came, however, on 12 February 1111, the terms of the agreement were read out and caused such uproar, especially among the German bishops, that Paschal refused to go ahead with the ceremony. Henry in turn renounced his side of the agreement and amidst turmoil in St Peter's, seized the pope and sixteen cardinals and carried them away to imprisonment. For two months Paschal held out, and then caved in and agreed to crown Henry. Furthermore he agreed that the emperor would have a 'privilege of investiture" allowing him to continue investing bishops throughout his territories. On 13 April 1111 Henry was duly crowned at St Peter's Basilica in Rome, and shortly afterwards returned to Germany to deal with troubles in his lands north of the Alps.

The 'privilege' was immediately denounced by the Church, protests being led by Archbishop Guy of Vienne, later to be Pope Calixtus, who demanded Henry should be excommunicated. Paschal hesitated to do this as he had sworn not to take reprisals for his ill-treatment by the emperor, but he did confirm the declaration of a Lateran Council the following year that held the agreement with Henry to be void.

In January 1114 the twelve-year-old Matilda was finally married to the thirty-two-year-old Henry. They had little time to establish a settled life, however, before further internal troubles broke out involving a war with Cologne, and barely had this been subdued than Italian matters once again needed attention. Matilda of Tuscany had died and reputedly (though no documentation was found) had left all her lands to the papacy. Henry V declared the lands belonged to his empire, and in 1116 once more crossed the Alps with an army, this time taking his young wife with him.

At about this time Pope Paschal formally declared his 'privilege' concession to Henry was invalid. He sent an envoy, Mauritius, Archbishop of Braga, to negotiate with the emperor, threatening excommunication if Henry continued to flout his laws. Mauritius, not always the most reliable supporter of the papacy, promptly defected. When, early in 1117, the emperor began to march on Rome Paschal fled, and on Easter Sunday, 23 March 1117, Henry and Matilda were crowned by the archbishop.

Matilda always claimed the title 'Empress', though this is the only possible coronation she received as such, and its authority is extremely dubious. Mauritius was certainly not a pope at the time, and it has been suggested this was more of a formal 'crown-wearing' than a coronation. It was enough, however, to have consequences. Paschal immediately sacked Mauritius and published the excommunication of Henry, which, of course, caused great delight in Cologne and led to a further falling away of support for the emperor in the German lands.

As soon as Henry and Matilda withdrew to northern Italy, Paschal returned to Rome and died there in January 1118. A successor, Gelasius II, was unanimously elected, and was briefly imprisoned by supporters of the emperor. Public outcry led to his release, but by then Henry and his army were looming, and Gelasius fled from Rome. Thereafter he refused to meet any representatives of the emperor or to hold any discussions on the matter. As a result, Henry declared his election invalid and set up the Archbishop of Braga as a rival pope, with the name of Gregory VIII. In reply, on 7 April 1118 Gelasius excommunicated both Henry and his pope.

By now unrest in his German lands meant Henry could no longer remain in Italy, but he left Matilda there as his regent. For the next eighteen months, the seventeen-year-old ruled in his name, but, of course, no contact with her husband meant no son and heir for the empire, and no grandson for her father.

Matters had moved on before Matilda rejoined her husband towards the end of 1119. Gelasius had died and been replaced by a new pope, Calixtus II, who despite his earlier opposition to the emperor, now seemed ready to negotiate. An embassy was sent to Henry V at Strasbourg, making enough progress for him to withdraw his support from Gregory VIII. The Council at Rheims in October 1119 that proved so useful to the English King Henry, was also intended to resolve the dispute with his son-in-law. When the emperor turned up with an army, however, he was again excommunicated, thereby achieving some kind of record in having been excommunicated by three popes in a row.

By this time Calixtus had achieved enough support to return to Rome and force out his papal rival. Gregory was duly taken prisoner at Sutri in April 1121 and spent the rest of his days 'imprisoned' in a monastery. Meanwhile the negotiations with Henry continued, finally resulting in 1122 in the Concordat of Worms, a compromise very similar to that achieved by Henry of England with Pope Paschal some sixteen years before.

Now, if ever, might be the time for Matilda and her husband to produce an heir but still no child came. Within two years the emperor was suffering from his final illness, generally identified as cancer, and on 23 May 1125 he died.

'On his deathbed,' says Vitalis, the emperor 'bequeathed the emblems of imperial power to the Empress Matilda.' What his intentions were we don't know. It is inconceivable in the context of the times, that he meant her to try and carry on ruling alone, and in fact her position was extremely weak. With no child, she had no chance even of a regency role. She was also put under the protection of his obvious heir, his nephew Frederick of Swabia, but if he intended her to use possession of the insignia to influence the succession in Frederick's favour, that plan misfired when Adelbert, Archbishop of Mainz, took charge of the election.

Somehow, we are not told how, he obtained possession of the 'imperial ornaments' from Matilda. Then, being a long-time enemy of Henry, he persuaded the assembled German nobles that there should be no hereditary right to kingship and that they could elect whomsoever they chose to be the new emperor. Vitalis describes, probably inaccurately, how three possible candidates were lined up and the archbishop's favourite selected. What is indisputable, however, is that Lothar of Saxony was elected as the next emperor, a move that sparked an immediate civil war.

There was no place in this for the young widow. William of Malmesbury suggests that she was 'recalled' to England by her father, and came reluctantly, not wanting to leave the culture and people she had grown up with, not to mention her extensive estates in the German lands. Nevertheless, it is likely she had no real choice unless she wanted to remarry immediately or enter a convent. For more than a decade, she had been an independent person of consequence. Now she was to again come under her father's governance.

They had not met since she was a child. She had attempted to visit him in 1122, possibly to discuss the consequences of her brother's death, but had been prevented by Charles of Flanders who would not allow her to cross his land. This probably had more to do with her husband than her father, since Flanders was not always on good terms with the emperor. Now she arrived in Normandy with what she had salvaged from her former state, namely her jewels, her own regalia, two of the crowns of Henry V and 'the hand of St James the Apostle'. This last, whose provenance can be traced back at least as far as 640AD, had been in the German Imperial Treasury since 1072, and it is not at all certain that Matilda had authority to remove it.

The Empress and her father spent a year together in Normandy and we don't know a great amount about their dealings, but it seems the twenty-four-year-old Matilda was not slow to give advice to the king. When in September 1126 they crossed to England, they brought with them prisoners of Henry's recent campaign, Waleran of Meulan and Hugh of Chateauneuf. Waleran was initially imprisoned at Bridgnorth and later at Wallingford, while Hugh was held at Windsor. At the same time, Robert Curthose was moved from the custody of Roger of Salisbury at Devizes to that of Robert of Gloucester at Bristol. The only explanation for these moves given by the Anglo-Saxon Chronicle is that this was done on the advice of the king's daughter.

The death of Henry V and the return of his daughter gave the English king another card to play in the matter of the succession, and it is clear that that and the remarriage of Matilda were uppermost in his mind at this time. How much Matilda was consulted, and how much she was simply instructed, is a matter for conjecture, but Malmesbury names two suitors, one from Lorraine and one from Lombardy, who were turned away because Henry had formulated other plans for his daughter.

It may be that he decided to spring one surprise at a time, or possibly the marriage was still only a vague idea, to be pursued more vigorously in the light of later events. Certainly the succession was uppermost in the king's mind when he called together a larger than usual court at Christmas in 1126. David of Scotland was there, the first time he had visited Henry since becoming king on the death of his brother in 1124. Possibly he had been consulted on the matter in hand, or it may have been as much of a surprise to him as to everyone else when Henry convened his council at Westminster immediately after Christmas and revealed his plan.

William of Malmesbury gives the fullest description of what happened. The king, 'having held much previous and long-continued deliberation ... now at this council compelled all the nobility of England, as well as the bishops and abbots, to make oath that, if he should die without male issue, they would, without delay or hesitation, accept his daughter Matilda, the late empress, as their sovereign.' It was, of course, a Norman tradition that oaths should be sworn and homage paid to the heir apparent during the lifetime of the reigning sovereign. It had been done for William Adelin when he was barely into his teens, but never had this been done for a woman, even one such as Matilda who had experience of ruling as a regent, despite her youth. There is no mention of homage here, and the word 'compelled' is instructive. Clearly there was some opposition to such a move, and Roger of Salisbury for one is likely to have opposed it, given his later comments. He it was, though, who had to outline and justify the plan, reciting the lineage of Matilda, whose 'grandfather, uncle and father ... were kings', while descent on her mother's side traced as far back as Egbert, king of Wessex.

Whatever reservations and reluctance there might be, the power and personality of Henry carried the day. Malmesbury is quite clear that, 'All therefore in this council who were considered as persons of any note, took the oath,' beginning with William Corbeil, Archbishop of Canterbury, his fellow bishops, then the nobility, with David of Scotland first, followed by Stephen, now Count of Boulogne; Robert, Earl of Gloucester; and the others in descending order. The last to take the oath were the abbots of the various monasteries. 'Thus,' concludes Malmesbury, 'All being bound by fealty and by oath, they ... departed to their homes,' no doubt with a great deal to think about.

There was now no longer any doubt. Son, nephews and all had been put aside in favour of a woman, and Matilda's marriage, for surely she would be married again, became a matter of vital concern to everyone in the country. More immediately, however, another marriage occurred, which may well have been prompted by Henry's announcement.

In January 1127 Louis of France again took up the cause of William Clito, having apparently taken no interest in the wanderer for several years. Possibly he had felt that while Henry had no obvious heir, the boy might have been in line for at least the Duchy of Normandy, if not the throne of England, should the king die with no legitimate descendant. The recent events in Westminster, however, made clear that that would not happen. Louis, therefore, called a meeting of his great lords and 'earnestly entreated them to take compassion on William the Norman and give him their succour.' Taking the lead in this, he arranged for William to marry Joanna de Montferrat, who was a daughter of Queen Adelaide's own mother from a second marriage. Having tied him close, but not too close, to the intimate royal family, Louis next provided him with lands, Pontoise, Chaumont, Mantes and 'all the Vexin' – that is if he could get it. Vitalis records, however, that before Lent William went to Gisors 'at the head of some troops to lay claim to Normandy, and the Normans paid him the respect due to their natural lord.'

The idea of William Clito in possession of Gisors, that key castle so often fought over, must have been a severe shock for Henry, as no doubt Louis had intended, but worse was to come. On 2 March 1127, Charles the Good, Count of Flanders, was assassinated at a church in Bruges. 'While praying to God, prostrate on the floor, he was slain,' says Vitalis, adding that 'almost all his attendants were cruelly massacred on the spot.' Charles had been trying to curb the power of a mighty family in Flanders and dozens of people were implicated in the plot. Violence broke out at once, as vengeance was sought for these sacrilegious murders, and this threatened to turn into civil war, since Charles had no son and there was no other obvious heir.

Of the immediate descendants of Robert the Frisian there was a legitimate grandson, Thierry of Alsace, through the female line, and another grandson, William of Ypres, who was the illegitimate offspring of Robert's younger son, Philip. Looking further back to Count Baldwin V brought into the picture Henry, King of England, and his surviving brother and sister and their offspring, including Stephen, Count of Boulogne, and William Clito. Charles the Good had inherited through the female line but he had been nominated by the previous count, whereas none of those now recognised as possible claimants had that advantage.

William of Ypres was first to put himself forward and, according to Vitalis, was active in pursuing the murderers. As well as his illegitimacy, however, there was also a strong suspicion he might have been involved in the plot himself. One account records that, when he was demanding that a prisoner should name his accomplices, he was told, 'You know as well as I do.'

As the chaos threatened to get out of hand, Louis of France arrived at Arras on 20 March and summoned the Flemish lords to meet him. As overlord of Flanders, he had a legitimate interest in the succession, and he brought with him his own candidate, William Clito. Under pressure from the king, Clito was installed as Count of Flanders before the end of March, and then by a mixture of threats, and promises to reduce rents and tolls, they advanced from city to city across Flanders, accepting homage as they went. At Bruges the 'bloody butchers' of Charles the Good were taken prisoner, and at Ypres, William of Ypres was besieged, and captured on 26 April. By early May, Clito seemed to be in complete control, 'having obtained the duchy by the king's gift and hereditary right,' as Vitalis puts it. He was, no doubt, delighted to be able, as one of his first actions, to give the castle of Montreuil to his faithful protector, Helias of Saint-Saens, but was destined to get far more trouble than joy from his new-found status.

Orchestrator of that trouble, of course, was his 'wicked uncle', Henry of England. Robert of Torigny seems to suggest that Henry only heard of the assassination and the takeover by William Clito at his palace at Woodstock at Easter 1127, but the news of the murder at least must have crossed the Channel long before. Henry's response was to call a council in London on 8 May, and then shortly after to send Matilda back to Normandy. She was accompanied by her half-brother, Robert of Gloucester, and by Brian FitzCount, illegitimate son of Alan of Brittany, who had become one of Henry's most reliable followers. If Matilda's remarriage had been only a vague idea before, it now became a vital part of Henry's reaction to events in Flanders.

Vitalis suggests that when William Clito was established in Flanders, Louis of France took back his earlier gift of the Vexin. Be that as it may, Henry now found himself with France as a traditional enemy on his south-eastern border, and a new enemy in Flanders to the east. He could not afford for the usual alliance to bring in Fulk of Anjou as an enemy to the south-west. Recent relations with Fulk had not been entirely cordial, but slowly and carefully Henry now set about negotiating a marriage between his daughter Matilda and Fulk's son Geoffrey.

Changes in Fulk's own situation helped ease his way. His earlier visit to the Holy Land had made an impression. While there he is believed to have joined the newly-formed Knights Templar, and he was still contributing to the funds of this organisation. At some point in 1127 he received a proposition from Baldwin II, King of Jerusalem, which would draw him back to the East. Baldwin had no son, and although his daughter Melisande was already taking a full part in ruling his kingdom, he knew she would need a strong husband to protect her interests after his death. He proposed that Fulk, whose wife had died the year before, should marry Melisande to safeguard her inheritance. Initially he proposed that Fulk would simply be a consort, but the count held out to be co-ruler and, for six months or so, seemed to be carrying on parallel negotiations with Henry and with Baldwin.

In the meantime, the English king could not let matters lie in Flanders while William Clito became stronger and more firmly in control. Initially he financed an intervention by Stephen of Boulogne, who had a claim of his own to the county. To undermine the Flemish economy, Henry forbade the export of English wool to the Flanders cloth trade. William, however, was being bolstered by support from Normandy and in August, according to Vitalis, he marched an army against Stephen and 'laid waste his territories with fire and sword in the most cruel manner.' Stephen was not long in suing for peace, and a truce was agreed between them.

By this time, Henry himself had crossed to Normandy. The marriage prospects were rapidly improving but it is possible he had to deal with Matilda's own objections to the match. She was an empress and she was being asked to marry the son of a mere count. Furthermore, she was a grown woman of twenty-five and Geoffrey of Anjou was barely fourteen. Nevertheless the alliance was agreed by their fathers and the lopsided betrothal took place.

By January 1128 the tide had begun to turn against William Clito. His actions in tracking down those involved in the murder of his predecessor were more enthusiastic than wise. Using all his efforts to search them out, Vitalis tells us, he 'spared no-one without regard to nobility, power, rank or penitence.' Nor did he seem too scrupulous in searching for evidence, with some 111 persons finally 'confessing' to the murder, and being condemned to punishments which, even at the time, drew comments about their cruelty. Not only people actively involved, but also their friends, families and sympathisers seem to have been drawn into this, and not surprisingly there was a backlash.

By now, too, Thierry of Alsace had launched his own challenge, urged on, of course, by Henry, fighting a proxy war with supplies of money if not troops. Thierry and his men were described as 'noble and powerful, distinguished for their courage and intrepidity, and formidable for their wealth ... and popularity with their countrymen.' Slowly but surely they began to gain ground. By the end of February St Omer and Ghent had turned against William. In another month Bruges had welcomed Thierry as Count of Flanders.

An appeal for help was sent to Louis of France, who initially responded by returning to Flanders and helping to besiege Lille, a hotbed of support for Thierry. Abruptly, though, Louis withdrew and hurried back to France where internal jealousies and expulsions within his own household had had the unlikely effect of driving Amaury de Montfort away from his allegiance to Louis and into the arms of Henry of England. Taking advantage of this, Henry had marched an army into France and occupied one of Amaury's castles at Epernon, where he sat for eight days threatening Paris, as securely as if he were in his own lands.

It was not a serious invasion. As soon as Louis returned with his forces Henry withdrew, but as a diversion to draw the French king away from Flanders, it had worked very well. Back in Normandy, Henry turned his attention to the imminent wedding of his daughter to the young Geoffrey of Anjou.

On 31 May, the Feast of the Ascension, Fulk of Anjou took the crusader's cross at Le Mans, intending to abdicate in favour of his son as soon as he had settled his affairs in Anjou. Ten days later, at Pentecost, Henry conferred knighthood on his prospective son-in-law, and a week after that, Geoffrey and Matilda were married in the cathedral at Le Mans.

Left on his own in Flanders, William Clito seemed to be holding back the tide of rebellion. On 21 June, with an army made up of Norman and French allies, he defeated Thierry of Alsace at the Battle of Axspoele, forcing his rival to retreat. Indeed, many of the chroniclers admired his prowess in the field, though Vitalis sounds a note of caution. 'He often marshalled his troops and commanded them like an able general,' he says, 'but still oftener he fought like a gallant soldier in arms.' This willingness to pitch into a fight alongside his men was to be his downfall.

On 12 July, in an assault on a castle at Aalst, Clito was wounded. According to Vitalis he was 'attempting to seize the lance of a foot-soldier who still made resistance,' and was 'wounded by the steel blade which he was endeavouring to catch in his right hand.' The blade entered the fleshy part of his hand between the thumb and the palm, and also pierced his arm. The wound as such was not serious, but from the description of its aftermath gangrene had quickly set in, 'and his whole arm up to the shoulder turned as black as coal.' A few days later, the twenty-five-year-old William Clito died.

An uncanny story is recorded concerning his father, Robert Curthose, still imprisoned in England. On the day of his son's death he is said to have dreamed his own arm was struck by a lance and rendered useless. When he awoke he cried at once, 'Alas, my son is dead,' and this well before news could possibly have reached him in his prison.

In fact for several days, the ever-faithful Helias of Saint-Saens concealed the fact that William had died. Only when the castle garrison at Aalst had surrendered did he let the news spread. When the lord of Aalst was taken to view the body he is said to have burst into tears, and then joined the party taking the young count for burial at St Omer. The eulogies recorded by the chroniclers make much of his nobility, the shortness and sadness of his life and his bravery. Henry of Huntingdon in particular, always a little partial to Clito and given to poetry, quotes a verse praising his refusal to retreat from a fight. 'Dauntless he turns to flight from no attack; no wingéd arrows pierce him in the back.' The same line is referred to by Robert of Torigny, while Huntingdon adds that William was, 'Himself the thunder's bolt, the lightning's flash.'

At some point in his last days the young man had dictated letters to be delivered to his uncle and long-time adversary, Henry of England. In them he asked the king's forgiveness 'for all the ill he had done him,' though some might think it should have been the other way around. He also begged him to pardon all those who had supported William against his uncle. This Henry was happy to do, no doubt feeling a great weight lifted from him by his nephew's death. Some at least, William Roumare among them, did return to Henry, while others took the cross and followed Fulk of Anjou to Jerusalem. It seems unlikely that Helias of Saint-Saens was ever reconciled with the English king, and he is believed to have died that same year. Whether William sent letters to his own father, and what they might contain, is not recorded.

The death of William Clito brought an end to all the rebellions. As Vitalis reports, 'with him departed the strength and daring of all who abetted him against his uncle.' In due course Thierry of Alsace was confirmed as Count of Flanders, making peace with Louis of France and renewing the traditional treaty of friendship with England. The other rebels being left without a focus, peace at last descended on Normandy.

In other places, however, the mood was not so tranquil. The Anglo-Saxon Chronicle recording the marriage of Matilda and Geoffrey notes: 'Howbeit, this displeased all the French and the English.' Many of those in England felt they had been tricked into taking their oath to make Matilda queen. Very few had known of the marriage before it had taken place, and the future status of Geoffrey seemed to have been left deliberately vague. Was he to be king or merely consort? Malmesbury writes that 'all declared, prophetically as it were, that after (Henry's) death they would break their plighted oath.' One particular opponent of the marriage seems to have been Roger of Salisbury. Again it is Malmesbury who tells us, 'I have frequently heard Roger, Bishop of Salisbury, say that he was freed from the oath he had taken for the empress; for that he had sworn conditionally, that the king should not marry his daughter to anyone out of the kingdom without his consent, or that of the rest of the nobility.' No-one, he claims, had advised that the match be made, and the only people who had known of the king's plans were Robert of Gloucester, Brian FitzCount and the Bishop of Louviers. Malmesbury adds that he knows Roger of Salisbury was 'a man who knew how to accommodate himself to every varying time,' so presumably the bishop was speaking out boldly after the king's death and not before, but he then adds, 'I write the general belief of the people.'

Certainly there was a long history of friction between Normandy and Anjou, which sentiment they had no doubt brought with them to England. Henry might have pointed out that the whole aim of the marriage was to bring a traditional enemy into an alliance. The fact remained that Anjou *was* a traditional enemy, and the marriage was not popular in England or in Normandy.

Nor was it popular between the couple themselves. It seems fairly clear that Matilda and Geoffrey disliked each other, and when their respective fathers had departed in 1129, Henry to England and Fulk to Jerusalem, it was not long before Matilda left her husband and returned to Normandy. No doubt, in her view, the death of Clito six weeks after the marriage had made the whole exercise pointless. It is possible it may not even have been consummated and she was hoping for an annulment. After all, Henry had freed the prisoners Waleran and Hugh whom he had recently locked up in England. Why should she too not be freed?

One account, that of the Durham monk continuing the Chronicle of Symeon of Durham, suggests it was in fact Geoffrey who threw out his wife, but gives no reason for this. The sixteen-year-old was now Count of Anjou, and there may have been trouble about Matilda's dowry, which was to consist, partly at least, of certain Norman castles. None of these had as yet been handed over, and indeed wouldn't be handed over in Henry's lifetime, causing further trouble later on. It may also be, of course, that Matilda simply reminded Geoffrey once too often that she was an empress and he a mere count.

For whatever reason, the couple were now living apart and Henry's hopes for a grandson seemed to be receding once more. This must have been all the more galling when he heard that Louis of France had had his thirteen-year-old son Philip consecrated as next King of France. Henry was by now more than sixty years old, and though surrounded by illegitimate children, still had no legitimate male heir on whom he could hope to bestow a crown.

It is around this time that there appears in the chronicle of John of Worcester what he claims to have been a series of nightmares suffered by Henry in the course of one night. In the first a band of peasants, complete with their farming implements, stood by his bed and began to rage and gnash their teeth at him, demanding their rights. In the second he was similarly threatened by a large band of knights, wearing armour and helmets, and carrying lances, swords and arrows. They threatened to kill him and cut him into pieces. Finally it was a group of archbishops, bishops, abbots and priors, who prodded him with their croziers and glared at him because of his plundering of Church lands. Between each of these dreams, apparently, Henry woke and leapt up to seize his weapons and defend himself, but found no-one there. The story is rather weakened by the chronicler then declaring that the three visions had been witnessed by one Grimbald, a skilled physician – skilled, indeed, if he could witness another man's nightmares – who advised Henry to redeem his sins by almsgiving.

Whether it was that or other intimations of mortality, Henry certainly became active at this time in supporting the Church. He had already founded a great abbey at Reading soon after the death of his son, 'for the salvation of my soul and the souls of King William my father, King William my brother, and Queen Maud my wife, and all my ancestors and successors.' He also began paying an annual sum of about £3,000 to the abbey at Cluny, which had got into financial difficulties over the building of a new church for the monastery. In May 1130 he was also present in Rochester for the consecration of the new Norman cathedral, during which time the town caught fire and was largely destroyed.

In the summer of 1130 he returned to Normandy. It was probably the first time he did so without being faced by an emergency, and also possibly the closest he ever came to taking a holiday. He travelled south, maybe detouring to visit the Abbey of Bec, and spent some time in Chartres as a guest of his nephew Count Theobald of Blois. It was there that he met the controversial new pope, Innocent II.

In February of that year Pope Honorius, successor to Calixtus, had died, and on the same day one group of cardinals had elected Cardinal Gregorio Papareschi to replace him. Gregorio took the name Innocent II and was consecrated the next day. Another group of cardinals, however, with strong Roman backing, claimed the election was invalid and elected their own candidate, Pietro Pierleoni, who took the name Anacletus II. Innocent was forced to flee Rome, but since he had been involved in the Concordat of Worms he had the backing of the Holy Roman Emperor, and soon others accepted him, too. The Anglo-Saxon Chronicle records that he was 'acknowledged by the emperor of Saxony, by the king of France, by Henry of England and by all on this side of the mountains,' while Robert of Torigny quotes a saying, 'Peter possesses Rome but Gregory has the whole world.' William of Malmesbury seems to have his doubts, giving the text of a letter written by Anacletus which claims Gregory was elected, 'in a corner, in a hidden place, in darkness and in the shadow of death.' When Henry met him at Chartres, though, he had no hesitation in prostrating himself before him, and later entertained him in some style at Rouen. There Henry is believed to have discussed with him the problem of his daughter's marriage, and the pope may well have communicated his thoughts to Geoffrey of Anjou.

Certainly when Henry returned to England in the summer of 1131 he had Matilda with him, and in September he called a council at Northampton. What happened there varies according to which account is read. The Anglo-Saxon Chronicle and Vitalis don't mention it at all. Henry of Huntingdon and Robert of Torigny, in more or less the same words, suggest the question was simply whether or not Matilda should be sent back to Geoffrey. 'It was determined that the king's daughter should be restored to her husband ... as he demanded,' they say, indicating that, if the count had thrown her out before, he had now changed his mind.

Again, however, it is William of Malmesbury who gives details of a more significant occurrence at the council. He says that 'the oath of fidelity to her was renewed by such as had already sworn and also taken by such as hitherto had not.' Clearly this refers to the earlier oath sworn at Westminster in 1126, and equally makes it quite clear that this was a second oath, taken after the unpopular marriage, and after that marriage was accepted as valid and ongoing. The oath-taking seems to be confirmed by the account of William of Newburgh.

Matilda was therefore again packed off to Anjou to resume relations with Geoffrey, 'and he received her with the pomp worthy of such an illustrious princess,' which may have made the reunion a little less frosty. Once more, no doubt, there was an anxious wait for a child, though the chronicles record only that Henry spent Christmas at Dunstable and Easter at his beloved Woodstock. They are more concerned with the pestilence in farm animals that swept the country in 1132, carrying off whole herds of pigs and stalls of cattle, and making meat scarce and expensive throughout the land.

Henry spent Christmas 1132 at Windsor, and for the first time it is recorded that the king was sick. No details are given about the kind of sickness, and he seems to have recovered quickly enough. Then in March came the news everyone had been waiting for. The empress had been safely delivered of a baby boy, to be named Henry. The sixty-four-year-old king was at last the grandfather of a potential male heir.

No doubt he was anxious to assure himself that the boy was healthy and strong, but he had affairs of State, and in particular affairs of the Church to settle first, and it was not until the summer that he would leave again for Normandy. Numerous chroniclers point out that he left on the anniversary of the very day he had become king, though they differ as to whether that was 2 August, the day his brother died, or 5 August, the day he was crowned and anointed. They also record all manner of 'portents' about this time, such as an eclipse and an earthquake and a warning from a recluse that he might go, but he would not come back. We might put these down to imaginative hindsight but for the corroborative detail added by Malmesbury that, 'at the time of the earthquake, the wall of the house in which I was sitting was lifted by two shocks and settled again with a third.' 'Notwithstanding,' says John of Worcester, 'King Henry crossed the sea, leaving England for Normandy.'

Almost as soon as he got there Matilda was pregnant again, and apparently went to pay a long visit to her father in Rouen. They would have been there in February 1134 when they heard of the death of Robert Curthose at Cardiff Castle where he had spent his final years. He was by then in his eighties, a fact that may have encouraged Henry to believe he might live long enough to see his grandson grow up. Robert was buried with all honours due to a crusader and a royal duke in the abbey of St Peter, Gloucester, later to become Gloucester Cathedral. It is intriguing to wonder whether Henry would have attended the funeral if he had been in England. As it was, he might have been a little relieved that the question did not arise. Nevertheless, he made a donation to the abbey to provide that a light would always be burning before the high altar in honour of his brother, and an effigy of the duke, made some time later, can still be seen in the Cathedral. This long, slim figure of a crusader is doubly flattering since Robert was always described as short and stoutly built and, like his father before him, he had become fat in old age, no doubt due to luxurious living and lack of exercise.

The birth of Matilda's second son, Geoffrey, at the beginning of June 1134 was not as straightforward as the first. She became extremely ill and it was feared she would die. It is maybe a mark of her character, however, that even in extremis she was arguing with her father about where she should be buried. He wanted Rouen, among her ancestors, while she favoured the Abbey of Bec. In the event neither was required, as she made a full recovery.

'During the whole of this year,' writes Robert of Torigny, 'King Henry lingered in Normandy, rejoicing in his grandchildren, Henry and Geoffrey.' The scene of domestic bliss, however, was not to last long. Already storm clouds were gathering in Anjou and southern Normandy, and when troubles came it may have surprised the old king that his daughter took her husband's part rather than his own.

There had been disturbances along the Welsh border in 1134 and it seems Henry was preparing to return to England to quell them with his presence, as he had done before. However Henry of Huntingdon says he was continually detained in Normandy, 'on account of sundry disagreements which had their origin in various causes between the king and the Count of Anjou, and which were fomented by the arts of his daughter.' He gives no more details, but as usual the matter is expanded on by Orderic Vitalis.

'Geoffrey of Anjou,' he says, 'coveted the wealth of his father-in-law,' and in particular wanted to get his hands on the castles that had been promised as Matilda's dowry. Another account suggests that both he and Matilda wanted the Norman lords to swear fealty to them while Henry lived. Perhaps during her stay at Rouen she had picked up on the suspicion with which her husband was viewed, and the unpopularity of her marriage to an Angevin. Geoffrey's status after Henry's death had still not been spelled out, and they may have felt a sacred oath was the only thing that would help them obtain the inheritance they had been promised. It would not, after all, be unprecedented. Such oaths had been sworn to her brother when he was only a child.

On the other hand, says Vitalis, Henry 'had no inclination to allow anyone, while he lived, to have any pre-eminence over himself, or even to be his equal. In consequence,' he adds, 'the arrogant young prince was so incensed that he gave offence to the king, both by threats and acts of violence.' One of his acts of violence involved besieging and burning down the town of Henry's son-in-law, Roscelin de Beaumont, who had married his illegitimate daughter Constance. Geoffrey also, says Vitalis, encouraged discord among the lords of Normandy and gave shelter and assistance to those in dispute with the king.

One such was William Talvas, son of Robert de Bellème. He had been restored to the Bellème lands in 1119, probably at the insistence of Fulk of Anjou, but had not been allowed to recover his castles. Now Henry repeatedly summoned him to his court and repeatedly he refused to come, being urged on by Geoffrey of Anjou and fleeing to him when the king finally lost patience and stripped him of his lands.

Through the summer there was a simmering unrest through south and central Normandy, kept in check by the king's presence as he journeyed from castle to castle, from Sées to Alençon, to Argentan. Fortifications were improved and garrisons strengthened, while Roger de Tosny, suspected of sympathising with the potential rebels, had his castle at Conches occupied by the king's troops. The storm, however, didn't break. Henry was still too strong to be openly challenged.

By November matters were calm enough for the king to plan a hunting expedition in the Forest of Lyons, some 20 miles from Rouen. On Monday, 25 November, the fifteenth anniversary of the death of his son, the king spent the day hunting, and arrived in the evening at a favoured lodging, the castle at Lyon-le-Foret. During the night he suddenly fell ill, and according to Vitalis, 'lay at the point of death from Tuesday to Sunday'.

Some accounts suggest that the recent stresses might have contributed to the illness, but it is Henry of Huntingdon who introduces the famous 'lampreys', though he says nothing about a surfeit. A lamprey is an eel-like fish, meaty-tasting, and therefore frequently eaten by the upper classes on the many days when, in medieval times, the Church forbade the eating of meat. Robert of Torigny, copying and expanding a little on Henry of Huntingdon, tells us that Henry 'dined off lampreys, a food which always did him harm, and of which he was exceedingly fond.' He adds, 'His physician had forbidden him to eat of this dish.'

He then describes in detail the aftermath, how the meal introduced to the king's stomach 'many an evil humour,' and excited those 'humours' already there. This 'chilled to a dangerous extent the old man's body,' and the chill was followed by an acute fever. It is only fair to lampreys to note that he could be describing a straightforward case of acute food poisoning.

During the long week of his illness Henry was able to order his affairs, directing Robert of Gloucester to draw money from the treasury to pay his household and his hired troops, and later, when it appeared he may be dying, to confess his sins to the Archbishop of Rouen and receive absolution and the Holy Sacrament. He gave the traditional instructions that exiles be allowed to return and prisoners be freed, though all of his most important prisoners except William of Mortain were already dead. Most importantly, according to William of Malmesbury, he was asked about the succession, whereupon 'he awarded all his territories, on either side of the sea, to his daughter, in legitimate and perpetual succession.'

For six days the king struggled against his illness while there gathered at his bedside some of the leading nobles from England and Normandy – his son, Robert of Gloucester; his son-in-law, Rotrou of Perche; Waleran de Meulan and his brother Robert, Earl of Leicester; and William of Warenne. Finally on the Sunday night, either 'early in the night,' according to Vitalis, or 'about midnight,' according to Malmesbury, 'unable to stand out the struggle, this great king died.'

12

The End of an Era

'The invincible monarch, the wise duke, the illustrious hero who governed so many nations under a just administration, alas is dead; and the sorrow for him is universal.' So says Orderic Vitalis at the beginning of his eulogy for Henry, and it is clear that his sorrow is not just for the death of the king but for the troubles that will inevitably follow it. It seems to have been abundantly clear that, despite their oaths and homages, the nobles of Normandy and England had not the slightest intention of following the path laid out for them by their king and duke. 'As soon as the death of her pious prince was known,' Vitalis writes a little earlier, 'On one and the same day, the Normans rushed like raving wolves to the prey,' and later he adds, 'It is as clear as light that peace is insupportable to these people.'

A quick glance at the names of those gathered at the dying king's bedside reveals some notable absentees. Geoffrey and Matilda were, of course, in Anjou and engaged in a face-off with Henry's army, so they were never likely to be in attendance at the end. Theobald of Blois was at home in his county, possibly watching out for Henry's interests in the area, and too far away to reach the king in time once it was clear he was dying. Theobald's brother Stephen, Count of Boulogne, was another who might have been expected to attend but who did not, and the reason for this quickly became apparent.

The anonymous writer of the *Gesta Stephani* – the Acts of Stephen – suggests that it was only when he heard of the king's death that Stephen was, in a moment, struck by its possibilities, and 'instantly conceiving a great design, he hastened to the coast, and embarking, with fortunately a favourable wind, he sailed for England on which his thoughts were fixed.' It seems unbelievable, however, that his bold bid for a crown could have been such a spur of the moment adventure. There must surely have been at least some sounding out of support in England, and possibly some longer term dreaming and planning on the part of Stephen himself. He may well have believed he was, as the *Gesta* claims, 'the best beloved by Henry ... of all his nephews,' but that didn't mean England would be ready to receive him with open arms.

At first it might have appeared he had overreached himself. Robert of Gloucester had garrisoned the towns of Dover and Canterbury, and one account declares that Dover would not let him land and Canterbury barred its gates to him. The Archbishop of Canterbury, however was more welcoming, and we find that within a week of Henry's death Stephen was happily ensconced in his own estate just outside London.

Stephen was lucky in finding something of a power vacuum in England. Those leading nobles, including the mighty Robert of Gloucester, who had been with the king at the end, had remained with his body to see it honourably borne back to Henry's chosen resting place at Reading Abbey. Delayed by the weather, it would be some weeks before they crossed the Channel, and meanwhile Stephen and his supporters lost no time in pushing his claim to the throne of England.

To succeed he would need support in London and in Winchester, and the backing of the leaders of the clergy and the administration. London came over to his side at once, probably in exchange for promises of privileges. They 'came out to meet him with shouts of joy, and received him in triumph,' says the *Gesta*, 'regaining in Stephen what they had lost in their protector Henry.'

Roger of Salisbury, who had never been keen on the succession of Matilda, now handed over the treasury at Winchester, while the Bishop of Winchester, who happened to be Stephen's brother Henry, persuaded the clergy that the oaths they had taken no longer applied in the changed circumstances. This was made all the easier when the royal steward, Hugh Bigod, claimed, in direct contradiction of Malmesbury's statement, that on his deathbed Henry had changed his mind and nominated Stephen as his heir. The result of all this was that, long before any serious challenge could be mounted, Stephen, son of Adela of Blois and grandson of the Conqueror, had been crowned and consecrated in Westminster Abbey as Stephen I of England.

In Normandy, too, the wishes of Henry were being ignored. Vitalis tells of a meeting of Norman nobles at Neubourg though he does not name those present. There the feeling was that Theobald of Blois should take over at least the duchy, if not England as well. Messages may very well have been sent to Theobald concerning this decision and it seems he set off to Normandy in response. At about the same time, however, news came from England that Stephen had been crowned king, and rather than suffer again from divided loyalties, the Normans now agreed to accept him as duke. Theobald, no doubt somewhat disgruntled at being upstaged by his younger brother, retired with fairly good grace to Blois and accepted the situation as a fait accompli.

All this time the body of the previous king and duke had still not been buried, and most of the chronicles give more or less gruesome details of his progress towards the grave. Malmesbury, for example tells us, 'The body, royally attended and borne by the nobility in turn, was brought to Rouen; where in a retired part of the principal church, it was embowelled, lest, through time, becoming putrid, it should offend the senses of those who approached it.' Vitalis says, 'During the night the body, which was very fat, was opened by a skilful surgeon,' though Henry of Huntingdon renders this as, 'slashed with knives.' Various organs were removed – brain, tongue, heart and intestines are mentioned – these being buried at the monastery of St Marie des Prees. William of Newburgh corroborated by Huntingdon, declares that the man who removed these organs subsequently died from an infection caused by the stench, though lack of hygiene is a more probable cause. Huntingdon adds a sour comment that, 'He was the last of that great multitude King Henry slew.'

The body was then 'embalmed with sweet spices,' according to Vitalis, or 'copiously sprinkled with salt,' according to Huntingdon, and then sewn up in ox hides and transported to the Abbey of St Stephen in Caen where it lay for some four weeks, waiting for the weather, which was 'very boisterous' at the time, to become calm enough for a Channel crossing. It was after Christmas before the monks could carry it to the coast and put it on a ship bound for England. There it was received with full ceremony by the new King Stephen – and one wonders what sort of atmosphere prevailed when he met for the first time those English nobles he had climbed above – and Stephen himself helped carry his predecessor to Reading, where the body was finally interred before the altar in the great church that Henry had founded there.

Sadly, following the dissolution of the monasteries in the 16th century and the destruction of the abbey, nothing now remains to mark the spot but a plaque on a nearby wall. Similarly, the magnificent tomb occupying pride of place in the choir at Winchester Cathedral, which was long thought to be that of William Rufus, is now believed to be more properly ascribed to Bishop Henry of Blois. Instead, one of the mortuary boxes kept near the altar bears the name of William Rufus, and may well have held the bones of that king until the time of the 17th-century English Civil War, when all the mortuary boxes, including those of King Cnut and his wife Queen Emma, were thrown about by the Parliamentarians. In collecting up the bones and re-packing the boxes, they are likely to have been thoroughly mixed up, so the remains of William Rufus may well be sharing space with those of Cnut, Emma and others, and be spread around in several different boxes. The only one of the brothers to have a lasting memorial is Robert, whose magnificent tomb, complete with effigy, can still be seen in Gloucester Cathedral. True, this was made something like a hundred years after his death, and may not mark the actual place of his interment, but it seems a little ironic that the brother who left the least in terms of personal legacy is the one with the most visible presence today.

It was during the later years of Henry I that Geoffrey of Monmouth produced a book known as the *Prophetiae Merlini* – the Prophecies of Merlin – in which he introduced the character of Merlin who would later figure large in his tales of King Arthur. Drawn from the Welsh Myrddin, and pulling in both Welsh and old British legends, the 'prophecies' were supposed to have been made centuries before and to relate to current and future events. The book was immensely popular at the time and the prophecies widely thought to be genuine. Both Suger and Vitalis clearly believed them, and the latter quoted a large chunk at one point and related it to the sons of the Conqueror. 'Two dragons shall succeed, one of whom shall be slain by the darts of malice, and the other shall perish under the shadow of a name. A lion of justice shall succeed, whose roar shall cause the towns of France, and the dragons of the island, to tremble. In his days gold shall be extorted from the lily and the nettle, and silver shall be scattered abroad by the hoofs of lowing kine.'

Quite clearly and correctly Vitalis identifies the two dragons as William Rufus, who was indeed slain by darts, and Robert Curthose, who still called himself Duke of Normandy even though there was no substance behind the title. It is interesting that Monmouth refers to 'darts of malice,' suggesting that he at least has not entirely swallowed the idea that William's death was an accident – or possibly he is simply being mischievous. The lion of justice is, of course, Henry, whose power did, indeed, eventually subdue both England and Normandy, and who was most adept at getting gold both from the nobility and Church (the lily) and from the common people (the nettle). The scattering of silver abroad, no doubt, refers to his liberal use of money in preference to warfare in obtaining the results he desired in Normandy.

Very ingenious, and if they were genuine prophecies they would be startling in the extreme, particularly when he goes on to say that the lion's children will become fishes – a clear reference to the White ship disaster. Furthermore he adds that 'the whelps of the roaring lion shall awake and leaving the forests shall hunt under the walls of towns. They shall make a great carnage among all who resist,' – no doubt referring to the troubled times after the death of Henry.

William of Newburgh, however, pours a very large dose of cold water over the whole business. In his preface to his own

History of Affairs in England, he writes that he is preparing this history in order to counter the lies and fictions of Geoffrey of Monmouth. In particular, he declares that Geoffrey 'has unscrupulously promulgated the mendacious predictions of one Merlin as if they were genuine prophecies.' He has drawn these, he says, from the 'traditional fictions of the Britons,' 'to which ... he added much from his own invention,' and then, the killer punch, 'Besides he so accommodated his prophetic fancies ... to circumstances occurring previous to, or during his own times, that they might obtain a suitable interpretation.' How easy it is to make correct predictions with the benefit of hindsight. Even the 'carnage' after Henry's death would be a fairly obvious guess in the circumstances. Yet the fact remains that people easily swallowed these 'prophecies', which argued that, as with modern political cartoons, they could see enough in them of their recent leaders to make the identification straightforward. Were Robert and William really 'dragons', then, and Henry a 'lion of justice' with a mighty roar?

Robert seems hardest to fit to the image, and yet even he had dragon-like moments. In his early defiance of his father, especially in the episode at Gerberoy, he certainly showed courage and ability. Similarly he played a full part in the First Crusade under the most difficult of circumstances, though his legend may have received a little polishing later. Yet after this he seemed to lapse into an entirely different character. 'Endeavouring to please all, he gave, promised or yielded what everyone asked', and 'abandoned himself to sloth and indulgence.' So says Orderic Vitalis who has no time for him at all, though it is hard to believe the extremes of the picture he paints of the duke's drunken and idle life. Nor was Robert blessed in his subordinates, particularly Robert de Bellême, while Normandy historically was a more turbulent land than England. It has even been suggested that fighting was the default mode of Norman nobles, and when they had no-one else to fight, they fought each other. Yet the fact remains that Normandy seemed in constant turmoil during Robert's time as its duke, and on many occasions he failed to act decisively, when doing so might have put an end to the trouble and re-established good order. He seems, certainly in his middle years, to have only wanted a quiet life – and signally failed to find it. Of the three brothers, Robert seems to have left the smallest mark on history and the least in terms of a lasting legacy.

It is easier to see dragon tendencies in William Rufus, though again we must bear in mind that most of the accounts of his deeds were written by clerics, and William's relationship with the Church was famously stormy. However, as one after another sums up his character a pattern does develop. 'He was very powerful and stern over his lands and subjects ... and much to be dreaded,' says the Anglo Saxon Chronicle. 'He was savage beyond all men,' says Henry of Huntingdon, adding, 'Whatever wickedness existed before was now brought to the highest pitch; whatever had no existence before sprung up in these times.' He was 'a warlike prince,' says Vitalis, 'Devoted to arms, making distinguished warriors his principal friends', while Eadmer's condemnation has already been recorded. This is the picture most commonly passed down through history, as evidenced by Roger Baker's 17th century summary. 'For he repented not more in time of sickness for the evil he had done in health, than being in health he repented of the good he had done in sickness.' Others, however, such as Geoffrey Gaimar and Wace, offer a more forgiving picture of the king, perhaps because they were writing popular 'romances' for a wider audience, rather than historical chronicles. They clearly approve of his military acumen, chivalrous gestures to those he considered worthy opponents and even encouragement of the military types boasting feats of arms who flocked to his court. It is not necessarily a character reference, though, when they both refer to how well he got on with Robert de Bellème, clearly a man after his own heart. William is also believed to have been Geoffrey of Monmouth's model for King Arthur in his History of the Kings of England.

Of those writing nearest the time of his death, perhaps Malmesbury comes closest to a balanced account. 'Greatness of soul,' he writes, 'was pre-eminent in the king, which, in process of time, he obscured by excessive severity; vices, indeed, in place of virtues, so insensibly crept into his bosom that he could not distinguish them.' In other places Malmesbury calls him noble and magnanimous, and when forced to recount his misdeeds, 'I blush to relate the crimes of so great a king.' He seems to attribute the change in William to the absence of Lanfranc's restraining hand after the archbishop's death in 1089. Then 'his liberality became prodigality; his magnanimity pride; his austerity cruelty,' and he sums up, 'I may be allowed ... not to conceal the truth; for he feared God but little, man not at all.'

It is in contrasting William and Henry that we can perhaps see the ending of one age and the tentative beginning of another. William clearly belonged to the earlier age, an age of robust military strength and conquest. We hear little of the gentler arts in his reign, possibly because he never married and these things were increasingly introduced by the noble ladies of the time. By contrast, however, we hear a great deal about his plans to expand his dominions, first to Normandy, and then into other French provinces and even France itself.

Gerald of Wales, a grandson of Princess Nest, writing in the latter part of the 12th century, tells a story of William visiting west Wales in 1097. Apparently – implausibly – catching a glimpse of Ireland across the sea, he at once declared his intention to conquer it. When told of this, the King of Leinster is said to have asked, 'Did he add, "If God wills it"? and being told William had not mentioned God, then stated that he had no fear of any such conquest. Although almost certainly apocryphal, the story seems to sum up William Rufus – ambitious, self-confident and with very little time for God.

The most lasting memorial of his reign, though he is seldom given any credit for it, is Westminster Hall. This mighty building was by far the largest hall in England, and probably in Europe, at the time. The span of the roof was so great that it is still a mystery how this was originally held up without the use of columns. Of course alterations have been made over time – the walls raised in height and resurfaced, the roof replaced in the 14th century – but essentially the internal space of this huge edifice is as it was at the time of the king's death in 1100, witness of so many historic moments since, and still in regular use today.

Perhaps William of Malmesbury's summary should be allowed to stand as the most fitting epitaph for William Rufus. 'He would, no doubt,' he says, 'have been a prince incomparable in our time, had not his father's greatness eclipsed him; and had not the fates cut short his years too early for his mature age to correct errors contracted by the licentiousness of power and the impetuosity of youth.'

If William's reputation suffered by comparison with the reigns on either side of his, Henry's certainly benefitted. Whatever the exact reality of William's rule, the complaints recorded in the chronicles got Henry off to a flying start, while his firm rule and glorious victory over the Normans at Tinchebrai carried him through the greater part of his time as King of England. More than thirty years of peace in that generally peace-loving country was also to his credit, and even though his plans for the succession were unpopular, by then respect for the king – and for his wealth and power – meant that no-one, in England at least, was prepared to challenge him openly on this.

Only after his death did his carefully laid plans begin to unravel, and it would seem harsh to blame Henry for that. He had done the best he could with what was available to him, and if he could have lived to the same age as his brother Robert, might well have been able to pass on his lands reasonably peacefully to his grandson. As it was, as soon as Stephen moved the first pebble the avalanche was almost certainly unavoidable.

It was against that rapidly deteriorating situation that most of the tributes to Henry were written. Thus Vitalis writes, 'He ruled the dominions divinely committed to him with prudence and success in prosperity and adversity, and was distinguished among the princes of Christendom for his love of peace and justice.' Furthermore, 'The common people among his subjects he indulged with equitable laws, and protected by his authority from unjust exactions and pillage,' and 'he obtained the favour of both the clergy and laity, who were delighted to find themselves governed by reason.' 'He was, as I think, the best of kings.'

For Malmesbury, Henry was 'active in providing what would be beneficial to his empire, firm in defending it ... Inflexible in the administration of justice, he ruled the people with moderation,' and 'If he could, he conquered without bloodshed; if it was unavoidable, with as little as possible.' Robert of Torigny calls him 'the father of the people, the protector of the orphan,' and declares, 'England laments him ... the people of Normandy weep for him.'

The acclaim was not universal, however. Henry of Huntingdon declares that, after the king's death, 'his character was freely canvassed by the people, as is usual.' Some, he says, declared that Henry was distinguished by 'three brilliant gifts' of wisdom, success in war and wealth, while others attributed to him 'three gross vices', namely avarice, cruelty and wantonness. Even during the king's life he had written in his famous *Letter to Walter* that 'the royal state is wickedness,' citing actions of the king to prove this. Thus he declared that Henry 'threw his brother ... into a dungeon and kept him there till he died', and that 'numbers fell into his hands by his breach of faith; numbers he put to death craftily,' Further, 'He was a slave to ambition and avarice.' He also declared that Henry's life was most miserable since all his triumphs were followed by disappointments, such as the White Ship disaster following his victories in Normandy. 'All I have said to his disadvantage is but too true,' he said in that letter, 'Would that it were otherwise.'

Where can we place Henry, then, between these claims and counterclaims? Was he truly a lion of justice, or was it just that his propagandists were more efficient and his reign a bright light, when viewed against the darkness that followed?

Certainly he preferred peace to war, but then so did his brother Robert who got no credit for this. Possibly the difference is that Henry's peace was accompanied by firm good government while Robert's was not. It is also claimed that the systems of justice and administration that became established in his time were not his invention, and possibly had their seeds in earlier times. This is probably true. What Henry did, though, was to encourage them and enable them to prosper, particularly by choosing the best men to nurture and develop them, whatever the background of those men might be. His success is shown by the fact that the systems were robust enough to survive the anarchy that followed, and to spring up afresh when more peaceful times returned. We might say that his gifts to England's future were the Exchequer and the English Common Law, neither fully developed in his time, but nonetheless an important part of his legacy.

These were certainly triumphs of Henry's reign, though some have questioned the king's personal commitment to justice when ruthlessness served his ends better. We will never be sure of Henry's involvement in the death of William Rufus, but his treatment of Conan in Rouen some years earlier was clearly cold-blooded murder. There was no trial for Robert Curthose, or for William of Mortain, although they might have been legitimately treated as prisoners of war, while in the case of Robert de Bellème in 1112, though he had a trial, it had many of the hallmarks of Stalin's famous show trials, with both the verdict and the sentence decided beforehand.

Henry has also been accused of vindictiveness in the way he relentlessly persecuted his nephew William Clito, something that Henry of Huntingdon surprisingly omits from his list of the king's wrongdoings. This persecution probably has a lot to do with Henry's perceived insecurity in Normandy, and possibly to his commitment to peace in the duchy. If he was to admit that Clito had any rights there, the implication would be that he himself was a usurper, which in turn would justify the Norman lords in uniting behind Clito to throw him out. As it was, the periods of violence were relatively short, and the majority of those who rebelled were later pardoned and reinstated.

By no means squeaky clean, then, by modern standards, we must recognise that Henry was a man of his times. The times themselves, though, were changing. A new, more cultured age was dawning, and the year 1100 is often quoted as a turning point, though the roots of this change stretch back into the earlier century. That was the time when Henry was receiving his education, an education that clearly had a greater effect on him than on his brothers. On the cusp of this great change, his reign must be seen as balanced between the old and the new, while Henry had one foot in each. Ruthless when he felt he needed to be, still his inclinations seem always to be towards something better.

Art, music and literature all underwent a revival at this time, and Henry's court, and particularly that of Queen Matilda, gave encouragement to all of these. 'Crowds of scholars, equally famed for verse and for singing, came over,' writes Malmesbury of the queen's court, 'And happy did he account himself who could soothe the ears of the queen by the novelty of his song.' Writers such as Malmesbury himself were also patronised, while Geoffrey of Monmouth with his Arthurian legends represented a whole new departure in the way of literature in England.

Architecture, too, was developing at this time, and again we find Queen Matilda showing an interest. She is reputed to have commissioned the first stone bridge over the River Lea at Stratford to the east of London. With three arches and a top shaped like a bow, the bridge gave its name to the area, first Stratford-le-Bow, and later just Bow, while Matilda herself is believed to be the 'fair lady' referred to in the chorus of the old song 'London Bridge is Falling Down.'

While we hear less of Henry's personal involvement in these developments, we know that when he had leisure he would retire to his favourite palace at Woodstock in Oxfordshire. There he had built a 9-mile-long wall around the park, not only to provide himself with a hunting ground, but also as a place to keep his collection of exotic wild animals. These, the gifts of other monarchs and travellers, are believed to include lions, tigers, porcupines and camels, the first known zoo in England.

Quite clearly Henry was by far the most successful of the sons of William the Conqueror. Both in terms of his achievements in life and in his legacy, he far outshone his brothers, and we can only speculate how much brighter his star might have shone had his hopes of passing on that legacy in peace and prosperity not been sunk with the White Ship. His death, said Robert of Torigny, robbed the world of a treasure and added to its sorrows. It was clearly the end of an era, and despite the king's obvious human faults and failings, that writer's tribute to the Conqueror's last son must be allowed to stand.

Here lies the reverend king Henry – the pride of the world – celebrated for his understanding, his riches, his condescension, his commendable firmness, his gentleness to the oppressed, his severity against the wicked, his excellency, and his humility.

With his death a light went out in England and in Normandy, and a time of darkness would follow, 'when Christ and his saints slept.'

A Note on Sources

The early twelfth century was a time when writing history was very much in vogue. Some attempted vast epics stretching back to the time of the Romans and beyond. Some wrote of more recent stirring events. Some recorded their own times. From this we have a great number of texts, written mainly in the first half of the twelfth century, covering the lives and times of the Conqueror and his sons. Especially important are the writings of William of Malmesbury and Orderic Vitalis, one in England and one in Normandy, who not only witnessed much of what they wrote about, but were also able to put it into its political context. The following are the main sources referred to in this book.

Ecclesiastical History of England & Normandy – Orderic Vitalis

The father of Orderic Vitalis was a Norman companion of Roger of Montgomery, 1st Earl of Shrewsbury, and it was he that prompted the earl to found a monastery in that place, whose church stands to this day. Orderic was born of an English mother in 1075, and at the age of five was sent to the abbey school. Six years later his father, feeling he had not made a large enough sacrifice in giving his son to God, sent him away to the Abbey of Saint Evroult in Normandy, where he spent the rest of his life. It was in Normandy that he acquired the name Vitalis as they claimed they could not manage his English name. Never quite losing the feeling of being a stranger in a strange land, Orderic always referred to himself as an Englishman, and tends to champion the English viewpoint. Nevertheless, living in a monastery in the middle of Normandy during the troubles of the late 11th and early 12th century, he had a ringside seat for the events he wrote about, and his bias against Robert Curthose is perhaps understandable. His *Ecclesiastical History* has a rather eccentric approach to chronology, but the later books, written between 1133 and 1141, are devoted largely to the lives of the Conqueror and his sons. He acknowledges his debt to other writers, including Eadmer, but much of what he writes is original, containing stories (and speeches) not found elsewhere. He is known to have travelled to France and England, and may well have been present at the papal council at Rheims in 1119 that he records so vividly. His monastery also became home to many retired soldiers who had fought in the Norman wars, or the crusades, from whom he is also likely to have gathered much information.

Chronicle of the Kings of England – William of Malmesbury

Born around 1095, William, like Orderic, had a Norman father and English mother, but he spent his adult life as a monk at Malmesbury Abbey in his native Wiltshire. He was a great scholar and lover of books, with an extensive library, and aimed to follow Bede in writing objective, factual history. Originally intending to cover the period AD449 to 1120, he later extended the work to 1142. Of all the sources, he gives the most balanced account of William Rufus, and the most detail concerning the oaths sworn to give the succession to Matilda. A note of caution should be sounded in that he dedicated his work to Robert of Gloucester, the noted champion of Matilda. It seems unlikely, however, that he would depart from a lifelong dedication to writing the truth, by inventing a lie to please his sponsor. Thus he gives little detail of Henry's last years in Normandy, since he declares he will not include anything for the more recent years at least, unless he has seen it himself or heard about it from a credible authority.

Anglo-Saxon Chronicle

Written in the English language, this is in fact a collection of chronicles, written at different times and places around England. Monasteries at Abingdon, Worcester, Winchester, Peterborough and Canterbury all copied and contributed local material, and there is almost certainly at least one version that has been lost, on which other writers in the twelfth century based their own work. Generally the closest contemporary record of the events described, the chronicle has the advantage of being unaffected by hindsight. It tends, however, to be fairly succinct and factual with little extensive comment, and is particularly interested in events, especially Church events, in England. Coverage of happenings in Normandy and elsewhere, tends to be brief and with little depth of knowledge.

History of Recent Events in England – Eadmer

Eadmer was an Anglo-Saxon, born around 1060, who became a monk at Canterbury. He became a close friend and assistant to Archbishop Anselm, whom he had first met when Anselm was Abbot of Bec. Eadmer's *History* covers the period 1066–1122, and has the huge advantage that, in a great many cases, he was an eyewitness of the events he describes. He is also a shrewd political commentator. It has the disadvantage, however, that he is hugely biased towards Anselm and against William Rufus, and in his summaries of that king cannot be regarded as an impartial recorder.

Chronicle of Henry of Huntingdon

Henry of Huntingdon was born around 1088. His father was an archdeacon in the Diocese of Lincoln and Henry grew up in the household of Robert Bloet. Succeeding his father as archdeacon in 1110, Henry was asked by a later bishop, Alexander, to write a history of England. He covered the period from before the Romans to 1154, relying heavily on the Anglo-Saxon Chronicle, including a version since lost. He does introduce his own comments here and there, especially when writing of his own time. His disillusionment with the world becomes increasingly apparent, however, thus explaining some of his more sour observations in later times. He is not a fan of Henry I, considering that he treated his idol, Robert Bloet, very shabbily at the end of his life.

Chronicle of John of Worcester

John was a monk of Worcester Priory who had entered the monastery at an early age. He was asked by Bishop Wulfstan of Worcester to copy and extend the Chronicle of Chronicles begun by an Irish monk, Marianus Scotus. John added a great deal, but with heavy reliance on the Anglo-Saxon Chronicle, particularly the lost version, and without a great deal of extra comment until the later stages. His chronicle ends in 1140 and it is thought he must have died soon after. Orderic Vitalis visited John and pays tribute in his own book to the way he carefully recorded the events of the reigns of the Conqueror and his sons.

Symeon of Durham

Symeon entered the monastery at Jarrow as a young man and transferred with it to Durham. He wrote two works, one a history of the church in Durham, which contains much detail about Ranulf Flambard, and another on the history of the kings of England. The early part of the latter is based solidly on John of Worcester, but from 1119 onwards, Symeon finds his own voice to give a more extensive independent view.

Life of Louis the Fat – Abbot Suger

Suger was given to the monastery of St Denis as a child oblate around 1090. He first met Louis when he was young, and then became closely involved with the king and his court, as both a friend and a counsellor. He was almost certainly present at the meeting between Louis and Henry near Gisors in 1109, spent time at the papal courts of Gelasius and Calixtus, and remained closely associated with Louis's court through the 1120s and beyond.

Chronicles of Robert de Monte

Robert was born at Torigni in Normandy, probably of a noble family, and entered the monastery at Bec when in his teens. He rose to become Prior of Bec and later Abbot of Mont-St-Michel – hence he is known as both Robert of Torigni and Robert de Monte. In his time Mont-St-Michel became a centre of learning, while Robert himself was both a pious monk, and a diplomat. He contributed to a range of works, and his chronicle copied and added to earlier material. He incorporated much of Henry of Huntingdon's chronicle, having been visited by Henry at Bec. He justified recording history as giving an example of the good to imitate, and of the wicked to avoid.

The History of William of Newburgh

William was born at Bridlington, Yorkshire, around 1135 and became an Augustinian cannon at Newburgh Priory. He was asked by the Abbot of Reivaulx to write a history of England, and declared that he did so in order to overturn the lies and inventions of Geoffrey of Monmouth, whose work was fashionable at the time. William covers the period from 1066–1197, aiming at a serious and precise narrative showing causes and effects of actions. Although making use of earlier material, he offers his own independent comments.

History of the English – Geoffrey Gaimar

Gaimar's *History* started as a translation of Geoffrey of Monmouth for the wife of Ralph FitzGilbert, who was presumably his employer. To this he eventually added a great deal of his own, so that the work ran from the Argonauts to 1100 AD, though a large part has been lost. Initially following closely the Anglo-Saxon Chronicle, after 959AD many sources are used, probably including his own imagination. While good on period detail, Gaimar was aiming more for a 'romance' or entertainment than a serious history.

Roman de Rou – Wace

Wace was born on Jersey, probably to a good family, and was brought up at Caen in Normandy. His *Roman de Rou*, written between 1160 and the mid-1170s, was commissioned by HenryII of England and was intended more as entertainment and propaganda. It covers the career of William the Conqueror and his sons, but ends abruptly just after the Battle of Tinchebrai, though briefly noting what happened to Robert Curthose afterwards. Wace explains rather huffily that he has to stop at that point because the king has asked someone else to write instead.

Select Bibliography

Primary Printed Sources

Anglo-Saxon Chronicle, ed. & trans. J.A. Giles (London: G. Bell & Sons, 1914)

Chronicle of Henry of Huntingdon, ed. & trans. Thomas Forester (London: Henry G. Bohn, 1853

Chronicle of John of Worcester, trans. Thomas Forester (London: Henry G. Bohn, 1854)

Chronicle of the Kings of England, Richard Baker, (London: George Sawbridge, 1670)

Chronicle of the Kings of England, William of Malmesbury, ed. & trans. J.A. Giles (London: Henry G. Bohn, 1847)

Chronicles of the First Crusade, ed. Christopher Tyerman (London: Penguin Classics, 2012)

Chronicles of Robert de Monte, trans. Rev. Joseph Stevenson (London: Seeleys, 1856)

Ecclesiastical History of England & Normandy, Vols. 2, 3 & 4, Orderic Vitalis, ed. & trans. Thomas Forester (London: Henry G. Bohn, 1854 & 1856)

Historical Works of Simeon of Durham, trans. Rev. Joseph Stevenson (London: Seeleys, 1855)

History of Recent Events in England, Eadmer, trans. Geoffrey Bosanquet (London: Cresset Press, 1964)

History of the English, Geoffrey Gaimar, ed. Alexander Bell (Oxford: 1960)

History of William of Newburgh, trans. Rev. Joseph Stevenson (London: Seeleys, 1856)

Journey Through Wales, Gerald of Wales, trans. L. Thorpe (Harmondsworth: Penguin Books, 1978)

Life of King Louis the Fat, Suger, trans. Jean Dunbabin (Internet Medieval Sourcebook)

Roman de Rou: Chronicle of the Norman Conquest, Wace, trans. Edgar Taylor (London: William Pickering, 1837)

The First Crusade, The Chronicle of Fulcher of Chartres & Other Source Materials, ed. Edward Peters (Philadelphia: Penn Press, 1998)

Secondary Sources

Aird, W.M., *Robert Curthose, Duke of Normandy* (Woodbridge: Boydell & Brewer 2011)

Ashley, M., *Mammoth Book of British Kings & Queens,* (London: Robinson Publishing, 1999)

Barlow, F., *Feudal Kingdom of England 1042–1216* (London: Longman, 1972)

Barlow, F., *William Rufus* (Abingdon: Routledge 1999)

Brookes, C., *From Alfred to Henry III, 871–1272* (London: Sphere Books, 1969)

David, C.W., *Robert Curthose, Duke of Normandy* (Cambridge: Harvard University Press, 1920)

Davis, H.W.C., *England Under the Normans & Angevins 1066–1272* (London: Methuen, 1921)

Davis, R.H.C., *History of Medieval Europe, From Constantine to Saint Louis,* ed. R.I. Moore (Harlow: Pearson Education, 2006)

Given-Wilson, C. & Curteis, A., *Royal Bastards of Medieval England* (London: Routledge & Keegan Paul, 1984)

Green, J.A., *Henry I, King of England and Duke of Normandy* (Cambridge: Cambridge University Press, 2009)

Hollister, C. Warren, *Henry I* (New Haven & London: Yale University Press, 2003)

Kiralfy, A.K.R., *Potter's Historical Introduction to English Law* (London: Sweet & Maxwell, 1958)

Lack, K. *Conqueror's Son, Duke Robert Curthose, Thwarted King* (Stroud: History Press, 2011)

Mason, E., *King Rufus, The Life & Murder of William II of England* (Stroud: History Press, 2008)

Maurois, A., *A History of France* (London: Jonathan Cape, 1949)

Poole, A.L., *Domesday Book to Magna Carta, 1087–1216* (Oxford: Oxford University Press, 1955)

Index

Adela, Countess of Blois 7, 8, 17,
  25, 130-1, 149, 163, 181, 185,
  200, 227
Adeliza, dau. of William the
  conqueror 7, 17-18
Adeliza of Louvain, wife of Henry
  I 226
Alan IV of Brittany 7, 18, 163,
  249
Alençon 12, 51, 65, 182, 189,
  191, 192, 194, 259
Alexander, king of Scotland 9,
  183, 184, 185, 211, 212
Alexius Comnenus, Byzantine
  Emperor 91-92, 93, 96, 97
Amaury de Montfort 10, 181,
  188, 190, 191-92, 194, 195, 197,
  198, 229, 230, 233, 234, 235-36,
  238, 250
Anglo-Saxon Chronicle 275-76
Anjou 15, 32, 78, 187, 201, 253,
  258
Anselm 81, 82, 83, 87-88, 89-90,
  102, 112, 123-27, 128, 129,
  130-31, 133, 145, 148, 149, 150,
  151, 155, 157, 159, 162, 185
Antioch, siege of 94-96, 211
Arnulf of Montgomery 11, 102,
  134, 135, 138, 141, 184, 214

Baldwin V of Flanders 8, 16, 248
Baldwin VII of Flanders 8, 181,
  186, 187, 189, 194
Baldwin I, king of Jerusalem 63,
  92, 96
Bertrada de Montfort 8, 10, 55,
  176-77, 181, 205
Bohemond of Taranto 92, 93, 94,
  95, 96, 210
Bourgthéroulde, battle of 12, 234
Brémule, battle of 12, 195-96,208,
  209, 210, 219
Brian FitzCount 163, 249, 253

Caen 16, 18, 37, 45, 121, 146,
  151, 166, 205, 207, 231, 264
Calixtus II,, pope 197, 198,
  199-200, 238, 242, 243, 244,
  255, 277
Charles the Good, Count of
  Flanders 8, 194, 199, 236, 245,
  247-48
church and marriage 164-65, 239
church reform 115-16, 118-19,
  123, 128
coinage 164-65, 239
Conan, citizen of Rouen 52, 53,
  54, 72, 271
courts 167-69, 170, 172

Crusade, First   63, 64, 76, 91-98, 101, 130, 210, 166
curia regis   165

David, king of Scotland   9, 183-84, 246
Domfront   12, 60-61, 62, 100, 105, 144, 159, 210, 211, 231
Donald Bane   9, 108-9
Dorylaeum, battle of   93-94
Duncan II of Scotland   9, 41, 107-8, 109

Eadmer   81, 88, 89, 90, 102, 123, 126, 276
Edgar, king of Scotland   9, 64, 109, 110, 183
Edgar Atheling   9, 58-59, 88, 107, 108, 109, 155, 156
Edith of Scotland,   see Matilda of Scotland.
Edward the Confessor   58, 59, 67, 85, 88, 106, 164, 169, 171
Eustace III of Boulogne   9, 45, 46, 47, 63, 92, 97, 138, 144, 145, 227
Eustace de Pacy, lord of Breteuil   10, 139-40, 144, 192, 195, 199, 209
exchequer   166-67, 271

Fulk IV of Anjou   10, 32, 55, 58, 65-66, 176-77, 205, 259
Fulk V of Anjou   10, 179, 180, 181, 182-3, 191, 194, 219, 229, 230, 238, 249, 251, 252, 253, 259
fyrd   103,136

Gaimar, writer of 'romance'   69, 75, 278
geld   163-4
Geoffrey of Anjou   7, 9, 10, 211, 249, 250, 253, 254, 256, 258, 259, 261
Geoffrey, bishop of Coutances   27, 44, 61

Geoffrey of Monmouth   264-66, 267, 272, 278
Gerald FitzWalter of Windsor   184, 185, 214-5
Gilbert FitzRichard of Clare   44, 45, 72, 75, 77, 102, 184, 185
Gilbert of L'Aigle   53, 190, 223
Gisors   12, 65, 178-79, 183, 199, 231, 232-33, 247, 277
Godfrey de Bouillon   92, 93, 96, 97
Gregory VII, pope   114, 116-19, 120,121
Gregory VIII, antipope   242, 243, 244
Gruffydd ap Cynan, king of Gwynedd   62, 64, 110-11, 184, 185, 228
Guy, archbishop of Vienne, see Calixtus II, pope

Helias, Count of Maine   56, 58, 65-67, 98-99, 149, 153, 154, 158, 179
Helias of Saint-Saens   40, 52, 61, 156, 180, 186, 199, 238, 248, 252
Henry I, king of England   7, 8, 9, 17, 28, 33, 34,35, 36, 37, 38, 42-43, 45-46, 49, 50, 51, 58, 60, 62, 67, 83, 99, 100, 101, 142, 199, 220, 221, 224, 225, 226, 248, 250-51, 255, 257, 263, 265, 268
   birth 18-20,
   education 23-24,
   appearance 40,
   Count of Cotentin 45-46
   defence of Rouen 52-54
   loss of Cotentin 56-57
   death of William Rufus 69, 72, 74-76, 78-79
   claims crown 73
   Coronation Charter   84-86, 169
   marriages 88, 90, 226
   Robert's invasion 102-105

lay investitures 127-131
and Montgomery brothers
134-138
and Normandy 144-45, 145-49,
151-54, 157-58 230-35, 237
court and household 160-61,
162-63, 165
and finance 163-64
and justice 167-70, 271
daughter's marriages 174-76,
245, 249, 250, 251
conflict with France 178-79,
180, 181-83, 187-97
and Scotland 183
and Wales 184-5
and William Clito 156, 179-80,
199, 252, 271
and Pope Calixtus 199-200
illegitimate children 202-3, 207
Matilda as successor 246-47
nightmares 254
illness and death 259-60
assessment of reign 269-72
Henry, grandson of Henry I 7, 8,
10, 256-7, 258
Henry IV, Holy Roman
Emperor 116, 119-21, 130, 132,
174-75
Henry V, Holy Roman Emperor 7,
9, 130, 174-5, 176, 233, 237,
241-44, 245
Henry of Blois, bishop of
Winchester 262, 264
Henry, Count of Eu 144, 189
Henry of Huntingdon,
chronicler 276
Henry Beaumont, earl of
Warwick 74, 86, 102, 138
Hildebrand, see Gregory VII, pope
Holy Roman Empire 112-14, 116,
117, 175, 241
Hugh d'Avranches, earl of
Chester 45, 56, 61, 62, 79, 87,
110, 123, 228
Hugh de Grandmesnil 44,45

Hugh de Montfort 230, 231, 232,
234, 235, 237
Hugh of Montgomery, earl of
Shrewsbury 11, 65, 110

illegitimacy 205-6
Investiture Controversy 116, 118,
120, 121-22, 126, 127, 128, 129,
131, 158, 162, 241-42, 243-44

Jerusalem, siege of 96-97
John, bishop of Lisieux 159-60,
166, 229
John of Worcester, chronicler 277
Juliana of Breteuil 10, 139,
192-92, 199, 209

King's Peace 85-86

Lanfranc 21, 26, 35, 40, 41, 43,
45, 46, 48, 60, 81, 121, 122, 123,
124, 268
lay investitures, see Investiture
Controversy
Leges Henrici Primi 169-170, 171,
172
Louis VI, king of France 8, 78,
146, 176, 177, 178-79, 180, 181,
182, 183, 186-87, 190, 192, 193,
194, 195-96, 197, 198, 200, 209,
210, 233, 237, 247, 248, 249,
250-51, 252, 254, 277

Maine 26, 27, 32, 41, 50, 54, 56,
58, 65-67, 78, 98-99, 105, 145,
179, 181, 182, 183, 194, 211,
217, 219, 229, 230
Malcolm, king of Scotland 9, 32,
42, 59, 64, 88, 89, 107-8, 109,
177
Maredudd of Powys 185, 228
Margaret, queen of Scotland 9,
59, 88, 89, 107, 108
Mary of Scotland, wife of Eustace
III of Boulogne 9, 89, 138, 139,
227

Matilda, Empress 7, 8, 9, 10, 140, 174, 176, 201, 208, 212, 226, 228, 241, 249, 261, 262
first marriage 174-76, 242
German education 176
Italian campaign 242-43
coronation 'as empress' 243
return to England 244-45
oaths 246-7, 256, 275
remarriage 245, 247, 249, 250, 251
and Geoffrey of Anjou 250, 253, 254, 256, 258
children 241, 256-57, 258
Matilda of Anjou, wife of William Adelin 7, 10, 183, 194, 229
Matilda of Boulogne, wife of Stephen of Blois 7, 9, 227
Matilda of Flanders, wife of William the conqueror 7, 8, 16, 17, 19, 20, 26, 29-30, 31, 32, 33, 88, 205
Matilda, countess of Perche 140, 210-11, 223, 225
Matilda of Scotland, (Edith) 7, 9, 32, 88-90, 104, 106, 138, 140, 143, 159, 174, 183, 188, 207, 211, 213, 218, 227, 272
Matilda of Tuscany 32, 242
Maurice, bishop of London 84, 86
Mauritius, archbishop of Braga, see Gregory VIII, antipope
Mont St Michel 12, 45, 98, 204, 277

New Forest 22-23
Nest, princess 214-15, 268

Odo, bishop of Bayeux 21, 41, 43-44, 45, 47, 48, 50, 51, 64, 82, 100
Orderic Vitalis, chronicler 17, 19, 274-75
Osmund, bishop of Salisbury 24-25, 32
Owain of Powys 184-85, 215

Paschal II, pope 127, 128, 129, 130, 131, 133, 145, 151, 175, 197, 241, 242, 243, 244
Philip, king of France 8, 10, 29, 31, 33, 52, 61-62, 78, 92, 101, 146, 174, 176-78, 205

Ralph II de Gael 10, 197, 210, 230
Ralph II de Tosny 10, 52, 55
Ralph III de Tosny 10, 139, 140, 144, 193
Ranulf Flambard 61, 64, 82-83, 87, 99-100, 103-4, 132-33, 159, 277
Ranulf Le Meschin, earl of Chester 153, 228, 231, 234
Raymond of Toulouse 63, 92, 93, 96, 97
Reginald of Warenne 53, 146, 151, 153
Richard, earl of Chester 138, 144, 184, 185, 193, 224, 226, 228
Richard of Lincoln, illegitimate son of Henry I 193, 195, 197, 199, 209-10, 220, 224, 230
Richard, illegitimate son of Robert Curthose 40-41, 76
Richard, son of William the Conqueror 7, 17, 18, 20, 22-23, 76
Robert Beaumont, 2nd earl of Leicester 188, 230, 260
Robert de Bellème, earl of Shrewsbury 27, 42, 45, 46, 47, 48, 49-50, 51, 52, 53, 55, 60, 61, 65, 66, 67, 85, 87, 100, 132, 134-38, 139, 141-42, 143, 146, 150, 151, 152, 153, 154, 155, 158, 167, 180, 182, 271
Robert Bloet, bishop of Lincoln 101, 136, 138, 161, 186, 208, 209, 276
Robert Curthose, duke of Normandy 7, 8, 17, 18, 20-21,

26, 27-28, 32, 36, 40, 41, 43,
44, 45-46, 47, 48-49, 50-51, 53,
54, 59-60, 61-62, 63, 76, 88, 99,
100, 135, 139, 140, 155-56, 157,
186, 207, 217, 245, 251-52, 264,
265, 270, 271
  appearance and character 39,
  rebellions against father 29-31,
  33-34
  illegitimate children 40-41
  treaty of Rouen 55-56
  attack on Henry 57
  loss of Maine 58
  First Crusade 63, 91, 92-98
  invasion of England 100, 103-6
  anarchy in Normandy 141-42,
  143, 144, 146, 147
  visits to England 142-3, 150
  loss of Normandy 148-50,
  152-54
  death 257
  assessment 266-67
Robert Fitzhamon 11, 49, 56, 71,
  75, 87, 101, 102, 133, 144, 146,
  148, 149, 208
Robert I, Count of Flanders 8, 29,
  248
Robert II, Count of Flanders 63,
  92, 96, 97, 101, 179, 180, 181
Robert of Gloucester, illegitimate
  son of Henry I 11, 75, 195, 203,
  207-8, 227, 231, 232, 241, 245,
  246, 249, 253, 260, 262
Robert de Meulan, earl of
  Leicester 73, 101, 102, 104,
  130, 133, 138, 139-40, 142, 144,
  145, 153, 178, 181, 188, 216,
  230
Robert de Montfort 86, 135, 139,
  144, 153
Robert, Count of Mortain 11, 43,
  44, 45, 47, 61
Robert of Mowbray 27, 44, 45,
  48, 61, 64, 108, 109
Robert of Rhuddlan 44, 62, 110

Robert of Torigny (Robert de
  Monte), chronicler 277-78
Roger Bigod 44, 45, 86
Roger of Montgomery, earl of
  Shrewsbury 11, 27, 42, 44, 46,
  48, 50, 51, 60, 65, 274
Roger the Poitevin 11, 100, 134,
  138, 141, 185
Roger, bishop of Salisbury 57,
  157, 159, 162, 163, 166, 173,
  186, 219, 239, 245, 246, 253,
  262
Rotrou, Count of Perche 140,
  144, 190, 198, 210, 211, 221,
  260
Rouen 12, 16, 29, 34, 41, 43, 45,
  50, 51, 52-53, 56, 61, 64, 65,
  150, 152, 156, 190, 193, 195,
  231, 256, 257, 258, 263, 271
Rougementier, battle of, see
  Bourgthéroulde

Scotland 64, 106-9, 183-84
Serlo, bishop of Sées 142, 146-47,
  159
sheriffs 84, 164, 165-66, 167,
  168, 169, 170
Stephen of Aumale 51, 64, 144,
  189, 199
Stephen, Count of Blois 7, 92, 93,
  95, 130
Stephen of Blois, count of
  Mortain 7, 8, 9, 162-63, 185,
  189-90, 191, 222, 225, 227, 246,
  248, 249-50, 261-63, 264
Sybilla of Anjou, wife of William
  Clito 7, 10, 230, 238
Sybilla of Conversano, wife of
  Robert Curthose 7, 76, 98,
  140-41
Sybilla, queen of Scotland 9, 183,
  211-12, 229
Symeon of Durham,
  chronicler 277

Tancred 92, 94, 96, 97

Theobald, Count of Blois   7, 8, 130, 181, 185, 187, 189, 190, 191, 198, 200, 221, 225, 227, 255, 261, 263

Thierry of Alsace, Count of Flanders   8, 10, 248, 250, 251, 252

Thurston, archbishop of York   186, 197-98, 199, 200

Tinchebrai, battle of   12, 152-54, 162, 181, 269, 278

Treaty of Alton   13, 105, 127, 132, 135, 138

Treaty of Rouen   12, 56, 61, 73, 105

trial, methods of   171-72

Urban II, pope   63, 91, 92, 124, 125, 126, 127

Vexin   34, 65, 66, 67, 76, 77, 78, 105, 178, 187, 193, 195, 231, 247, 249

Wace, chronicler   70, 74, 278,

Waleran de Meulan   7, 188, 212, 230, 231, 232, 234-35, 237, 245, 254, 260

Wales   64-65, 109-11, 184-85, 228, 258

Walter Giffard   51, 86, 141, 193, 195

Walter Tirel   66, 68-70, 72, 76-78, 79

White Ship   220-224

William I (the Conqueror), king of England   7, 8, 15, 16-18, 19, 20, 30, 31, 32, 33, 34-37, 107, 121, 157-58, 165, 177, 186, 205, 206

William II (Rufus), king of England   7, 17, 18, 21, 23, 26, 28, 31, 32, 33, 34, 35, 36, 37, 44, 49, 58,59, 61, 83, 89, 110, 167, 171, 177, 207, 264, 265, 271
appearance and character 39-40
accession 41-42

Odo's rebellion 44-48
attacks on Normandy 51-52, 55-56, 61-62
attack on Henry 57
obtains Normandy 64
conquest of Maine 65-67
death and funeral 68-79, 80
and Scotland 64, 108-9
and the church 81, 84, 122-23, 124-26
assessment of reign 80-83, 267-69

William Adelin   7, 8, 9, 10, 140, 182, 186, 187, 194, 195, 200, 201, 218, 219, 220-21, 223, 224, 246

William Clito   7, 8, 10, 140, 156, 179-80, 186, 187, 188, 193, 196, 199, 200, 228, 229, 233, 238-39, 240, 247, 248-49, 250, 251.52, 271

William Giffard, bishop of Winchester   86, 158, 161

William Talvas, Count of Ponthieu   11, 182, 183, 194, 259

William of Breteuil   10, 27, 69, 73, 139

William of Eu   44, 45, 48, 55, 64, 171

William, count of Evreux   10, 139, 144-45, 153, 181, 183, 188

William of Malmesbury, chronicler   17, 275

William, count of Mortain   11, 100, 132, 134, 138-39, 143, 144, 150, 151, 152, 153, 155, 156-57, 260, 271

William of Newburgh, chronicler   278

William of Roumare   231, 252

William of St. Calais, Bishop of Durham   43, 46, 48, 125

William of Warenne   100, 101, 134, 142, 143, 146, 153, 193, 195, 199, 260

William of Ypres   8, 248

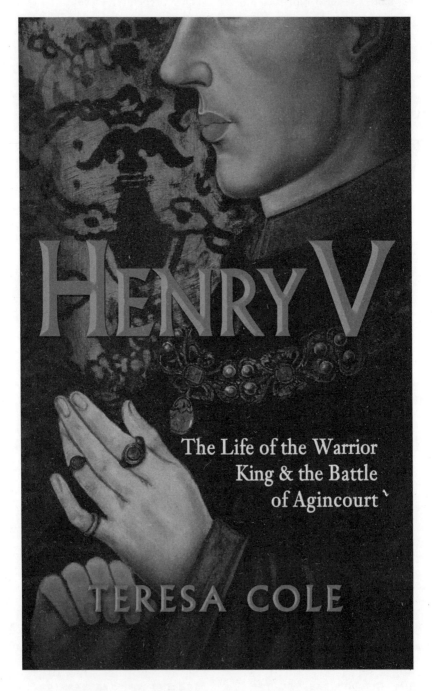